W9-DCG-490

Boys at War, Men at Peace

Ed McBoyie

Boys at War, Men at Peace

Former Enemy Air Combatants
Meet to Remember and Reconcile

Compiled and Written by
E. D. McKenzie

Contributions by

Kenneth J. Kurtenbach, leader of German stalags
Hans G. Berger, Luftwaffe fighter pilot
Richard P. Anthony, Flying Fortress pilot
Ralph E. Lavoie, prisoner of war, repatriate
John Cran Blaylock, Flying Fortress tail gunner
Edward J. Kolber, Flying Fortress engineer
Klaus Zimmer, German historian, author, teacher

VANTAGE PRESS
New York

FIRST EDITION

All rights reserved, including the right of
reproduction in whole or in part in any form.

Copyright © 1998 by E. D. McKenzie

Published by Vantage Press, Inc.
516 West 34th Street, New York, New York 10001

Manufactured in the United States of America
ISBN: 0-533-12466-2

Library of Congress Catalog Card No.: 97- 90735

0 9 8 7 6 5 4 3 2

Contents

Part II

Foreword by Klaus Zimmer
Hassel, Saint Ingbert, Germany

"Die Fliegende Festung bei Bubach im Ostertal. 24 April 1944" was published in the *Westricher Heimatblatter: Heimatkund-liche Mitteilungen aus dem Kreis Kusel,* a periodic publication of the Kusel County Authorities. This documentary was the sole subject of the issue of volume 26, number 4, in 1996:

> What brought the giant bomber to the Buberg hill near the lit-tle village of Bubach in Saarland, Germany? What of the men who had flown her? What of the strange name painted on the nose, "Toonerville Trolley"? We knew it had been shot down by a Luft-waffe fighter, but who was its pilot and what were his experi-ences? Did he survive the battle, the war? And the ground witnesses, what did they observe and report?

Neither those who witnessed what happened on April 24, 1944, nor even those who were directly involved knew all the answers. But now local historians were determined to learn all, even though fifty years had passed, and they have been success-ful beyond anything they might have imagined.

In Germany, the Saarland Association of Regional History and the Oster Valley Cultural and Historical Association became involved when Dieter Bettinger noted to Pres. Hans Kirsch that he had heard records existed of an American bomber who was attacked by German fighters and forced down at Bubach in 1944.

Time was shrinking the ranks of survivors and fading the recollections of those who had knowledge, so if the task was to be done it had to be done soon. As a local historian and author, I was called upon to take charge.

Within a few months we had done archival research, con-ducted interviews, discovered pictures and documents, and made key contacts in Germany and in America. I enlisted the aid of

Werner Eckel, researcher and author of *Air War over Saarbrucken*. He had found among documents obtained from the National Archives in Washington, D.C., a "Missing Aircrew Report" in which were references to the Bubach Flying Fortress incident. In it were the names of those who had parachuted or were still on board the plane when it made its fiery descent and came to a crashing halt on the hillside in Bubach.

I also sought the aid of Roland Geiger of Saint Wendel. His research of aircraft crashes of World War II led to valuable information contacts in the United States with authorities and archivists, and through them I learned that some of the crew of the Flying Fortress at Bubach were alive and active. With the help of the U.S. Department of Veterans Affairs in Saint Louis, Missouri, and Robert D. Elliott, historian and archivist for the Ninety-second Bomb Group of the Eighth Air Force, I found the names of the six surviving members of the ten-man crew. Four of them answered the letters that were forwarded to them and provided information about the crash and events that followed.

Thus encouraged, we Ostertal historians increased our efforts. Walter Harth, of Bubach, and Hans Kirsch interviewed people in the region, then visited the Buberg hill and found the exact site of the landing, placing it above the Saubosch wood in a field called im Hofland. It is quite near the center of the little village of Bubach, and people there joined in to mark the site for the international ceremonies to be held in May 1996.

Family photographs and details about the aircraft on the ground continued to turn up. More eyewitnesses came forward. What appeared as contradictions between crew members and witnesses were soon reconciled, and the full story was learned. Only the German fighter pilot's story was still unknown when our book was published.

To our astonishment, soon afterward I was able to select from among hundreds of personalities in Germany the correct Hans Berger, ex–Luftwaffe fighter pilot of Jagdegeschwader One, and he had in his possession a certificate of *Abschuss*, or "shootdown," of a Flying Fortress at the time and location that made it a certainty it had been Bubach's *Toonerville Trolley*. Hans G. Berger agreed to join in the historic project.

In May 1996 two bomber crewmen and the Luftwaffe pilot met on the very site where the giant plane came to its end. Supported by an emotional gathering, which included schoolchildren, military officers of three countries, many people of the Oster Valley villages, news cameramen and reporters, the three clasped hands together while their countries' national anthems were played. These aging veterans of the biggest air war in history, men who had been deadly enemies, were now meeting as friends and comrades. The scene was captured by international news media and was shared with people in many countries around the world.

All of the questions posed have been answered, and Ed McKenzie now has put them together in this book, which is far beyond the historic record we published earlier. It is a fascinating story about major events and unique experiences and happenings during the war.

Acknowledgments

Beyond the major contributors of material for this book and its forerunner in Germany, "Die Fliegende Festung bei Bubach," there are others whose research and helpfulness were appreciated, including:

Werner Eckel, of Limbach, Germany, air war expert; Roland Geiger, of St. Wendel, Germany, World War II aircraft archaeologist; Walter Harth, of Bubach, Germany, historian, musician, and farmer; Hans Kirsch, of Selchenbach, Germany, president of the regional historic association; Ewald Neu, of Pfeffelbach, Germany, artist and eyewitness to crash; Uwe Benkel, of Kaiserslautern, Germany, World War II aircraft archaeologist; Eugene Sebeck, of Vanderbilt, Pennsylvania, POW "escapee who got back in"; Robert Elliott, of Newbury Park, California, Ninety-second Bomb Group historian; Richard Bowen, of Plaistow, New Hampshire, World War II aircraft historian; Luther Victory, of Baytown, Texas, Stalag Luft XVIIB historian; Albert Clark, of Colorado Springs, Luft III leader and historian; and Roger Freeman, of Essex, UK, author and World War II air war historian.

Archival resources utilized included: Boeing Aircraft Company, Seattle, Washington; Werksarchiv Dornier-Werke, Friedrichshafen, Germany; National Archives, Washington, D.C.; and Kreisarchiv Kusel, Germany.

Boys at War, Men at Peace

PART I

1

"You Must Come Back to Bubach"

My brother and I had each flown the Atlantic several times. I began with a wartime flight to England in a Flying Fortress. One of his important crossings was when he brought home a wife from Germany a few years after the war. Now they have children and grandchildren living near their home in Florida.

But two years ago Dan and I both decided we would never again fly to Europe. It is just too many time zones away from home, and the comfort of long-distance air travel in coach class might be compared with that in traveling by covered wagon in the last century. We had been on a tour of Scotland to see the marvelous scenery and to find our ancient ancestral castle.

On arrival at London, however, to connect with a flight to Manchester, we were told there would be a five-hour delay.

Time to tour London? It would seem like it. But British Customs insisted we remain locked in a secure area the whole time, with only the barest of conveniences.

Now, no one with differing views of world affairs should be so enclosed with my brother Dan, especially when enduring severe symptoms of jet lag. As Dan's misery level rises, then so does that of anyone else nearby. We called our malady "terminal jet lag" because of where we were but also because it might be termed a near-death experience. It is true that we intensified the discomfort by our failure to follow advice to "sleep on the plane; avoid caffeine or alcohol." His wife had added, "And do not get into any discussion of politics or economics."

Then why were the two of us now on this Delta jetliner, off the coast of Newfoundland and en route to Frankfurt, Germany?

Well, just as some of the awful memories of the events of the war fifty-two years ago had faded, so, too, have the memories of more recent events.

Planning for this trip began recently with the arrival of a

3

letter from Klaus Zimmer, a youthful German historian. While working on his second volume of history of the Oster Valley in Saarland, he discovered in several family photo albums pictures of an American bomber lying on a hillside near the little village of Bubach. He was told that three parachutes had blossomed from it before its wild crash-landing on the twenty-fourth of April 1944, a date more firmly fixed in my memory than my birth or marriage date.

Herr Zimmer's research revealed that those who had run from that crumpled airplane were soon rounded up and made prisoners by villagers. Some were still alive who had watched the air battle between the Luftwaffe fighter and our Flying Fortress, then seen us dive toward the earth with two engines on fire. They had provided their recollections of the events of that day and wanted to meet us.

Thus the movement began. We surviving Americans would be invited back to Bubach for a reunion, a mission of peace and reconciliation.

Klaus and I found five of the crew, including Dick Anthony, the pilot who had somehow gotten us safely to earth that day. But only tail gunner John "Cran" Blaylock was able to make this trip. He would meet us at a country inn near Bubach tonight.

I had not seen Cran since we marched across Austria together near the end of the war. Worried German guards were urging us onward, to avoid being overrun by the advancing Red Army.

But then there came an almost unbelievable discovery.

The German fighter pilot who was certified by the Luftwaffe to have shot down our B-17 had been located. His name was Hans G. Berger, and he would drive over from Munich and meet us at the Wildpark inn later tonight.

When I flew down to Florida from my home in New Hampshire a few days ago I was able to seek out and talk with Emil Karl Demuth, now living in Saint Petersburg. Karl flew a Focke Wulf 190 in the same *Jagdgeschwader* as Hans Berger. They were and continue to be friends. Karl was a bit apprehensive about talking at first, but when he learned of my admiration for the fighter pilots on all sides in World War II we had a great con-

4

versation. In my flight bag I have brought his greetings to Hans, along with greetings from the governor and a congressman of my state of New Hampshire to the people of Bubach.

The Flying Fortress on which I was the ball-turret gunner in April 1944 was named the *Toonerville Trolley*. My bomb group had just completed a successful bombing run on the Dornier Aircraft Works near Munich when we came under attack from two or more *Staffeln* of German fighters. During the ensuing battle Hans Berger and two of his comrades shot down three of our bombers. I have a copy of a Luftwaffe document indicating that Hans was credited with an *Abschuss* or "kill," at a time and location matching the American reports of where the *Toonerville Trolley* had gone down in flames, no chutes sighted.

Dan's wife, Rita, was born in Uberlingen, Germany, speaks three languages, and wonders if what Dan speaks is really German. However, by use of hands and a loud volume he seems able to make people in that country understand him, as he has done in Turkey and Japan.

What little German I speak was learned in a prison camp and is not suitable for general conversation. I needed Dan's help, and I also needed it with the U.S. Air Force, from which he retired several years ago. People at the Ramstein air base were helping with the arrangements for our visit, and there had been some confusion about transportation from Frankfurt, where we would arrive in a few hours.

Public greetings and ceremonies were scheduled, starting with a welcome at Ramstein, then continuing at city halls, a parish church, restaurants, the hillside crash site in Bubach, and Baumholder, now a giant U.S. Army base but a giant Wehrmacht base in 1944 when we were thrown into the guardhouse there.

"You must make the speeches for the American flyers," Klaus Zimmer had written, "and have something ready for each situation, including planting of the cherry tree to replace the one torn from the ground by your airplane."

Ex–Luftwaffe pilot Berger would speak also. I was sure we would both put emphasis on the peaceful relations our two nations had enjoyed for more than half a century. When we last met, in the skies over Kaiserslautern, we were each doing his best to destroy the other. What in the world would we say to each other when we met tonight?

Perhaps we would simply shake hands and exchange some pleasantry like, "How good to meet you again." Tail gunner Cran asked me in a letter: "Are we really up to such a meeting? At our age and in front of a whole lot of people?"

It sure would be great to see him again. But for his actions while our plane was going down I probably would not have survived.

Cran is a quiet man and won't say very much unless prompted. He lost his first wife a few years back. They had done very well developing a few supermarkets in California; then he sold out and bought a cattle farm back home in Oklahoma. He was married again and will be bringing Jo Ann with him. She was much his junior and more excited about the trip than he was. I am sure that the plan to tour France and Italy after our ceremonies was not Cran's idea, even though he was still quite an active man for his seventy-seven years.

Cran never asked for nor did he ever get anything from the U.S. government in connection with his war service, not even his medals. He never joined a veterans' organization, nor did he submit to the physical examination that all ex–prisoners of war were urged to undergo a few years back. He felt that nobody owed him anything.

I was anxious to meet Klaus Zimmer, the young teacher, historian, and author responsible for this trip and all the activities connected with it. How he found us is an amazing story all by itself. It was Klaus who told Cran and me and our pilot, Dick Anthony, that the plane we flew that day was named *Toonerville Trolley*. All the people of Bubach had known it for three generations. They could see the name in many photos in their family albums.

After the publication of our story in Germany, Klaus was able to learn many more details of the *Toonerville Trolley* incident. I was astonished at the volume and detail of German records that are available for research. Hans Kirsch, president of the Oster region's historical association, used the word *indefatigable* in describing Klaus Zimmer. With that characteristic he was able to find, out of all the "Bergers" in Germany, the Hans G. Berger who had flown that Focke Wulf 190 on that day and was credited with the "victory."

"Don't worry about what to say to Hans when we meet him tonight," said Dan. "He is wondering what in the world to say to you and Cran."

In our huge jetliner a movie screen hung about midway in the center section. Dan and I had chosen a double seat on one side, since he liked a window seat. I liked to be on the aisle, which has something to do with wanting a clear route to an exit. Also, before they began wearing pants suits and aprons it was enjoyable to watch the stewardesses walk up and down the aisle from such seats.

On the screen were projected some cockpit instrument readings: "210 miles off Newfoundland, airspeed 668 miles per hour, temperature 46 degrees below zero F."

My Atlantic flight of fifty-two years ago was much slower and not nearly so high. The American coast was blacked out. German submarines were sinking hundreds of our ships down there, though it was not being reported in the newspapers. At our destination in England German planes were still dropping bombs, which would go on for many more months. There was little threat of German invasion anymore; in fact, there were huge preparations being made for an invasion in the opposite direction. British and American planes were continually taking off to cross the Channel to bomb targets inside German-occupied Europe.

The Boeing B-17 was cold, noisy, and not pressurized. Relative to the comfort of this Boeing 747 jet-liner, the B-17 was about as primitive as you could get, except for closed cockpits.

I nudged my travel partner with my elbow. "Say, Dan. Do you remember when Dad brought you to Grenier Field to see me?" We had stopped there for refueling before the next leg of our overseas journey. "How old were you then, twelve or thirteen maybe?"

He remembered and grinned. "Yeah, that was really something. Dad felt pretty important, getting clearance to go onto an air base that was sealed off to the public. Can you imagine me, a young kid who just loved to talk, ordered not to mention that I had been there? Some of my pals didn't believe me when I told them I'd seen you, even saw your bomber out on the flight line."

I sat back with my eyes closed, smiling at the picture of Dan spreading the news, forgetting about all the German spy warnings.

When I opened them again he had pulled his sleep mask over his eyes and stuck the earphones in his ears. Unusual for him not to have a drink with me and talk half the night. But he was recalling all the things we did wrong on that last air trip. He wasn't about to repeat them and suffer "terminal jet lag" again.

The screen now read: "Airspeed 598 miles per hour, altitude 38,000 feet, and temperature 57 degrees below zero F."

Our Flying Fortress was rated for that altitude, but only rarely did we get above 30,000. I should be sleeping, too, but an aching hip was giving me almost as much trouble as did that earache back in 1944. Actually, it was the ear problem that brought about Dan's secret trip to the air base in Dad's '36 Chevy, along with Doris, our older sister.

That flight had begun in Kearney, Nebraska. After crew training in Iowa, we were sent to the army depot to pick up our new B-17-G, just delivered from the Boeing factory in Seattle. The "Fortress" part of the name came from all the machine guns mounted in her, supposedly providing total defense against any fighter attacks.

There were eleven fifty-caliber Brownings mounted at five locations. Four were dual mounts, at top, tail, belly and nose. The nose turret was new. Head-on fighter attacks were causing big losses, and this new "chin turret" was to discourage them.

2

The B-17 Called *Toonerville Trolley*

It was more than half a century after the event when historians closely examined photos of the *Toonerville Trolley* as it lay on the *Buberg*, then used the markings on its tail to locate those survivors of the crew who had flown in it on April 24, 1944.

The "B" inside a triangle indicated that the bomber was from the First Division and the Ninety-second Bomb Group, stationed at Podington in England.

Below the "B" was the Boeing company's serial number: 297218. That plane was found to have rolled off the assembly line at Seattle, Washington, on February 9, 1944, and turned over to the Army Air Corps on March 11. That was close to the date when the Anthony and Wallace crews had each picked up their new B-17-G airplanes at the Kearney, Nebraska, depot.

The letter "G" below the serial number on the tail identified the particular plane in its squadron, and the "JW" just behind the waist window indicated the squadron to be the 326th.

When the new plane arrived at Podington, it may have been the ground crew chief who gave it the name *Toonerville Trolley*. Numbers one and two engines, visible in one of the photographs taken by the Germans, showed names painted on them: Mary on one and Ginger on the other. They are thought to have been names of characters in a comic strip drawn by Fontaine Fox during the 1930s. He featured a little old operator, "the Skipper," whose trolley car always appeared to be out of control.

The bomb bay held four or five tons of bombs that could, by use of a top-secret computing Norden bombsight, be dropped somewhere in the vicinity of a target. The claim that we could drop a bomb into a pickle barrel was a gross exaggeration.

Gunsights in the top and bottom turrets also used computers. In those days computers worked with gears, shafts, and cams and not chips, transistors, or even vacuum tubes.

The B-17 to be named *Toonerville Trolley* had come off the assembly line in February, almost the very first G-model made. It was all silver, with no camouflage paint. That airplane was so pretty that Boeing featured it on the cover of the company magazine that month, sitting outside the factory with all props turning, straining at its wheel chocks.

Dick Anthony and the crew's other pilot, Ray Raney, decided to flip a coin to see who would take the right seat, and Ray "won" that position. Both had the same skills, but this coin toss put Dick in the left seat, in command of the plane and its crew. He had joined the Guard at age seventeen and was called up before Pearl Harbor for an Air Corps assignment. Pilot training began at Freeman Field, Indiana; then he went on to multiengine flying. Now his orders read that they were to fly the Southern Route to England. That meant heading for Brazil, refueling, and crossing the Atlantic to Dakar, Africa, before making the final leg of the journey to an air depot in England.

My crew, led by a Texas horse wrangler named Guy Wallace, was picking up its B-17 a week or so later. Each of us was issued a tropical survival pack, so we assumed we would be following the Anthony route. That gear, however, was only to fool any Nazi spies that might be hanging around the supply room. Our orders were: "Fly the Northern Route." The first refueling stop would be in New Hampshire, twenty miles from my home.

New Hampshire senator Styles Bridges was head of the Senate Armed Forces Committee, and he may have used some influence to get a bomber base in Manchester, just in case someone might need to stop there on the way to England someday. It turned out he was right, of course, and the New Hampshire voters were glad to re-elect him. Today it is a large commercial airport. I could have used it for my flight to Florida; however, our retirement home in the White Mountains is closer to Portland, Maine, than it is to Manchester.

Unfortunately, when we arrived there on that late-winter day in 1944 Grenier was socked in, and we were diverted to what was then the East Boston Airport, now Logan International. The clouds were just as thick there.

Narrowing in on their radio beacon, we dropped into the cloud tops at about ten thousand feet after being informed that there were a few hundred feet of clear area above the peak of the highest building in the city, the Custom House. Pressure in my right ear began to build up, and none of the usual tricks of opening it would work.

Normally I would ask the pilot to level off or take us back up a bit until I could clear the ear, but now we were committed to follow that radio beam to the bottom of the cloud cover.

Sure enough, there was some open sky and it was easy to pick out the field lying out across the harbor. When we touched down, the runway kept looking shorter, and we passed midfield going much too fast for wheel brakes to do much good.

"Short runway. Balls to the wall!" said the horse wrangler, and he thrust the throttle-handle balls toward the fire wall for a go-around. The same thing happened on try number two.

"Pilot to Radio Op," he called. "Dick, call Grenier and see what they've got for a ceiling now."

Dick was back in a minute, "Grenier Tower says they've got a few hundred feet under the cloud cover, and if we're already under it then we may as well hedge-hop up there."

By now my ear had cleared with a soft pop but no pain associated with it, only relief.

Now we were flying in my home territory. Pilot Wallace told me to stay up in the nose with the navigator and point out landmarks for him. We unrolled a map, but the only things marked were the hangar at Haverhill, Massachusetts, and some big chicken houses over in Kingston, New Hampshire. We were too far west to see either of those items. I thought I knew every pond, lake, and meadow in the area, but the only recognizable feature was the Merrimack River.

Where I expected to see familiar villages and streets I could see nothing but woods. Going over them at 200 miles an hour we might as well be in Wisconsin for all I could make out.

Wallace was worried. "Pilot to nose. Ed, are you damned sure there are no mountains or towers between Boston and Manchester?"

Under my breath I said, "Oh Lord, I sure hope not!" but on the intercom I reassured him as the navigator winked at me. He had been trained to never let anxiety show in your voice when you didn't know the answers.

We had permission for a straight-in landing, and when the Grenier runway appeared dead ahead of us they gave me full credit for it.

Before putting the map away, I pointed out to the navigator that our flight path took us directly over the Civil Defense aircraft spotting station in the town of Atkinson. Just two years earlier I was reporting there for three shifts each week, scanning the skies with binoculars. There were many of us who never saw even one airplane fly over, never using the official field phone for anything but the daily test call to headquarters.

Now I was picturing one of my friends down there frantically cranking that phone and reporting, "A giant four-engine Flying Fortress going right over our heads, at low altitude, heading north!"

It was the high point of World War II for someone down there on the afternoon shift.

The Grenier air base looked totally different from those I had been used to in the western states. The barracks were on pine-covered hillsides above the runways and flight line, and there was a light cover of snow on the ground. Manchester lay just beyond, with no building taller than the city hall on Elm Street.

What we thought was to be an overnight stop would turn into an eight-day layover. My eardrum had burst and was becoming infected.

We were "jeeped" to the transient combat crew quarters and spent the evening talking about what we might be facing within the next week or two. Newspaper headlines read: "German Industries Suffer Heavy Bombings," but also, "Many U.S. Planes Lost."

Later Hamilton woke me up and told me I was talking in my sleep and if I didn't knock it off he would put me out in the snow. Then he noticed I had a high fever. He woke up one of the others, and they decided to get me over to the base hospital.

The corporal on duty wasn't convinced that help was needed until they let go of my arms and I collapsed onto the floor. With no doctor on duty he finally agreed to find me a hospital bed and give me some APCs (aspirin tablets). The whole staff seemed to be suspicious of combat crewmen who claimed they were sick.

"We're going back to bed," Hamilton said. "Probably be leaving for England in the morning without you, and we've got to get some sleep." When I tried to get up to follow them, the bed spun around the room a few times and I barely caught it as it went by.

The next morning a lucky thing happened. Lieutenant Wallace, my pilot, was brought in with acute appendicitis. He was back from the OR in a few hours, in no condition to go out and fly an airplane. His crew would be going nowhere. What a wonderful guy, to make a sacrifice like that for me.

On the third day of our recuperation, an orderly came to my bed and announced, "Sergeant McKenzie? The base sergeant major wants to see you. He's on the way over from headquarters."

Oh Lord, I thought. *What in the world could I have done to attract his attention? Am I being classified as a deserter?*

Then in walked Sgt. Maj. Robert Herrick. Our two families had been good friends for many years, and he had just read my name on his Morning Report. We swapped stories for a while before he said, "You know, Eddie, you being here is a military secret. But maybe I can think of some reason to let your father know you're here and arrange a visit."

By the next afternoon it was happening, after only one little hitch. Father had to apply to the local War Rationing board for a travel permit and an extra gas stamp in order to drive as far as twenty miles from home. They came up with a very important reason for it, however. Dad was chief air raid warden for the town of Plaistow, and I suspect that he and Bob convinced the administrator that his presence was required at the air base for special action.

Showing a special pass to the alert guard at the Grenier main gate, Dad was saluted and waved through. With him was little brother Dan, now sitting beside me in the 747 headed for Germany, and our older sister, Doris. Without attempting to describe Doris, when she came walking through the recuperation ward with long blond hair touching the shoulders of her snug angora sweater, wearing heels and perfectly aligned seams on her silk stockings, every man on both sides of the aisle suddenly became radiantly healthy.

We had a happy reunion, each having thought our good-byes

of the previous November may have been the final ones. When they left us, we were well supplied with chocolate bars and copies of the latest *Life* and *Esquire* magazines.

In a couple of days I was able to sit up without toppling over and Wallace could support a suppressed sneeze without popping any stitches. A young doctor we hadn't seen before walked in, looking at his clipboard. We appeared far too comfortable.

"You men are classified 'ready for combat,'" he said as he flipped through some papers. "I hope you don't think you're going to avoid going overseas by hanging around this hospital."

We couldn't believe our good luck. The last thing in the world we wanted was to be hanging around his hospital. He wrote something on some forms and without so much as a "let me look at your scars" handed us our discharge papers.

The happy crew members were called in, and they helped us into our flying gear before we staggered out to the flight line. As one of the guards unslung his rifle and challenged us, I could read his mind: *Oh boy. More of those crazy flyers who've been out on an all-night toot.*

After crawling into the waist hatch, I made my way up to the nose, where a stack of comforters were spread out. The boys had thought of everything. The copilot, Corky, was running up the engines. As I plugged into the intercom, pilot Wallace was saying, "Tell Ed to leave some room for me. I'll be down as soon as we get the gear up."

"Welcome aboard, you malingerers," announced Corky. "Now let me fly y'all to where the war is!"

3

The Cold, Gray North Atlantic

Now the movie screen in our jetliner showed our position to be far out over the ocean, headed for Iceland, just as we had been fifty-two years earlier. But this time we would not stop in Labrador or in Iceland to refuel.

Dan peeked up through half-closed eyes. "Fifty below! Was it this cold at high altitude when you guys were flying over Germany?"

"Some claimed it was, but who could really discriminate between ten below and fifty below? You'd get frostbite if you exposed anything for more than a minute," I told him.

It was a long flight to Europe in 1944, as it was now in 1996. Then, of course, there was no stewardess to bring us a snack and no movies were shown. At our Goose Bay, Labrador, stop there was nothing to see but high snowbanks and a gasoline truck driven by what appeared to be an Eskimo. Heading out over the Atlantic, we were told to keep a close watch below for any airplanes that may have had to ditch for some reason or other.

"If you have trouble, don't bail out," was the advice. "You won't survive long enough to get out of your chute. Ditch near a fishing boat if you can find one."

I saw no boats of any kind and wondered what we would do if we managed to survive a ditching and crawl out of the icy water into our life raft, assuming we got it deployed. Waves were ten feet high, and there were many icebergs down there.

Hours later as we approached the landing strip in Iceland the cross-wind was so strong that Wallace had to look out his side window to see the runway. Then the wheels grabbed and straightened us around. Plenty of room on this runway for a roll-out; then we trailed a "Follow Me" jeep to a parking hardstand.

Our B-17 could not be left unprotected, so while the rest of us spent the night in a tin hut, the bombardier stayed in the plane. He borrowed our loaded pistols to supplement his own, "in case the Icelanders attack." We had been warned they might not be friendly, not having invited the Americans to be there.

In the hut, noise of the hail on the roof was so loud we could do little sleeping. Huddled on the cots in our sheepskin flying clothes, we nibbled on cheese and crackers from cartons of K-rations from the airplane.

As soon as it was light enough to see, we were out "walking the props through," anxious to get going again. On this leg of the journey the turret guns were loaded and we stayed alert. German fighters had been known to come out this far to knock down unsuspecting bombers before they even got near England.

After a few hours the navigator reported a beautiful green island lifting above the horizon. "By the color," he said, "it's got to be Ireland and it must be spring there."

After we landed and taxied into position with a row of other B-17s, we got a shock. That shiny new Fortress we had picked up at Kearney, Nebraska, was going into action right away, but we were not. It seemed that more airplanes than men were being lost. Some wrecks they had managed to fly back to their bases would never fly again, good only for spare parts.

We cleared out our bags and left our B-17 at the Nutt's Corner depot. Loaded into the back of a lorry, we were driven to a ferry landing and taken to Scotland. The train ride down into England was a wonderful introduction to that country, and it made up somewhat for the loss of our airplane.

4

England . . . and the Air War

At Podington Bomber Station 109 a sign over the gate told us that we were "Fame's Favored Few."

Ground crews worked around-the-clock repairing battle damage and changing engines, doing whatever was needed to get a full group into flying condition for the next day. The Ninety-second had lost lots of people and airplanes lately, it was claimed. It had been "maximum effort" every day.

One crew chief told us the pressure was pretty strong on him to make everything flyable. "We patch 'em up and put 'em up," he said, laughing. But we were not laughing. Such talk was not what we wanted to hear about those B-17s, some of which looked like they could be out of service for a good long time.

When the noncommissioned officers were shown to the Nissen hut barracks at the 326th Squadron area there were only a few men around. Many of the beds were stripped of bedding and the mattresses rolled up.

"Take any one you want!" someone yelled. "Those guys won't be needing 'em anymore." That kind of talk was not what we wanted to hear, either.

After unpacking, we went out to check on important things, like the mess hall, latrine, orderly room, briefing rooms, and hangars. Some of the ground crew guys didn't mind talking. One said, "You sure are lucky the weather's so bad. You'll be standing down for a while 'til the fog and clouds go away."

His buddy wasn't so sure. "Hey, they'll have you climbing right up through this crap. We seen 'em go out in lots worse weather 'n this."

Checking in at the orderly room, we were told by the first sergeant to come back later with a five-pound note. This was the equivalent of twenty bucks, and it was the going price for a bicycle. There was a row out front, each one with a name tag tied to

17

the handlebars. We were to pick one, remove the tag, and bring it back in to him when we had the five pounds.

He said, "I'll mail the money to his next of kin and give you a new tag with your name on it to tie on the handlebars." Was this another way of telling us we might not be around very long?

The bomber base was spread out over a large area of farmland, and the bike was considered necessary. The gate near us, we were told, gave access to the little town of Wollaston, only a ten-minute bike ride away.

It was actually a few days before the crew's first mission, hitting aircraft facilities in the area of Lechfeld. Afterward, at debriefing, the fighters and flak were described as "moderate" but heavy enough to convince us that the Continent was well defended. The "ack-ack" gunners and fighters surely wanted to kill us.

My buddies went through some "alerts" and "scrubs" for a few days. I had real concern about being sent on that long haul to Berlin. Although I didn't get sent to Berlin, one day we went beyond that city to Oranienburg. After completing that one, I knew that the odds of doing enough missions to be rotated back to the United States were definitely not favorable.

The English weather wasn't quite as bad as had been predicted, and missions came every couple of days after that. Someone said, "You might gain a lot of experience, but you'll never get used to it. No matter how many antiaircraft shells have exploded around you, it is the one *about* to explode that keeps your heart pounding and your anxiety high."

The Anthony crew went to Frankfurt, then to the "Big B," Berlin, fighting off attackers all the way. Their ball-turret operator was incapacitated, and I was pulled from my regular crew to fly with them about this time. There were only short rest periods between hits on aircraft and transportation targets. We went to Belgium, then to Kassel and Hamm, in Germany.

When was it, I wondered, that flyers went into town and drank beer and played darts in the pubs? I had heard a lot about American airmen making friends in the English villages, but schedules weren't going to permit it for us. There were pubs in both Podington and Wollaston, but I never got to see the inside of one, which wasn't that important, because as a teenager my

18

drink was more likely to be a milk shake than a beer.

Sometimes fog or drizzle would mean difficult takeoffs, and casualties could be heavy before even getting to the Channel. It was always a relief to see a "scrub" flare go up before we started our takeoff roll.

The way things were going, I might never get a chance to see some of the sights I had heard so much about, so early one morning Bill and I hitched a ride into London on one of our supply trucks.

"Let's see if we can find Buckingham Palace, London Bridge, and Piccadilly Circus," I said.

We had all heard stories about the ladies of Piccadilly and how nice they could be to the "Yanks." Female companionship was very scarce on the air base, and it was impossible to get close to one of the Red Cross girls. When I considered the odds against having many more opportunities to make contact with the female of the species, I was anxious for this trip.

It was disappointing. The London air was heavy with fog and smelly with soft-coal smoke and the smoke from smoldering bomb ruins. We saw lots of ruins, some old and some quite new. We lunched on a few pennies' worth of fish and chips, presented in a rolled-up newspaper cone that left black marks on our hands and on the chips.

Piccadilly turned out to be just a big traffic circle or "square" with a giant Bovril sign and double-decker buses making up most of the traffic.

Ladies scurrying around with kerchiefs on their heads were all much older than I was, and they didn't seem eager to stop and chat with a couple of American soldiers.

When it got dark in London it got really dark. We felt our way along the streets, apologizing as we bumped into people. Only dim lights showed here and there, and we had been warned that if we lit up a cigarette out in the open a "bobby" or an air-raid warden might whack us with his baton.

We hadn't been warned about the public toilets. They were unlit, and as the evening progressed people began relieving themselves nearer to the entrance. We were clearly not having a "wild night on the town," so we headed for the USO, where most of the sensible guys went.

By ten o'clock we'd had enough. Finding our truck at the appointed place, we were soon headed back for the comfort and security of the air base. Later, when the others asked what kind of a time we had, we told them stories about the great girls we had met. It was a part of the military ritual. Everyone did it.

5

The Cook Who Longed for Combat

Seven miles above the Atlantic in the jetliner, Dan came back to his seat after a walk up and down the aisle for exercise. I asked him if he remembered a boy named Walt Warren from back home when we were kids.

"Oh sure," Dan said. "He was one of the few guys who survived all of his combat missions and came back home. Right?"

"Well, not really, Dan. He never did any flying," I told him. It was so many years ago now that it couldn't make any difference if the story got out or not.

"I had gone to a training area in what had been an English resort area called The Wash for two days of shooting at tow targets. RAF pilot trainees pulled sleeve targets out over the water, and we fired at them with thirty-caliber machine guns mounted on swivel posts, never knowing whether or not we had hit them.

"I ran into Walt in the chow line one afternoon. He was dipping hot chocolate out of a big bucket and into our metal canteen cups. I had heard about his combat flying adventures in England and was really surprised to see him here and doing this kind of duty. I wondered what the hell a combat veteran like Walt had done to be busted to buck private and put on a chow line. Without making a big deal out of it, I asked him, 'How come?' and he told me that he wanted desperately to fly but never had been given the chance. He said that after I had been at Podington for a while I might be able to help him work something out.

"It occurred to me that he may have spent as much time training to be a cook as I had to be an armorer gunner, but I told him that I would sure do my best.

"It turned out that Walt's real job was in food service, Dan. He was a permanent KP."

Dan was as surprised as I had been. "Was he embarrassed?"

"No, I don't think so. We didn't hold up the chow line to talk right then, but he asked me to come back after they were through serving. Walter wanted to know all about people we both knew back home, and I was eager to learn what he knew about England, so I hung around and chatted with him while he took care of the pots. He'd been here for a year and had made friends in Kings Lynn."

"'Why don't you come into town with me, Eddie, and I can show you around?' he asked. [Some people who had known me when I was a little kid called me Eddie instead of Ed.]

"It sounded like a great idea, and I didn't need to worry about permission. I just had to be in that truck for the return trip to Podington next day.

"After Walt had helped to clear mess that evening, he got on his Class A's and we started to walk. He was carrying a package, said it was part of the U.S. 'Bundles to Britain' campaign. In it was a pound of butter and a little bag of sugar. He told me it was also to be sure we'd be welcome company at the home of one of his lady friends in Kings Lynn.

"An older woman—oh, maybe thirty—answered the door. I got the impression that Walt's package wasn't really needed to earn her warm greeting. She introduced me to a teenage girl who had been helping her keep a little twig fire going to boil some tea, then sent her out front to bring in a bench so we could sit down. There wasn't much in the room except for a small table.

"We sat and sipped tea for a few minutes; then, leaving him to share the benefits of his gift with the cook, the girl and I went outside. She led me on a casual stroll alongside a canal where there were rows and rows of bright red and yellow tulips. We talked and laughed together at our difficulties with each other's language, and we held hands as we walked.

"The memory of the flowers, her soft hand in mine, and her happy laughter were tucked away in my mind and I would draw on them from time to time over the many long months ahead. End of story, Dan," I said.

"You mean that's it? Nothing else?" Dan would never have quit at just holding hands. "Whatever happened to Walt?" he wanted to know.

"Well," I said, "Walt had to open the kitchen at 4:30 every morning, so we walked back and said our good-byes. Do you know I kept my promise not to say anything about his military career to folks back home? But I also promised him that we would meet again real soon and I would try and get him onto a combat mission somehow. It was the last time I ever saw him."

"That wasn't your fault. You can lay all the blame for that on the Luftwaffe fighter pilot you're going to meet tonight."

We laughed at the thought of my telling Hans Berger that story.

6

"The Air Force Will Meet You at Frankfurt"

The airline stewardess was approaching with her aisle-blocking cart to serve breakfast, and I couldn't recall closing my eyes for more than ten minutes to compensate for the eight hours of sleep I was missing.

Dan reminded me to set my watch ahead six hours, then asked me once again about transportation from Frankfurt.

"Are you certain that the air force is actually going to be there and pick us up and not just expect us to catch one of the blue bus runs they use for transient airmen?"

The blue bus, he explained to me, was today's equivalent to our old "six-by" trucks with benches in the back. A busy place like Ramstein probably ran two or three buses a day from the terminal. They had suggested, at first, that we carry our bags to the USO and await a bus run. We had politely but firmly rejected that idea. If we couldn't afford first class, we could at least rent a car or take a cab, but no bus.

Once again I read to Dan the words in Egon Keller's fax, received just before we left Florida. His message was reassuring: "You will be met at the gate by a man holding a sign reading 'McKenzie' and he will take you to his vehicle and drive you to Ramstein for a reception and a brief rest at the Ramstein Protocol Office."

"Well, OK," said Dan, "but I wish we'd accepted Klaus Zimmer's offer to meet us there in his car and drive us right to the Wildpark inn at Hassel. Can't help but think that getting the air force in on it is a mistake. There's bound to be a screw-up."

We had also been offered a ride with my tail gunner and his wife in their rental car. But their plane arrived two hours after ours and Jo Ann had brought a truckload of suitcases, since they planned to tour the Continent after our ceremonies at Bubach. There'd be no room for us.

The landing at Frankfurt was smooth, Customs was a breeze, and there was only a short wait for the bags. We loaded them onto one of the available carts, pushed for a ways, and then off-loaded them to a conveyor belt, on which they disappeared for a few minutes. When they reappeared our cart had been taken. Now I was glad to have the little wheels on my larger bag.

Ah! There was a man holding a MCKENZIE sign over his head. We waved, and he came over and introduced himself, "I'm Mr. Browning and I will be your driver."

He would not, however, be our "sky-cap," since he took off into the crowd empty-handed, motioning us to follow. I looked desperately for a porter or a cart, but to no avail. Dan has a stride like that of a racehorse and was right on Browning's heels. My stride was more like that of a plow horse as I dragged one bag and shouldered the other. Somehow I kept Dan and Browning in view, with the knowledge that in a few moments we would be stepping into a comfortable staff car or at least a jeep or lorry.

But we rushed right on past nearby parking and headed for the bus area. *Why would Browning park in the bus area?* I wondered. Now I saw. It was because he had brought a bus and he was a bus driver. That was his job. There stood one of the infamous blue forty-passenger buses.

Dan simply clapped his hand to his forehead and said, "Good grief!"

Browning explained that he had brought a load to the airport earlier and had been ordered to await our arrival and bring us back with him. We dragged in our bags, braced ourselves on the benchlike seats, and headed for the autobahn. Later we learned that the old days, when the air force provided cars for guests, were gone, unless you happen to be a general or congressman. Our choice was, after all, arrange your own ride or take a bus. But at least the bus had windows and not canvas sides like the six-by trucks of the old days.

Taking advantage of his captive audience, Dan sat behind the driver and for the next hour and a half swapped stories with Browning. Dan learned what has been happening in the region since he left it many years ago and told Browning how great it was in the Wiesbaden and Munich areas when there were only a few cars on the autobahns.

At least there was plenty of space on the empty bus, and I got up and moved about to keep my joints from locking up. It was a long ride to Ramstein from the Frankfurt terminal.

And then came a new problem.

The guard at the air force base did not know that we were expected, and Browning had no orders that might authorize him to bring us inside. Our bus was ordered over into a waiting area while we entered the sentry house to make an appeal.

Identification was required; however, the passport, credit cards, and even Air Force Association membership cards were not recognized.

"You need a pass or positive ID," said the young man in the blue uniform. His courtesy and broad smile only added to our frustration.

"Perhaps word from the commanding general's office would suffice," I suggested. "We are supposedly here at his personal invitation. Would you please call General Stevens?"

"I do not call generals," said the private first class.

Browning simply lounged by his bus and looked bored. We would get no help from him. Our joking about the possibility of being spread-eagled against the side of a blue bus didn't seem so funny now. Finally Dan noticed a man who looked much more like a terrorist than either of us. He simply waved some sort of card as he drove up and was waved right on through the gate.

"What sort of ID was that?" Dan asked the sentry.

"Sir, that is a Retired Air Force ID card."

"Well, Good Lord. I have one of those right here!"

With only a quick glance at it, the guard said, "That's fine, sir. Just have your guest sign in and go ahead on through." So now Dan was the invitee and I was the guest.

As we dismounted from the bus, a lovely lady stepped out of the building marked BASE PROTOCOL OFFICE, greeting us with a broad smile and handshakes. "Don't worry about the bags," she said. "Browning will take care of them."

We were led into a comfortable conference room where coffee and snacks were laid out. "Relax and let me pour you a cup," she said, "and your German hosts will be along in just a few minutes."

Soon Herr Doktor Professor Egon Keller strode into the

room with a broad smile, extended hand, and effulgent greeting. Egon would be our guide, interpreter, and good friend during the coming week of ceremony and activities. He was exactly as I had pictured him during our phone calls. He introduced Klaus Zimmer, "the young man who is responsible for all this." I had looked forward for months to this moment.

A video cameraman was recording our greetings, and we were presented with printed brochures about the country, district, and villages where we would be their guests.

With Dr. Keller and Herr Zimmer was president of the Oster Valley Historical and Cultural Association Hans Kirsch. Perhaps of equal importance was Hans's primary occupation. He was general of police for the Landstuhl District, where the USAF Ramstein base was located. A tall, young, handsome man, Mr. Kirsch introduced Mrs. Kirsch, a tall and attractive woman who held a young baby in her arms.

Cran Blaylock would be happy to learn of Hans's police position. We wanted no risk of being arrested and thrown into prison in any of these towns as we had been the last time we were here.

When Dan learned that the Kirsch family spoke no English, his eyes lit up. He had been practicing his German ever since we decided to make the trip, and he went right to work on it with them.

"Please call me Egon," said Dr. Keller, and he began one of the many history lessons he would provide during our stay. He was brimming over with facts and statistics about the region and its people, and we were eager listeners. Barely a teenager during the war, he had been drafted into the military to serve with an antiaircraft gun battery during the year after our plane had been shot down. He had lost family members during the bombings and seen some of his comrades killed as the Allies fought their way in.

Since the Wildpark inn is in Herr Zimmer's village of Hassel, Dan and I rode with him as we left Ramstein. We had much to talk about, and it was a pleasant ride. We diverted briefly and drove past his home, a relatively new one but fitting in beautifully among the old ones with their red tile roofs and lovely flowers. The purple lilacs and other spring flowers were in full bloom everywhere throughout this region, as they had been back in

27

New Hampshire before I left. It was cool and a bit drizzly here, too.

Klaus had anticipated our need for some rest and planned it into the schedule. We were shown to our rooms without delay. Through my window I could see a reason why the inn was called the Wildpark. There were deer grazing in the field.

After a short nap, Dan and I decided to go downstairs to see what we might find for lunch. The restaurant had a fine reputation in the area. There was an adjoining banquet hall, and it was said to be a very popular place for social gatherings and meetings.

The *Speisekarte* (menu) was Dan's responsibility, since the only words recognizable to me were *Käse, Wurst,* and *Brot* (cheese, sausage, and bread).

We only wanted a light lunch. Sandwiches would be ideal, but they were unheard of here. The English innovation of meat, cheese, or jelly between two slices of bread just never caught on.

Dan ordered a plate of *Käse, Wurst, und Brot,* along with some mustard and butter. We'd create our own sandwiches. Of course, beer was the primary beverage, but the local wines were promoted also. I knew better than to ask for milk, and caffeine had reached critical proportions in my system over the past several hours.

We inquired about running a tab for meals on our hotel room bill, and Herr Bullacher said that would be "gut." Dan had brought Visa, while I had MasterCard. Dan's guess was the correct one. Innkeeper Bullacher took only Visa, so it would be "divide by two" when the bill arrived back home. Prices here seemed reasonable, even expressed in Deutschmarks, exchanged at a rate of three for two dollars.

7

"So, We Meet Again, Hans Berger!"

The day was cool and cloudy, but the fresh air and exercise were helping us to reestablish routines. When Dan and I were together we generally had a scotch and soda at about five in the afternoon. Fortunately, it was not an addiction, since scotch seemed to be unknown here, as was soda water. Anyway, our busy schedules over the next several days made no allowance for a "five o'clock pause." Also, most restaurants seemed to have fine brandies.

When the dinner hour arrived but still no sign of the Blaylocks, we were becoming anxious. Cran and Jo Ann had reserved a rental car at Frankfurt, planning to tour France, Italy, and Monte Carlo after the affairs at Bubach. Not knowing Jo Ann, except for a few phone calls, I imagined what she might look like striding into a posh Monte Carlo casino wearing a ten-gallon hat and snakeskin boots and dominating a roulette table.

Klaus Zimmer had mapped their trip from Frankfurt to the inn with great attention to detail several months ago. "If they follow my map they cannot get lost," he said.

Meanwhile he drove us over to his home to meet his wife, Christa, and their daughters, Claudia and Bettina. The three-story Zimmer house was modern yet traditional and comfortable in appearance. Klaus pursued his avocation of history in a spacious studio on the top floor.

As we returned to the inn, Dan and I were amazed at Klaus's ability to make U-turns while completely disregarding curbstones.

The inn's parking lot was across the street. It had no ramped access, and those who used it just bumped up and over the four-or five-inch curb. An American driver would rush his car to the garage for a front-end alignment after such a bump. It didn't trouble Klaus.

Through a large window in the dining room I could see Hans Berger at one of the tables, easily recognized from the pictures I had received from him. He stood when he saw us come in and waved us toward his table.

Although not really needed, Klaus made a formal introduction. The old Luftwaffe fighter pilot said to the old American air force gunner, "Ed, it is very good to meet you." Then, with a smile, "So much more pleasant than the last time, eh?" He was a strong and healthy–looking man, and his smile drew my smile in return. As we shook hands, my greeting was similar to his.

"Although I didn't get to know you that day in 1944, Hans, it is as though we are old acquaintances." Then I turned toward Klaus. "We are surely indebted to Klaus Zimmer for bringing about this meeting."

Klaus only nodded. He was much happier arranging such things than participating. He introduced my brother, Dan, to Hans, who said, "I had no doubt that you two were brothers." Although I was seven years Dan's senior, we were often mistaken for one another.

All were aware of our state of exhaustion, that we had had little sleep since getting out of bed yesterday morning in Florida. Although eager to sit down together, we made plans for meeting early in the morning, said, "Auf Wiedersehen," and climbed the stairs.

Meanwhile, concern about the Blaylocks was growing. Cran and Jo Ann had not yet arrived, and no word had been received from them. Egon had contacted the airline and learned that they had "deplaned" on time. The car agency confirmed that they had picked up their rental some seven hours ago.

Klaus felt a heavy responsibility for them. He had developed a condition Dan called "terminal nervous stomach." Klaus's carefully drawn map and written instructions as to the precise route from the airport to the inn had gone to Calvin, Oklahoma, weeks ago. Where could they be? What could possibly have gone wrong? He had heard about a few German tourist "car-jackings" in Florida. Could it happen here?

Egon contacted our police general host, Hans Kirsch, on the cellular phone he always had at the ready. "Will you please alert your officers on the autobahn?" he asked.

30

Now there was nothing else to be done and all became quiet at the Wildpark.

Much later, I was awakened by sounds in the corridor outside my room. There were sharp-toned voices, noise, and confusion as someone was trying to fit a key to a door. The room keys were large and it was not an easy task. A woman's voice was giving instructions.

Since the only vacant room on our floor was for the Blaylocks, I concluded they had arrived. There were the sounds of the large key hitting the floor, then at last a door opening and the moving in of a number of suitcases before the door slammed shut.

Wildpark was quiet once again, but I heard a voice from the next room, which could only be Dan: "Thank God that's over!" He was obviously greatly relieved that Cran and Jo Ann were safe and sound at last. Klaus had been informed at his home, and now he could go to sleep. In the morning we would get the differing views from them as to how they could drive for six hours on a three-hour trip from Frankfurt to Hassel.

Dan had warned me not to attempt oral communications in their own language with the staff at the inn or restaurant. "You'll only confuse them," he said. "They'll be expecting you to speak English, and this is fixed in their minds. When you insert what you might think is a good German word or phrase it makes their minds go blank." In spite of his warnings, I went ahead and experimented with my meager knowledge of German.

The rooms at Wildpark were neat and clean but austere. It was a country inn, after all, and there were none of the modern hotel luxuries such as writing desk, comfortable chair, dresser, telephone, or tissues. Neither was there any bedding.

In our exchange of letters about accommodations there had been a meeting of the minds on toilets. When we had to "get up during the night" Klaus understood that it was not to wash our hands, and so a "bathroom" was not what we need. We needed a water closet, "WC," or toilet. An American who says to his host, "Oh, I really must go and wash my hands," may find himself directed to a room in which nothing else can be done.

Due to some reservation overlaps, we knew that we had to

move to rooms without toilets for one night only. Otherwise we each had the proper facility appropriately located.

However, my comments concerning how distressed I had been with featherbeds on a previous visit to Germany had gone unnoticed. Perhaps I was too subtle, or to be fair, it may be that some cultural differences are just too great to be overcome. Nevertheless, our Wildpark country inn provided only featherbeds and no sheets or blankets.

One lies either between or on top of the two featherbeds. There was no other option. If between, then it was too warm except in midwinter. If on top, then it is much too cool, at least for this time of year.

It was not yet summer in Germany. Room heat was not provided nor was it easily requested when the staff spoke only German. When I asked Dan's help with the maid, I learned that my failure might be improper use of the word *heiss* when I meant "heat."

"The way you say it," Dan explained, "you are more likely to get a glass of ice water, the maid's name, or a cough drop than you are to get the steam radiator turned on. Listen closely:

"Wie heissen Sie?" What is your name?

"Heisere Kehle! Sore throat. Verstehen sie meinen Bruder?"

It made me think of the time when Dan, at a sausage kiosk, asked for a *Heisser Hund*. He thought he would get a hot dog but found out he was asking for a "dog in heat."

I know better than ask for a bedsheet or blanket that would make sleeping more comfortable. That would be improper here in southern Germany, as I recalled from a visit to the Bodensee a few years ago. I remembered thinking how embarrassed my hostess would be when it occurred to her that she had put me in a bedroom with no sheets or covers on the bed.

After making do with two bath towels, in the morning I was greeted, "Ah, guten Morgen. Gut geschlafen?"

"Ja, ja. Gut, danke Schön. Aber . . . aber . . . die Leintuch?" I stammered, perhaps asking about a napkin or toilet paper and not a bedsheet.

8

Getting Friendly with the Enemy

Our first day in Germany had been set aside for recuperation from jet lag, according to Klaus Zimmer's schedule. Beyond that there was a full schedule for the next four days.

I got up early to take advantage of the time to talk with Hans Berger but found that he was already up and out for a walk in the countryside. Dan remembered the fine walking paths provided throughout Germany, and he left to explore some of them.

It was cool and drizzly out there, so I awaited their return in the lobby area while reading some of the material that had been provided by our historical and cultural society hosts.

As Hans returned, he seemed pleased to see me and asked for a few moments to retrieve something from his room. Before mounting the stairs, however, he was able to convince innkeeper Bullacher that there should be a pot of coffee brought to a table for us, even though it was before the usual opening time.

When the ex–Luftwaffe pilot returned, he was carrying a box and a bag, and he set them under the table while we started on the coffee.

My first questions were about his experiences flying Focke Wulf 190 "hunter" planes against our Eighth Air Force bombers and escort fighters. His No. 1 *Gruppe, Jagdgeschwader* 1 (1 JG/1), included many senior pilots with combat experience in Poland and Russia before assignment to the "Defense of the Reich" campaign.

He was identified as "Weissĕ Acht," since his FW-190 was marked with a large white number 8 on the fuselage, behind the *Tatzelwurm* on the cowl. He explained that this squadron insignia was really a glowworm, but one with a gaping mouth full of teeth. I recalled that the famous "Red Baron," von Richthofen, had flown his red triplane as a member of 1 JG/1 in World War I.

Hans's *Jagdgeschwader*, he said, was originally made of up

three groups, each with three squadrons. Each squadron had twelve fighters and four staff planes, making a total of a 112 aircraft in the JG.

A few months after his battle with the *Toonerville Trolley* this was increased. Then there were four groups of four squadrons, each having sixteen fighters and four staff, for a total of 260, or more than double the previous size.

Losses in his *JG* were very heavy during 1944. Two hundred and ninety-seven pilots were killed in action. Their names are recorded in the book *Defending the Reich,* written by his friend Eric Mombeek. Hans had mailed a copy to me just last month, written in German but easily readable, with its many illustrations.

Beyond the KIAs, 171 were wounded and 49 were missing or made prisoners of war. That added up to 517 casualties for the one year of 1944 alone. We both shook our heads as Hans said, "What a terrible toll it was of brave young men."

Many months after his victory of April 24, an event I remembered more clearly than he did, he was captain of the Third Squadron of JG/1. Before the end of 1944 he was moved to airfields in lower Saxony and, as the Allies advanced, to different fields in France, under continual bombing and strafing attacks.

"The group was built up with inexperienced pilots when we were moved to Greifswald during the 'Defense of Berlin' campaign. It was at this time we knew that defeat was inevitable.

"But then we were surprised by an order to move to Leck for some special He-162 retraining. The days of interception and attacking bombers were over for me," said the veteran fighter pilot.

Hans told me of having been shot down on two occasions and of parachuting to save his life, but not without some injuries.

My one jump had not been as dramatic. It was after a mission when our landing gear hydraulic system had been hit and the wheels would not lock down. From the ball turret I confirmed that they were not fully extended before scrambling up into the radio room to take my crash position.

The pilot, however, decided that he would not risk ten men in his belly-landing attempt and ordered everyone but his copilot out. We were close to our base, and it was all open farmland below.

Outside of the shocking silence as the B-17 flew away from me and the slight wound to my buttock as I was dragged over a wire fence, I could recall no unpleasantness. A farmer added a funny ending to the story, thinking that I was a German paratrooper and not recognizing what I spoke as English. "Oh, a Yank!" he finally said.

Hans called a crash landing a *Notlandung*. This was what our *Toonerville Trolley* had supposedly experienced only a few kilometers from where we were now sitting, after three men had bailed out.

Hans's Luftwaffe service began in 1941 with basic military training not too different from our own. Then he was assigned to officer training at the *Luftkriegsschule,* after which came the flight training that led to piloting a Messerschmitt 110, a twin-engine "destroyer" aircraft.

The growing need for single-engine fighter pilots, Hans told me, resulted in retraining in both the Me-109 and FW-190. He was rated as cadet until his assignment with 1 JG/1, then was promoted to the rank of *Leutnant Ingenieur.* Our B-17 pilot, Dick Anthony, I told Hans, had moved from single-engine to multi-engine aircraft. Some flyers who had long dreamed of being fighter pilots might not feel that was "advancement," but Dick told me that he was not at all disappointed to be assigned to a Flying Fortress.

After a year on the ground as a prisoner of war, Dick again picked up his air force flying career. He gained experience flying the big cargo planes along the Berlin "corridor" back when the Russians were trying to isolate the city from Western support.

When Hans said, "I hope he was able to experience jets during his career," I mentioned the T-33 jet trainers Dick had flown during the Korea period. It was about the same time that we were converting from P-47s to F-94s in the 133d Fighter Squadron. Our pilots were using the T-33s for familiarization about the time when I turned over my armament chief duties to a younger man and went back to civilian life.

"Dick and I will have plenty to talk about when we meet, besides looking down each other's gun muzzles on that day." Hans could tell Dick of his experiences during the final month of the war, flying the revolutionary Heinkel 162 Volksjager. I made

35

a note to get that whole story later, having been primed by Karl Demuth just before leaving Florida. Karl had been Hans's company commander, and they had surrendered to the British together in May 1945.

We commented on the renewed popularity of the leather jackets worn by both air forces, and I joked, "You know, Hans, those A-2 jackets wore like iron and we might see mine being worn by someone in Bubach when we go there later on."

I had last seen it inside the fuselage of the *Toonerville Trolley,* covered with earth we had plowed up from the orchard. It was with the GI shoes I retrieved before running for the woods to avoid capture.

This was the opening Hans needed. Reaching into the bag he had brought, he pulled out a leather flying jacket, that vital piece of flight apparel for all flyers. On the breast of this jacket was a patch where the Iron Cross medal had been pinned. It occurred to me as he showed me the medal, with its small swastika in the center, that it may well have been the *Abschuss* of our Flying Fortress that earned him that award. The number of sorties flown was a part of the formula for the Iron Cross to Knight's Cross series; however, the numbers of "kills" or certified victories was vital also.

"We pilots were told," Hans said, "that we would achieve higher rank with completion of future studies and awards. But after I had earned the Iron Cross with Front Line Clasp we learned that the rules were changed, and another condition added. Further studies for advancement could only begin after final victory for the Reich."

The wry grin on his face seemed to me to indicate a mixture of humor and sadness. We sat for a moment, staring into our coffee cups.

Can this really be happening? I thought. *Would anyone have dreamed that I someday would be sitting with the man who had shot me out of the sky, calmly discussing it with him?*

When Klaus Zimmer had called me from Germany to tell me he had found the Luftwaffe pilot who might well be the one who had hit us on April 24, 1944, there was excitement in his voice. Klaus had called the *Toonerville Trolley* men "needles in a haystack" to be found, but finding the fighter pilot, with the certificate of *Abschuss* in his possession, was finding a much smaller needle in a larger haystack. The time and location shown on the document tied it to information on the "missing air crew report" he had retrieved from the U.S. National Archives. The burning engines were noted, but not the three parachutists, whose departures came after the dive.

"I must admit," I told Hans Berger, "that I was surprised to learn you had survived the war. Our fighters must have greatly outnumbered yours toward the end of 1944. We must have had you with odds at ten-to-one."

"Well, you are right," he said. "But your ratio is too low. The records show that the odds were nearer forty-to-one against us on many occasions."

Although he credited his survival to luck, it was certainly the skill and experience he developed during his many sorties. But also he told of some special measures he took to avoid getting destroyed while landing and taking off for refueling. That was the critical moment when a great many Luftwaffe fighters "bought the farm." Hans would mark some out-of-the-way landing strips on his map, seek them out, and avoid the regular aerodromes where Allied planes were waiting to make an easy "kill."

Reaching down beside his chair, Hans brought up a box. Carefully he opened it and removed a model of his FW-190 fighter plane, explaining that he had made it for me. It was carefully packaged with foam pellets, to protect the extended landing gear and three-bladed propeller, during the drive from Munich in his BMW. For a moment the significance of the gift made me choke up.

"Now, to make this totally unique," I asked, "would you be willing to write your name under the wing?"

He turned it over and inscribed: "In memory of our first encounter on 24 April 1944, Hans Berger."

What a treasure it will be for my young grandson, Jacob. As a small token of thanks I removed the small replica of my World War II wings from my lapel and insisted he accept the gift.

Appropriately, brother Dan walked in with one frame left on his camera film at that moment, after using most of it on the deer out in the field. He snapped the picture that tells the whole story of our extraordinary morning conference and exchange.

"For all this long time," said Hans, "I have not thought too deeply about the wartime experiences. But at our present advanced ages, and with all of the historic interest developed by Klaus Zimmer and the Oster Valley association, I was moved to come to Bubach and join you and to bring along these few mementos."

"Wunderbar!" I said. "Since we all survived our experiences, then we have no reason to be anything but thankful we are able to meet like this and share our memories."

When Cran came down I wanted to get some of his recollections of that aerial battle we fought with this man across the table. For all these many years I had had only my own memories.

9

Tail Gunners See Where They Have Been, Not Where They Are Going

At long last, down the stairs came my old buddy Cran Blaylock. Yes, the added fifty years were showing just a bit. It was the first time I had seen him since we said good-bye at Reims in May of 1945, just before boarding the Liberty ship for America.

"Last time I saw you," said Cran, exhibiting the sense of humor I remembered, "we were having lunch with General Eisenhower."

This was true. "Ike" had been visiting the temporary camp where returned prisoners were being fed and deloused, to welcome them all back into the U.S. Army, and he went through the chow line. He was far ahead of us in line, and by jumping we could just make out the top of his shiny head as he took off his cap.

Dan had returned from his walk by now, and we all decided to move into the dining area before the breakfast buffet disappeared.

What a joy to meet "old Cran" again. I use that term because he was the elder of the crew at age twenty-five, while some of us were still teenagers. There had been no conscious desire to forget old friendships from the prison camps, but we were spread over the whole USA after the war and each had a life to get on with. Time just slipped by, somehow.

We talked for only a few moments about the cold, crowded, and noisy barracks and the double eight-foot-high barbed-wire fences that surrounded us for eleven months, the guard towers and smelly latrine, and the gaunt, ragged crowd of POWs who seemed perpetually to be walking the perimeter wire, talking about food and making wild escape plans.

Before Klaus arrived to take us in hand for the day, Jo Ann

joined us at the breakfast buffet table. Now we learned the details about the Blaylocks' delayed arrival. It turned out there was a simple explanation. When leaving the Frankfurt airport they turned right instead of left. Later, stopping to ask—in English of course—how to get to Hassel, they found that there were many towns in Germany with names that sounded like "Hassel" when pronounced by Americans, especially Americans who had lived in Oklahoma most of their lives.

Much later the Blaylocks decided to stop and find the map Klaus Zimmer had sent. It was, of course, packed in their luggage. Then they went back and began over again. Although Jo Ann was acknowledged to be the driver, there was some question about who was to be navigator.

"Hans," I asked, "do Germans also have the habit of only reading instructions after all else has failed?"

He laughingly agreed that it was probably universal.

Klaus Zimmer, our anxious director of schedules, said to me, "Ed, you must reserve one and one-half hours so that I may review your book material with you. There are some corrections to be made. Also, I will give you some originals of maps and photographs you will be using."

While waiting for Dr. Egon Keller and other guests to arrive and join the tour on which we were to embark, Cran had a chance to sit in with a few questions for the German fighter pilot.

"How many of our airplane losses were you responsible for during the war?" was his first one.

"Well," Hans summed up, "my final record was forty sorties flown, five Flying Fortresses shot down, and two more forced out of formation. There was also a credit for one British Spitfire and some aircraft destroyed on the ground."

Now Cran had an important question: "Were you ever shot down yourself, Hans?"

"Oh, yes. I was a casualty on several occasions. There were two crash landings and two parachute jumps, and once I nosed over while landing. That usually resulted in explosion, but I was lucky it did not. I did spend some time in hospital, however."

We looked over his pilot wings and medals as he continued, "Two good friends who flew with me on April 24, 1944, each scored a four-motor American bomber. They were *Oberfeldwebel*

Toni Piffer and *Leutnant* Gottfried Just. Toni was shot down and killed during the invasion and was awarded the Knight's Cross posthumously. Gottfried was killed over the Ardennes at Christmas during our offensive you called 'the Battle of the Bulge.'

"One of the losses that affected me deeply," Hans continued, "was that of Johannes Rathenow. He was a *Feldwebel,* sergeant, in our *Staffel.* For a reason I do not recall we called him Bulette; you Americans would say, 'Meatball.'

"When I first got to 1/JG 1 as a young cadet I was assigned to him as his *Katschmarek.* A fine fellow, he proved to be an excellent flight instructor, teaching me all the tricks of the trade. He was helpful, too, in getting me settled as a newcomer to the *Staffel,* and we developed a personal friendship that continued after my advancement to *Leutnant,* even though our senior officers frowned on fraternization between commissioned and noncommissioned officers, just as yours probably did.

"On a sortie on November 3d, 1943, I was again flying beside him. As we attacked a group of *Vier-mots*, heavy bombers, our wings were not far apart when he was hit and his Focke Wulf was suddenly turned into a giant fireball. There was no chance of a bail-out.

"All we ever found among the wreckage that fell to earth was one of his shoulder straps. It was a painful experience for me.

"But my pain was not over. I was assigned to accompany the coffin to his hometown for the funeral. His mother wanted desperately to open the coffin to take one last look at her son and say good-bye. The whole experience became deeply engraved in the memory of this young man of only twenty birthdays.

"From that day there was an awkward feeling of anxiety with me as a companion in all my sorties. It happened to many, of course, and may explain the intensity of emotion we Luftwaffe pilots felt when we would hear the announcement on our PA system. 'Enemy bombers assembling over southeast England'!"

10

Return to the "Scene of the Crime"

After slipping his cellular phone back in his pocket, Dr. Egon Keller told of the arrangements for us to visit the huge U.S. Army base at Baumholder. But first we had to see our crash site and the square where we spent our first several hours on the ground in Germany in 1944. Baumholder then belonged to the Wehrmacht. We had "done time" in their guardhouse after leaving the dungeon at Kusel.

"Ed, please call me Egon," he said, running his hand over his head as though to smooth the hair no longer there. He was our guide, interpreter, and director, with expert aides Zimmer and President Kirsch to help. He looked and sounded, however, like one who ought to be addressed by his full title, *Herr Doktor Professor Keller*. Not only did Egon interpret what was said to us, but he also supplemented and expanded until there was no chance of an uncomprehended phrase. Of course, when appropriate, he could also delete with the same alacrity. There was a keen sense of humor behind his sparkling eyes, and with an easy smile, he was attentive to any comment we might make.

The travel party now included Walter Harth, native historian, musician, farmer, railroadman, and more. Another man of the same surname kept a videocamera running constantly, and a strange man who wore sandals and no hat in spite of the cold rain, and about whom we guests knew nothing, joined us, as did a young cameraman and reporter for the *Stars and Stripes* newspaper. Finally we were off for the nearby village of Bubach.

Cran and I talked a bit in the car.

"Nothing," he said, "in our training had prepared us for what we faced on that day in Bubach. Not knowing what might happen next was especially hard. Our fate was totally in the hands of the enemy, and we had all heard tales about their cruel treatment of non-Germans."

Klaus had been eager for Cran and me to walk with some of the villagers from the crash site into Bubach along the same route we were taken fifty-two years earlier. A sudden increase in the rain helped our protest, and we stayed in the cars until parked just below the open area we had remembered as the "village square," now inexplicably enclosed by chain-link fencing.

We stood in almost the precise location where we had stood as prisoners. Now our hosts held umbrellas over our heads while we looked about. It had been sunny on that day, but we remembered the chill that had crept in with the evening shadows.

Cran recalled a few other long-forgotten details.

"Isn't that the house where the woman went to get us water?"

While Egon was snapping pictures, Klaus responded, "Yes. That is the house. It was the *Burgermeister*'s niece who got the water for you."

As I pointed out the stone-faced building nearby, Cran remembered being marched inside, where we were made to take off flying clothes.

"Hamilton thought they were going to put us up against that wall and shoot us," I told Egon. Today as we looked out over the red roofs to the hill where our Flying Fortress had sat, I could tell by Cran's face that he, too, was reliving those hours we spent where we now were standing, fifty-two years and twenty-two days ago.

Others spoke to us, but we did not hear them. Dan was studying the area carefully. He had carried a picture of this village in his mind ever since I described it for him many years ago. During his air force occupation assignments he had driven through hundreds of small Bavarian and Saarland villages, wondering if one of them might be the one his big brother had described.

It was a relief to get back into the car and drive away. Bubach was a beautiful town, and its people today were warm and friendly. But the memories were too vivid. Even squeezing into Egon's BMW brought back thoughts of that last ride down the hill and out of town and the hardships to be endured during the year that followed.

Klaus had been right. It was not more than a half-hour drive to the city of Kusel, even though I had told him it seemed like many hours to me. Kusel had been the seat of district government in those days, but after postwar redistricting that seat was now at Saint Ingbert.

When we arrived at the Kusel *Rathaus,* or city hall, the *Burgermeister* was waiting to greet us. There was a small gathering of officials and a coffee reception laid out. I seemed to be alone in my enjoyment of the coffee and wonderful pastries, and I wondered if there was some protocol I might be violating. Apparently not, for others were just too busy with pictures and speeches.

Cran and I and ex–Luftwaffe pilot Hans were each requested to sign the ancient logbook of the city. Egon explained that it held notes of every major event in Kusel's long history and that this meeting would be forever preserved in its pages. We were each given a photocopy of the page and a city coat-of-arms plaque as gifts.

With the urging of the *Stars and Stripes* cameraman, we found the door to the dungeon across the street from what had been the police station. When several reporters invited Cran and me to go inside for a photo op, he asked me if we really ought to do it.

"Only if we feel bayonets in our back," I suggested.

We compromised by standing on the steps down which we had fallen or were pushed on our visit half a century earlier.

Riding back to the Wildpark, we arranged for a meeting with Hans after dinner, to exchange recollections of how Monday, April 24, 1944, had begun and what events had led up to our aerial confrontation.

11

April 24, 1944: How It Began

It was a Monday, and the predawn wake-up call came as a surprise to some of us. We thought we had a couple of days of "standdown" coming after surviving a few recent missions. When the CQ, charge-of-quarters, shook Hamilton's bunk, Bill told him he had the wrong bunk or maybe even the wrong barracks.

"Briefing at oh five hundred!" was the only response Bill got.

"Oh what the hell," someone said. "At least we get to have bacon and eggs for breakfast."

The thought of food made me a little nauseous as I considered facing German flak and fighters again so soon. We all believed that they only fed bacon and eggs to those who probably would not show up for breakfast the next day.

Bill and I would be subbing today for two gunners missing from Lieutenant Anthony's crew. We had not been with our own crew in over a week, but I could see that at least two of them had gotten the wake-up call, too. I would talk with them later, after briefing.

The ball turret was my assignment. It seemed to go with the "aircraft armorer" designation. Bill would not get his regular tail gun position. He objected when he saw that he was to handle a waist gun for this mission.

Sgt. John "Cran" Blaylock seemed to be the senior member of Lt. Dick Anthony's crew, and Bill said to him, "Hey, I'm a tail gunner. That's my job. Don't put me in the damn waist!"

After listening to his complaint, Cran said, "Well, you see, Bill, this plane already has a tail gunner and it's me. Take the waist."

I don't know why Bill liked the tail position. There was a lot of motion back there, and after some training flights I remember he had to scrape his frozen vomit off the fuselage.

Anthony's bombardier was assigned to the lead ship for this

mission. Sergeant Fields would move up to the nose-guns, and Bill would replace him. Navigator Bill DePaoli would release our bombs when he saw the leader's bombs go. Dick Anthony said his copilot, Ray Raney, was a good flyer who might have been aircraft commander if he'd called "tails" instead of "heads" when positions were assigned back in the States.

Ed Kolber was flight engineer and top turret gunner. Chalmer Wildman was radio operator. Irving Blank was the other waist gunner.

Sergeant Blank was a bit nervous about flying over Germany with an "H" stamped on his dog tag, rather than a "P" or "C" like we others had. This was the imprint to show what kind of last rites to administer when you were killed in action. We had heard about what was happening to Jews in the Third Reich, and no one was sure if we would each be identified simply as "American" if we became guests there.

Before the day was over and during the next many months this would be put to the test. We would all know a whole lot more about Germany and the war on the ground than we had learned in our briefings or read in the newspapers.

Before leaving our hut to head for breakfast and briefing, I put a letter to sister Doris in the outgoing mail slot. Some of the guys left farewell letters on their bunks, to be mailed if they didn't come back. I thought it would be bad luck to actually prepare to not come back, so I wiped it out of my mind.

"We're seasoned veterans, now, after only a few missions. Lady Luck seems to like us," I told Doris. She would be reading that letter in about three weeks, about the time the MIA telegram would be sent from Washington.

It was very dark and very damp as I followed the other bikers to the mess hall. Even though I had no appetite, I would force down enough to last until late this afternoon. I usually carried a Clark candy bar in my flight bag but never got a chance to eat it. We got the idea that the ground crews envied us our "hearty breakfast." Some actually envied our assignments and offered to change places with us.

Army coffee was described in a song as "good for cuts and bruises and tastes like iodine," but it was always hot and strong.

I had learned not to drink more than one cup before a mission. Whatever I drank had to stay with me until we got back and broke formation for landing. Only then could I climb out of the turret and use the relief tube, if it wasn't frozen solid, that is.

Inside the briefing hut, visibility was near zero from all the cigarette smoke. About a hundred men were milling around, but soon they all settled down and the voices softened. Someone near the door shouted, "Ten *hut!*" and we all jumped to our feet as the group CO walked to the front.

He gave a cheery greeting before motioning his S-2 officer to pull back the curtain covering the huge wall map of Europe. A long red string, starting at Podington, was attached to a series of pins. The string headed off toward Holland, then swung down into Germany, I couldn't see exactly where, but it seemed like a long way. The groans from the front rows meant that this would clearly not be classified a "milk run."

We were rapped to silence by the long pointer stick of the S-3 officer; then the whole mission was spelled out for us.

Earlier this month German transportation facilities and aircraft manufacturing plants were chosen as targets by those who set strategy for the Eighth Air Force. Down the line, targets for divisions and wings were selected and assigned. Some of the guys in my squadron had heard of the Dornier aircraft company, our target. None, however, had ever heard of Oberpfaffenhofen, the town near Munich where the huge plant was located.

Over fifty years later the "Obey" plant would be better known when "mission control" for Germany's space program was put there. As the Allies were unaware of how much of the facility had been placed underground, it was reported "destroyed" several times after attacks in 1944 and 1945. The structures and airfield facilities there are today's targets for our bomb group and for one other.

Now we got the weather forecasts, expected winds at various altitudes, and cloud conditions. The sites of antiaircraft batteries were marked, as were the locations of Luftwaffe "hunter" bases that would be put on alert by the time we became airborne.

As briefings ended there was often a little pep talk.

"We will strike a powerful blow against the German war machine and the German aircraft industry today. If you are successful, then the war will undoubtedly be shortened by months!" Some were even bold enough to state the number of months.

Another S-3 officer told about recent Luftwaffe fighter tactics, as reported at debriefings after recent missions. "It's going to be a long mission," gunners were told, "so conserve your ammunition."

The chaplain offered a special prayer for us, then announced that he would be available right up to takeoff time for any who needed his services. Last procedure was the "time-tick," when our watches were all synchronized. "Coming up; four, three, two, one . . . hack!" Now we felt we were all cogs in the same machine.

The noncoms were dismissed to go to the ready rooms. Pilots, navigators, and bombardiers had to stay for special briefings, so they gathered in the front to huddle over their maps and aerial recon photos.

With only a few missions behind me I still tried to learn by watching the men with more experience. It was a bit troubling that the newer ones were beginning to watch *me*. Some were putting on the electric suits right over their underwear, but I wore my wool OD shirt and pants. I used two pairs of socks under the electric felt shoes. The white scarf was tucked in tight to keep oxygen mask condensation from running down my neck. I pulled on the new "browns." This was the pants and jacket set designed for wear over the electrically heated liner. I wrapped my woolen scarf around the jacket collar so no skin would be exposed to that way-below-zero air up there.

Some of the men put on their leather flying jackets, but with the limited space in the ball turret I had no room for any more clothing. I tossed it into the flight bag.

By the time I strapped on the parachute harness and the Mae West life jacket, I was sweating. Picking up glove liners, electric gloves, sheepskin helmet, goggles, oxygen mask with built-in mike, and a throat mike, I placed them in my zippered flight bag, along with my GI shoes, sheepskin jacket, flak vest, and steel helmet. I couldn't wear the armor in the turret but might want it if I had to evacuate while over Germany. This is not intended to be a double entendre, but I had heard that the steel helmet was sometimes useful to "evacuate" when a guy was unable to wait until he got back to base or perhaps had it "scared out of him."

Before heading for the parachute shop to pick up the chest pack, each flyer got a package called an "escape kit." It had all sorts of items that would come in handy in case we went down in enemy territory, including money: French francs and German marks. "It makes a nice present for the Germans when they capture you," someone commented.

I had earlier sewn two compass needles into hems of my OD shirt and pants as my own personal escape kit. We were told to check in personal items that the enemy should not see. I kept only my wallet with a picture of a girlfriend. There was no name or other identification showing.

Assigned to the Anthony crew, Hamilton and I tagged along as our new comrades headed out to a lorry and climbed aboard. The driver threaded his way to the hardstand where our assigned Fortress was parked. It was a new G model, just like the one we ferried over (could it be?) all shiny aluminum and with a new gun turret in the nose.

Crawling under the belly, I pulled down the ball-turret door and took a look inside. The two guns had been cleaned and were sitting by the turret, and I examined them carefully to be sure they were assembled right. Mounting one in each side, I leaned in to connect the gun charging cables and the ammo chutes, admiring the turret's compactness. It was the last time I would ever have this view of the ball turret, because within a few hours it would be ground into scrap metal.

The other gunners seemed to be all set with their guns, so I had plenty of time to do the armament checklist inside. The eight quarter-ton bombs were all mounted in the bay, and I examined them closely to be sure that each shackle was solidly mounted on the rack and that all of the release and arming levers were in their slots. "There is no such thing as a completely 'safe' bomb," was one lesson I had drummed into me at the Lowry Field armament school. All of the safety pins and arming wires were just where they should be, and the bomb bay doors were secured.

Back outside in the dim light of dawn I looked up at the four Wright Cyclone engines for reassurance. We called them "Wright

Rattlers" in fun. They were really dependable and powerful engines, with their huge nine-foot propellers. On this dim and damp morning if any of us noticed that the nose of Boeing's number 297218 airplane was inscribed with the name *Toonerville Trolley* then it has long since been forgotten. We all remembered that there was no figure there, such as the scantily dressed or undressed girls that were painted on some of the Fortresses.

I know that the name was clearly painted there, because I have seen a fifty-two-year old picture of it, sitting on its crushed belly on a hillside near the little village of Bubach, in what used to be Bavaria.

The crash landing there was the major historic event of the war for people of the nearby villages. Historian Klaus Zimmer was able to find many pictures in family albums as he collected material for a documentary publication named "Die Fliegende Festung bei Bubach." For three or more generations everyone in the village recognized the name *Toonerville Trolley* as a part of their history.

Numbers on the tail were used by Klaus to find out about this B-17-G Boeing bomber and that its flight had originated at bomber station number 109 in England, with the Ninety-second Bomb Group and 326th Bomb Squadron. Missing air crew reports are accessible when one can provide numbers and dates. From this report Klaus learned the names of the ten men aboard and the report that it had been last seen near Thallichtenberg, going down with two engines on fire. Then he doggedly sought out those of the *Toonerville Trolley* crew who might still be alive.

To many Americans of our generation, reading the "funnies" was often the high point of each Sunday morning. One of the popular strips was by Fontaine Fox, and the title was *Toonerville Folks*.

Featured in that strip was a rickety old streetcar, or trolley car, that seemed always to be jumping off the tracks. Its mad little driver, with a corncob pipe clamped in his jaws and his engineer's cap, was called "the Skipper."

Lt. Dick Anthony was anything but a "mad little driver." He was a strong, handsome guy with plenty of piloting skills, and so far, the B-17s assigned to him had been kept "on the track."

Today all of his strength and skills would be needed to get us to the aircraft factory that was our target, then safely to the ground.

The three officers were the last out to the hardstand. The two pilots did their preflight checks, walking around our Flying Fortress and pulling at all movable surfaces, kicking tires, and checking to be sure the cover was off the Pitot tube and caps were on the fuel tanks.

Pushing their packs up through the forward hatch, each man grabbed the rim, pulling himself up and in, feet first. There is a scene in the old movie *Twelve O'clock High* where group commander Gregory Peck, after some rough missions, finds himself psychologically unable to pull himself up and into that hatch and has to be replaced for that mission. Many experienced the feeling, knowing they might very well be struggling back out of that tiny hatch, high over enemy territory, rip cord in hand, before many hours had passed.

The crew chief slammed the door shut behind them, then backed away to a point where Dick could see his signals through the open cockpit window by his left shoulder. All ten of us were on board now. The pilots' checklists were reviewed, and we awaited the precise second for starting engines. But racing against the clock, one of the crew leaped out the waist door for a final bladder emptying, or perhaps to throw up that special breakfast he had just enjoyed.

Finally a green flare went shooting up from the little balcony on the control tower, and one by one our engines turned over, blasting clouds of smoke and dirt rearward.

The sounds grew to an overwhelming roar, and we were able to talk with one another only on the intercom system. I plugged my headset into an outlet on the bomb-bay wall of the radio room, where I was stationed during takeoff. When copilot Raney said, "Here comes our number," he meant the airplane we were assigned to follow had left its hardstand and was moving toward us.

Chocks were pulled, wheel brakes released, and we started bouncing along out onto the taxiways, joining up with the wingmate who would take off with us. We lined up offset so as to avoid each other's prop wash.

The takeoff roll began with all four engines under full power, but our slow rate of acceleration was not reassuring. We couldn't help but think of those tons of bombs and gasoline on board and that line of trees out at the end of the runway. There were some landscape scars and filled-in craters out there to remind us that some had not made it into the air. I'm sure that all ten of us were heisting our bottoms a bit to help the bomber lift off and become converted from a rolling express train into a flying machine.

Finally I could feel that the wheels were no longer contacting the runway and I heard. "Gear up."

As the long climb toward the departure altitude began there was time to go in and arm the bombs. I did it by pulling the tagged safety pins from fuses at either end, pocketing them carefully because each must be accounted for later. Now only the arming wire, controlled by the bombardier up front, was keeping the bombs "safe."

Before we got to oxygen altitude, 10,000 feet, I moved back to the waist, unlocked the ball turret, and moved the hydraulic controls to bring the door inside the fuselage. Through the open door I looked straight down at the earth. That first step into the turret was what took an "oh, what the hell" attitude, and it might be a reason why there was rarely a contest for the position. Settling in, I bent forward and secured the two latches behind my head, plugged myself into the oxygen supply, then the electrical and intercom systems.

The ball turret had a bad reputation for casualties. If the plane went out of control or if power was lost, there could be a real problem in getting out. It was a tight fit, and I couldn't wear my parachute, armored vest, or steel helmet. After many hours in this position my feelings sometimes went beyond discomfort and approached pain. But at least I could move the turret so as to either sit up straight with head bent or lie back with legs horizontal.

Top gunner and engineer Ed Kolber's turret was also hydraulic. He was in a semiseated position with a sling seat. He could get down and use a walk-around oxygen bottle when he had to transfer gas or help the pilots out with something. Ed used a computing gun sight like mine.

Cran Blaylock, back in the tail under the high rudder, had twin fifties, hand-operated, and a ring-and-post sight. It was not a very relaxing position back there, either squatted or half-kneeling on a bicycle seat. If the waist was open then there was a blast of subzero air behind him.

Pilot Dick Anthony asked for a response from each position and a check to make sure we were on oxygen. I reported, "Ball turret OK," then settled back to watch the gathering of the squadrons into group, and group into division, before our whole formation wheeled and headed for the enemy coast.

12

"Defenders of the Reich" Getting Ready

German "hunter" planes were alerted as soon as our groups were detected forming over East Anglia. The Luftwaffe pilots were up and making preparations even while we were still at briefing.

One of those pilots, Hans Berger, tells how the day begins to unfold for him on that April 24, 1944:

> At Jagdgeschwader 1 in Bad Lippspringe we got up at about five o'clock and were taken out to our "berth." This is a wooden hut alongside the landing field of the aerodrome. Sometimes we sit here on alert all day long, but today it will be only a few hours. We fifteen pilots in our squadron have our own cook at the berth and we are served breakfast without getting very far from our airplanes.
>
> The FW-190s are lined up at a distance of only fifty yards away. A mechanic is assigned to each plane, keeping it ready for takeoff on very short notice.
>
> My assigned plane has a white number 8 on the fuselage. Pilots do have some superstitions, and I always feel a bit uneasy when I fly an airplane other than this one. If my "Number 8" needs repair and there is no spare, then I will stay on the ground.
>
> On this Monday morning there is a blue sky and bright sunshine. When the weather is bad— "QBI," we call it—then we cannot fly. Our Focke-Wulfs are not equipped for instrument flight. There have been times when we were sent up in bad weather, but we had much difficulty in getting back down safely.
>
> We pass time playing cards or chess, reading, or just chatting and sleeping. Our first warning this morning comes about half past seven. As we listened to soft pop music over the loudspeaker, it was interrupted by an announcement.
>
> "Accumulations of enemy bombers are over southeast England."
>
> This means action!
>
> When the bomber formations have crossed the continental

coastline we are ordered into our aircraft and to stay ready.

There is a popular song, "Sing nightingale. Sing a song of bygone times..." and when this is played over the PA system then we know that takeoff will follow right away. For many young Luftwaffe pilots, it is the last music they ever hear.

At 12:42 P.M. the order comes. The takeoff sequence will be group staff, First, Second, then Third Squadrons. We start our engines.

When a red signal cartridge is fired, off we go, side by side. Each of the squadrons takes off right from its berth, regardless of the wind direction. When one is airborne then a green flare is fired and the next squadron takes off, but in the opposite direction, and so on until all are in the air.

We are to head for Mannheim, the aerodrome closest to our intercept location. I get an awkward feeling in my stomach because one or more of our deck chairs are sometimes empty when a squadron returns from such action. One is always afraid that the empty deck chair may be his own.

13

Under Way and under Fire

The gatherings and dividings of groups and wings were visible to me from my position in the B-17 *Toonerville Trolley*. After "wheels-up" it took more than an hour to climb to our assigned altitude and assemble into the "Angel's Ladder" pattern. Today there was no thick ground fog or cloud cover to penetrate as we climbed. I noticed only one or two B-17s aborting, turning back to base. There were supposed to be spares waiting to fill in, but I didn't happen to see them.

As we moved out over the English Channel, the crew chatted a little on the intercom, helping to reduce the tension. I had not yet gotten used to this crew and was not sure about their procedures, so I kept quiet. Every crew developed its own pattern of chatting and communicating, and they recognized each other's voices on the intercom. Only waist gunner Hamilton knew mine.

As we went on oxygen at 10,000 feet, the pilot had each position check in, then said, "OK to clear your guns any time now."

We had not yet loaded shells into the guns' chambers, for safety reasons. Now we did it by pulling the charging handle on each gun. I felt the vibrations as the others fired quick bursts of five or six rounds. Then I made sure there were no B-17s in my line of sight, snapped on the gun safety switches, and pressed the thumb buttons on my control levers. There were explosions beside my thighs, and empty brass shells flew out exit ports under the receivers. But the metal links that bound them together spilt inside and down onto my viewplate. Picking them up, I poked them out through the holes under each gun where the link-ejection chute had been removed. It seemed that a ball-turret gunner recently got a "link-jam" in one of the chutes, so all were removed. I thought that for the next mission I would re-install mine, to save this clutter and to stop that tiny blast of frigid slipstream that hits my legs when my turret is turned toward either side.

As we crossed over the French coast we seemed to be standing still, even though our ground speed was well over two hundred. There was a good tailwind now, but I would prefer to have it on the way home.

As we went inland, black puffs of antiaircraft fire dotted the sky ahead. When they began to appear close to our squadron I tried to shrink my body into a smaller target. One or two showed red centers, meaning that they were close. None had been reported hitting our plane, so far.

A whole lot of big guns were firing at us, but I couldn't see where they were from this height. Soon the black flak clouds faded away behind us and it became easier to concentrate on watching for the tiny specks that might turn out to be enemy fighter planes ready to pounce.

It was now 11:05 and all the Eighth Air Force bombers were reported to have crossed the French coast between the Somme and Seine rivers. All were headed for Luxembourg up to this point.

But now we divided into two streams. One headed north toward Stuttgart, while the second split, half heading toward Augsburg. The other half, including the Ninety-second Bomb Group, steered for the Munich area.

We were all after aircraft facilities, one group even striking for the Zeppelin Works at Friedrichshafen. One unit got diverted to a secondary when the Germans put up a smoke screen at their primary target. They would bomb the NSU Works at Neckarsulm, instead.

There were some B-24 Liberator groups along, and they struck at the Augsburg area and the airfields at Gablingen and Leipheim. They had some high explosives, but they would also be dropping half a million leaflets. (Over fifty years later I was shown some of the leaflets in a German scrapbook and wondered if they really convinced anyone on the ground that the war was lost.)

An hour after we had crossed the coastline, hundreds of our fighter planes began crossing also. They provided an escort for us "heavies" but also were to provide a "screen" to keep defensive fighters up north. They were mostly made up of P-38 Lightnings and P-47 Thunderbolts.

We had been told that our strategy was a part of a long-range plan to reduce German air power and to gain air superiority before the Allied forces dared to begin the invasion. Hitler and Goering had to be familiar with such a plan. It was not too different from theirs of four years earlier when hundreds of Luftwaffe bombers and fighters struggled for air superiority over England so that Operation Lion, the German invasion, could begin.

Our group and the 384th, of the Forty-first "Triangle B" Wing, were now committed to a beeline for the Dornier Aircraft Works at Oberpfaffenhofen, near Munich.

Looking straight down, I could see the symmetrical patterns of towns and farmlands four miles below. I wondered what people thought when they heard the thunder of our engines approaching. Back in England, even when I knew they were "friendlies" the sound raised the hair on the back of my neck. Ernie Pyle, reporter for the *Stars and Stripes* newspaper, once said, "The sound is deep and all-encompassing, with no notes in it, just a gigantic, faraway surge of doom."

Each of our Fortresses left four spinning streams of vapor behind, and all of them merged far to our rear. The vapor trails got so thick that the whole sky appeared overcast behind us.

Unfortunately, those trails were also long white arrows, each pointing directly at one of us.

Time seemed to stand still as we proceeded deeper into Germany and toward our target. I could see only eighteen bombers in my field of view. Some American fighter escort planes I had seen earlier were nowhere in sight. We might have gotten beyond their range and they went home. Continuing to sweep the lower half of the sky, I heard the nose gunner reporting fighters far out ahead. Top Turret reported some might also be between us and the sun. Sergeant Fields was twitching the chin turret nervously from side to side. We still had not come under direct attack, except for the heavy antiaircraft fire that came up in great clouds.

Bombardier Bill DePaoli finally said that the target was in

view, and he took control of the plane for the bombing run. Now was the "sitting duck" part of the mission, as we had to stay straight and level for the sighting procedures, which seemed to take hours. Flak bursts got heavier as we approached the Dornier works. The black puffs looked impenetrable. I reminded myself that it was mostly from shells that exploded while we were still approaching. It was only those that had not yet appeared that could hurt us.

The bomb-bay doors swung down right in front of me. Suddenly the big iron bombs with their square fins dropped within only a few feet of my viewplate.

"Bombs away!" was the welcome call, and I felt a little bounce as the plane became a couple of tons lighter. Tilting the turret down, I counted them, just to be sure there were no hang-ups in the bay. There were eight, and each of the fuses had become "armed" as the little propellers spun off. The bombs tipped downward and drifted far to our rear.

As Dick Anthony took back control of the plane I watched the bomb-bay doors close. Someone said, "Let's get the hell out of here!" As we gently banked away with the formation, I moved the turret to keep the bombs in view for just a bit longer before they became too small to follow.

My search of the sky for enemy fighters was so intense that I needed to rotate the turret continually to change perspective. Now I rotated downward to check on the Dornier aircraft factory we had targeted. There were huge explosions occurring down there, and I could see where the bombs were striking among the many structures.

Giant shock rings shot outward and upward. One blast sent a perfect smoke ring rolling into the sky. Most bombs seemed to be striking in the factory and airstrip complex, but some of them were opening craters in nearby vacant fields.

Pressing my mike switch, I gave a quick description of the damages being created below, adding, "Someone wasted the trip. His load only rearranged some turf out in a field!"

Another pilot with whom I had flown might have said, "Thanks for sharing that with us, Ed. Now let's get back to our jobs." Dick Anthony was a little more direct. "Keep quiet and watch for fighters," he said.

U.S. Air Force historical records say it was a good job: "The attack by the 92nd and 384th bomber groups of the 41st Wing on 24 April climaxed about fourteen hundred hours and was considered by the German high command to be the heaviest against the Dornier works to date, possibly because of its high precision."

The rearranged turf in the field was not mentioned.

Beyond the USAF report, in 1996 Klaus Zimmer provided details from the Dornier company's archives in Friedrichshafen, including aerial photos of this day's bomb damage. Their forty buildings had been widely dispersed to limit the damage, he learned. All utilities were installed in concrete tunnels below the floors and thus were not destroyed.

The complex was hit on nine different dates, including strafing by fighters throughout the war. Many completed aircraft were destroyed before they could be shipped out. The number of Dornier 217s, 335s, and Messerschmitt 410s "shot down" without ever having gotten into the sky totaled 367. Overall bombing damage was calculated at over 35 million Reichsmarks.

14

"Attack the Four-Engine Bombers"

Hans Berger and his *Staffel* of 1 JG/1 were now back in the air. This is how he described it:

By 1425 hours we have refueled and gotten takeoff orders from Mannheim to attack the four-engine American bombers. They are by now on a westerly heading. We will be guided by our ground station while we climb to their altitude and until we make visual contact.

Hardly anyone says a word on the radio now. Sitting here in our cockpits, each man alone, we are tense and anxious about the massive firepower we are about to challenge.

Climbing to over 25,000 feet, we keep an intense lookout; then someone calls, "Thick autos left ahead." *Autos* is our code word for the *Vier-mots,* or four-motored bombers. Now the ground station remains silent and we hear only the voice of our commander:

"We turn left to attack. Don't start firing too soon. Don't dive off too late. We pull to the right and will reassemble five minutes northeast of the bomber formation."

There is no time to be afraid anymore. Although I am aware of the shells swishing by to the right and left, I try to shrink inside myself, tucked in behind the bulky engine of my FW 190. My entire aircraft must be aimed at the enemy, since my cannons are rigidly mounted, meaning I must stare through my reflector sight right at his guns.

Fixing one of the B-17s in the lighted circle of the gunsight, I pull the trigger. At the same instant the thought flashes in my mind, *Good God, it's too late.*

With a desperate push of the stick I dive below it, my plane shaken like a leaf by the bomber's prop wash.

Just as suddenly comes a feeling of great relief. They didn't get me! Not this time at least. With that relief comes a terrible lonely feeling, because there is no sign of the others of my squadron.

After a while I can make out a few metallic dots far off in the sky, but how can I be sure if they are friend or foe? Approaching very cautiously, it is a great relief to recognize them as my own "Little Brothers" (our fighters) and not "Indians" (enemy fighters).

We are all accounted for, and we have taken a toll of the bombers.

Official 1 JG/1 records show that Hans Berger's hits on the *Toonerville Trolley* were witnessed by comrades and coordinated with the reports of witnesses to the *Notlandung* at Bubach.

Two other 1 JG/1 pilots also hit bombers of the Ninety-second Bomb Group that day, and each would eventually be credited with an *Abschuss* on his record.

Eighth Air Force historical records show that a second wave of American fighter planes was dispatched to meet us after the bombing run, to escort us back to England. German air defense units reported sightings of P-47 and P-51 type aircraft between Verdun and Malmedy beginning at 1345 hours and directed their hunters to interception courses.

Antiaircraft guns were creating hundreds of bursts around the B-17s in the general target area, and the gap in the escort did not go unnoticed, now the first wave had turned back toward England. Luftwaffe Central Control directed the German fighters to move in while they had this advantage.

What an opportunity Cran and I now had, with Hans Berger here, to get the Luftwaffe point of view. Hans was an active "hunter" in his FW190E as the techniques evolved and through most of the final months of the air war. Why had they decided to attack "head on"? He leaned on his elbows for a moment, then began with these recollections:

How should we attack the American bomber formations? In the fall of 1943 there was much debate about this. I think that it was about the time of your experience in the *Toonerville Trolley* that the frontal attack was determined to be especially effective.

Obviously it would be best to climb to a higher altitude and then come out of the sun to dive down on you from behind. But on your way to Germany from England your bombers were heading east, flying toward the sun. Coming from behind meant attacking from the west and being seen very early. And that meant plenty of aiming time for all the many gunners in your formation. Our losses were accordingly high when this happened.

When Maj. Emil Schnoor, the commanding officer of the First Group of *Jagdgeschwader* 1 suggested we should attack from the front, many at first said it was a crazy idea. From a distance of half a mile, the maximum range of our 20mm cannon, we had only about four seconds in which to aim, fire, and then dive away to avoid collision.

Well, this Major Schnoor came from the north of Germany, and some people from that area are said to possess a certain "perseverance." Others just say they are stubborn in pursuing something that is already settled in their minds. So he made us fly a few sorties that way and, indeed, the more experienced pilots did succeed in marking a few hits. But above all, our death toll was lowered remarkably.

The tactic proved to be even more advantageous, as the bombers got long-range fighter escort. Gaining good altitude a hundred miles or so farther to the east, we could launch our first attack with the sun at our backs, thus having one pass at you before you could see us. If your "four-mots" were without escorts we were usually able to regroup, move around forward, and make a second attack.

Our 20mm cannons had a longer range than your fifty-caliber machine guns. Much American ammunition was fired at us before we came into range, but we cannot underrate the effect on the German pilot of seeing tracer bullets streaking out at him as he begins his attack. Even though not accurate, they could rattle a fighter pilot into using faulty judgment.

It was about the time of your final battle in April 1944 when things got worse. As American escorting fighters increased their range, the Thunderbolts, Mustangs, and Lightnings came down on us like birds of prey, and each of us was left to his own devices.

We asked Hans if any of the rare collisions of fighter and bomber may have been intentional. He thought it improbable.

"As your air raids grew ever more devastating during 1944," he said, "we Luftwaffe pilots heard about a new order coming from very high up in our command.

"We would be required to ram the four-mot if we did not succeed in shooting it down!

"Oh, there were rumors that a few pilots had actually tried it, but probably the majority of us lacked the necessary kamikaze mentality. Later we learned that some of the very highly decorated Luftwaffe aces had persuaded the Supreme Command they should not pursue this idea further."

15

"Abbeyville Kids" Join the Attack

The Luftwaffe fighter pilots of Jagdgeschwader 26 were known to flyers of the Eighth Air Force as the "Abbeyville Kids," a name used with deep respect. They were highly rated by both sides. When our route took us across the Channel anywhere near the Abbeyville Aerodrome then we knew we were in for trouble, whether or not we were escorted by our own fighters.

On April 24, 1944, they were not there. However, our relief was temporary. They had been relocated to the Munich area, right where we were going, because Berlin had suspected the Allies might remember that it was the birthday of the Nazi Party, which had been born in Munich.

JG/26 generally flew Messerschmitts, but their historians say that Hauptman Herman Staiger flew a Focke Wulf 190 on this particular day. It had a thirty-millimeter cannon in its nose instead of the customary twenty-millimeter weapon. He ordered his men to prepare for direct frontal attack on the bomber group as they dropped their bombs and approached his sector.

This would be the first such attack for one pilot, and he claimed that the sensation of going straight through an enemy formation, with all those machine guns firing at him, was totally frightening and indescribable. With closing speed well over 500, the prop wash of the "Viermots" tossed him about as he went through their tight formation.

There were only a few seconds in which to aim and fire at any individual airplane, and as with Hans Berger, the loss of contact with his *Staffel* and the sudden loneliness of the empty sky far behind the bombers were unnerving.

Through the intercom system in *Toonerville Trolley* came the sudden warning from both nose and top turrets:

"Here they come! Fighters! Twelve o'clock! Right at us!"

Many Focke Wulf 190s swept in with all guns firing, either

passing straight through or doing a snap roll to dive under us. Two that did the roll showed me their armored bellies for just an instant and then were gone, much too fast for my turret to move and for me to frame one in my sight and fire. That didn't prevent me from squeezing off a burst in their general direction, futile as it might be.

It seemed incredible there were no collisions, especially since we suddenly dropped about fifty feet in reaction to all those guns blazing at Dick's windshield. As we did, I became weightless and the loose belt links in my turret became flying projectiles around my head and in my gun sight.

Others in the squadron were taking evasive action, too. I hoped they were coordinated, as one B-17 seemed to be only twenty or thirty feet below me. If he suddenly evaded upward then I would be the filling in a sandwich.

Up front, Fields had spotted even more dark specks out ahead at one o'clock, starting a turn to make a pass at us. In the top turret Kolber was keeping an eye on some Messerschmitt 109s that might come at us out of the sun any minute.

Our formation was anything but tight right now. There might be some adjustment going on to fill a gap left by one lost B-17, the one I could see drifting back below us leaving a trail of smoke. I hadn't seen any bodies or chutes coming out of it.

More fighters coming straight in, "twelve o'clock." As one rolled down and away I was able to track him briefly and fire a quick burst. At the rate of twenty per second, then I probably sent thirty or forty projectiles in his direction. Half my bullets were armor-piercing, and half were incendiaries. I saw a little dark smoke trailing him; then what appeared to be his cockpit canopy flew off and he pulled up almost vertical. For a split second the black crosses on his wings were clearly in view. He was way out of range now, and I quickly spun forward again.

"Who's that firing?" I thought it was the pilot asking, and one of the waist gunners answered, "That was the ball turret."

I realized that I should have announced what I was doing, but things were just happening too fast. Maybe my breach of crew etiquette would be forgotten by the time we got back to base and were debriefed.

Even as the arrival of some of our "Little Friends" was reported there was yet another frontal attack by the Focke Wulf 190 fighters. Ed Kolber saw some breaking in from two o'clock, and as the pilots spotted them they could see flashes along their wings. More explosive projectiles were coming at their windshields, and Dick reacted by shoving the control column forward hard. Too late; we were hit.

Copilot Raney and waist gunner Blank could see flames shooting from the engines on the right side, and those two props were "windmilling." Ed Kolber and his top turret had been hit.

Something slammed into my ball turret and dazed me. Was it a cannon shell or a piece of one of our engines? I must have seen something coming, since my hands went up in front of my face. Now my fingers were numb and my gloves were torn. There was a blast of wind hitting me, and I was not able to grip the control handles to move the turret. Some objects went streaking past me, and one of them was a huge three-bladed propeller, certainly from a B-17.

Moving the controls with my wrists was ineffective. The turret was stuck with guns pointing at twelve o'clock and my door wouldn't open into the fuselage unless they were pointed straight down. I had to move it manually. Slapping some feeling into my hands, I reached behind my head for a crank, taking what seemed an eternity to mount it on the shaft and begin turning it. If I could stop that numbing blast of slipstream then maybe I could do other necessary things.

In my state of semicontrolled panic, did I only imagine I heard the "bail out" order? One of those objects flying past me may have been a man curled around his chest-pack parachute.

In the cockpit Lieutenants Anthony and Raney had front-row seats as Hans Berger and his *Staffel* mates came boring in. This is what Anthony has remembered about the experience all these many years:

For the pilots, frontal attacks are more nerve-wracking than those from side or rear. I am sure the German fighters' gun sights are projected right onto my windshield. As they ripped through our formation and down under I had looked directly at the gun flashes on the wing edges of one of them. I am sure he was looking at the flashes from our nose, top, and ball turret guns also.

There are explosions. We are hit bad this time.

In an instant we have lost all power on the right wing. There were hits right above my head someplace. Raney and I both reach for the controls as flames begin to shoot out of numbers three and four engines. Two urgencies: get those flames out and feather those props. It is surprising how much thinking can be done in only a few seconds, when that is all one has. I run down a list in my mind: assess our injuries, ability to stay in the air, and danger of blowing up. Will the Germans attack again? The crew is told to throw overboard anything not essential to staying in the air, guns, ammunition, radios, tools . . . and I decide to try and blow out the fires in the engines.

Two of our P-47s pull alongside and I wave them off, struggling to keep the right wing up and pushing the nose down as steeply as I can. We quickly gain speed. Raney hasn't been able to get the props feathered, but the fires are going out. Now the men can be given an option.

"Bail out, or stay with it and we'll try for a ditching!" I order.

Cran Blaylock has checked on my engineer, Ed Kolber, who got blasted out of the top turret, and has gone back to spread the word. It will be a risky try with power only on the left wing and a poor selection of landing sites below. I have no intention of bailing out myself as long as I can keep the plane moving toward France.

We have few options left for a crash-landing site. We need to see not only an open approach but a run-out area to stop us before we rupture the tanks or come apart. It is hilly and there are scattered trees. We are using brute force on the rudder now and fighting to keep the nose up. As I make a shallow bank toward a fairly open hilltop another engine quits.

We touch ground just before reaching the brow of the hill, lose some parts, bounce up over the crest, and go sliding down the back side with no ability at all to control direction. Only later did we see what had pulled us to the left, away from the woods and disaster which lay at the bottom of the hill.

A large cherry tree was lodged in the wing, next to the cockpit.

Long afterward, Raney told me that he recalled us sliding past a farmer with ox and plow, looking straight ahead of him and making a nice neat furrow across the hill.

Eyewitnesses in the towns below, according to the research

of Klaus Zimmer, reported what they saw as the Fortress came down:

"At 1507 hours, one of the bombers is dropping out of its formation, north of Thalichtenberg. Two engines are burning."

"From outside Pfeffelbach we saw a body come out of the bomber; then a parachute opened and drifted over the town of Kusel."

"A second and third parachute are seen opening behind the crippled bomber and now three are in the air. The airplane's heading will take it over Herchweiler."

"A bomber with two of its four engines stopped is now passing between Reichweiler and Pfeffelbach, flying very low over the Stauderwald forest. It is heading toward Herchweiler and is continuing its descent."

This last could have been the report of woodcutters Ewald Neu and his grandfather. Ewald later made a drawing of what he saw and in 1996 he presented it to the historians for use in their publications.

16

A Most Unusual Day in Bubach

In the little Bavarian village of Bubach it was a lovely spring day, the Monday afternoon of April 24. Many of the people of these Oster Valley towns were working in the fields that lay on the hillsides surrounding their homes. It was clear, warm, bright, and pleasant.

But a distant thunder could be heard. Many heavy airplanes were approaching, but only their vapor trails could be seen, miles up in the blue sky. Such things had been seen before, and it was expected that the enemy would pass on toward faraway aerodromes and factories. German "chaser" planes were up there, too. Tiny dots left their own curving vapor trails, making watchers below aware that an aerial battle was under way.

But soon the villagers saw and heard something startling. A four-engine American bomber was diving downward, fire and smoke streaming behind it. A parachute was seen emerging, then another and another. Nearer and nearer it came, losing altitude rapidly and finally touching down on the nearby hill called Buberg. There was a tearing, crunching sound from the hillside; then all was still.

Field workers were awestruck. People ran out from the village, and news of the event spread like wildfire throughout the Oster Valley. A migration of people began, all hurrying from every direction toward the Buberg hill, on foot and via bicycle and wagon, to marvel at this strange happening.

What German Witnesses Saw

Another view of the *Toonerville Trolley*'s crash landing, is taken from the Bubach village history, enlarged upon after research by Walter Harth, grandson of the man who was a leader

70

in capturing some members of the crew and marching them to the square.

Notlandung auf dem Buberg [Emergency Landing on the *Buberg*]

[It was 3:15 P.M. when the farmers in the fields] near the Buberg looked up to see a huge airplane gliding down on them. It was an enemy bomber. Skimming over the Klingelberg hill, it seemed that it must touch down there.

It did barely clear the hill however, and the plane with only one of its four engines working rushed toward the Buberg hilltop at a sharp angle, hitting the ground on the upward side toward the village of Marth, just in front of the path which passed over the hilltop. As it struck the earth a propeller was torn off one of the right side engines, along with some other pieces.

The plane was airborne again for only a few seconds; then it struck on the downward side of the hill. One of the cherry trees on the hill was torn out of the ground and swept along with the left wing. It turned to the left as it slid, finally coming to a stop, and all was still for a few moments .There was a long furrow plowed in the earth where it had slid. The swing to the left caused by the cherry tree, may have stopped the huge plane in its downhill plunge toward the nearby Saubosch forest. Watchers later remarked on the extraordinary skill of the pilot, but also on the extreme good luck contributing to the survival of those still inside the crippled bomber.

* * *

Seated against the bomb-bay bulkhead, with hands clasped behind my head, I felt a giant slam from below. My head was driven down onto my parachute. *Can we be down?* I thought.

But then came a prolonged crash that seemed to go on and on. We had bounced off the hilltop and become airborne for a couple of seconds. We four were tossed around and ended sprawled together in a heap. The sudden silence was almost shocking.

A thick cloud of dust filled the fuselage. We had scooped up bushels of earth from the field, folding back the blades of the three remaining propellers as we slid down the hill. We were aware that there was a lot of high-octane gasoline still in the wing tanks and were expecting fire or explosion at any second.

Scrambling for the open hatchway overhead, we pushed the first man out; then he turned to help the others. The fires had been on the right wing, so we slid down the left side of the fuselage, right into the branches of a tree.

For all these years I thought we had destroyed a whole orchard. The local people with pictures taken by their older relatives point out now that it was just a single cherry tree. We had uprooted it when we struck the hilltop and dragged it along. The escape hatch up front, under the *Toonerville Trolley* lettering, was jammed into the earth, along with the chin turret. But the two men in the nose had already gone, bailed out. The pilots, and wounded engineer now had to crawl back through the bomb bay and radio room. The dust was settling now, and they could see that there was a clear path, past the crumpled ball turret, to the open waist hatch on the right side of the plane.

Dick took a good look at Kolber's injury and told him to stay near the plane and surrender to the Germans, since he needed more medical help than he could get from men on the run. Noting some of us heading down the hill, Dick and his copilot, Raney, dodged around the tail and ran for the woods in another direction. I was just returning to the plane to get my shoes when I saw them disappear. (That was the last time I would see Dick until 1996 in Tennessee.)

And now the shock of reality hit me. I was alive, but on the ground deep in the heart of Nazi Germany, and would not be going back to my base, nor to my home in New Hampshire, probably ever again.

Hanging the GI shoes around my neck, I headed at a trot across the hillside shedding what was left of my equipment as I went. There were trails of chute harness, life vests, helmets, headsets, oxygen masks, and goggles accumulating in the field. A woman farm worker was standing not far away taking it all in.

Klaus Zimmer learned, in his research, that someone had approached her and asked, "Are you French? Are we in France?"

She had stared at him without understanding, but placing the bucket she carried between herself and this strange creature who was making strange sounds.

Others could be seen in the distance, approaching with some speed, and I set my course for a small pile of branches that was only a few hundred feet away. I would never make it into the woods.

In research for the 1996 documentary, members of the Oster Valley association interviewed many eyewitnesses to the crash.

Mathilde Schlemmer had been spreading dung on the field. Never in her life had she seen such a giant airplane. Seeing it swooping down over the hillside, tearing up earth and ripping out a tree, was terribly shocking. "It left me speechless for two days," she claimed.

Mathilde saw four men run from the aircraft. It was to her that the wounded man went out to surrender. Frightened at this strange being holding onto his injured arm, she held her tin coffee jug out toward him. "He accepted it and stood with me while taking a sip of the coffee," she said.

Adolf Becker was in the *Schinderwiese* field, located on the hill opposite the Buberg, and witnessed the crash. He stood in amazement watching as two of the men (believed to be the two pilots, Anthony and Raney) ran into the woods and disappeared.

"I hurried up to the edge of the woods, carrying my whip in my hand," he reported, "cracking it several times as a threat to them, but they did not respond and my attention was drawn to others who were still in view."

From all directions people came, carrying hoes, rakes, and pitchforks, all wanting to help to apprehend the enemy soldiers. *Burgermeister* Lensch arrived on a motorcycle after only a few minutes. Adam Harth, local leader of farmers, carried an old rifle with him and waved it in the air to emphasize his direction in apprehending the flyers.

Two men (Blaylock and Hamilton) had not yet reached the woods and as they were approached by the Bubach men made no further move to escape. They were quickly moved out onto the road from Bubach to Krottelbach.

Another man (radio operator Wildman) had somehow avoided contact and was seen heading deeper into the woods where the two pilots had disappeared. Another (Ed McKenzie) was seen running away but had not yet been caught.

Adolf Becker said, "It quickly turned out that the hiding

73

place which he had chosen was not enough to screen him for very long. We saw him and drove him out right away. We accepted his surrender and made sure that he did not carry any pistol, then brought him along with the others."

Becker said they spoke no German, but he helped them to understand they were not in France, as they seemed to think, but were in Germany. "We thought they were English, but one of them told us they were Americans," he said.

Beadle (Deacon) August Anton and thirteen-year-old Fritz Spater, both of Marth, had been plowing not far away, and they soon ran up and became involved. They claim to have assisted the wounded man and "bound up his arm with a shred of his parachute."

Ernst Buttner of Bubach admitted to some knowledge of first-aid techniques, and he took further care of the injury, moving Kolber back into the airplane to find the crew's first-aid kit. (Ernst was killed a few months later during an air raid on Ludwigshafen.)

Emil Schneider, a young soldier on leave, was cycling toward his home in Bubach when he saw evidence of something big happening. He pedalled directly to the crash site, arriving just as Ernst was taking the wounded man back into the plane. Emil had never seen the inside of a plane and looked around carefully. Then he helped *Burgermeister* Lensch and Adam Harth to march the four captured American flyers down the hill and into the village of Bubach.

Fifty-two years later, the same Emil Schneider was interviewed before the television news cameras at the hillside ceremonies and told about his experiences. In answer to the question, "Why did you help out an enemy soldier?" he shrugged and said, "Mensch ist mensch" (people are people). Adam Harth's grandson, Walter Harth, was one of the historians who helped bring about the 1996 reunion of Germans and Americans at the site.

17

"Kamerad!...I Surrender"

Angling away from the others a little, I dashed for the small pile of brush or tree prunings back a bit from the edge of the woods. I practically dived into it, wiggling around to try to make it cover me. I desperately needed a few minutes to see if I was wounded and try to get my breathing passages open again. My nose was blocked solid with blood and dust.

Scraping some of the dirt off my hands, I could see that the pain was caused by some small pieces of glass and metal driven into the flesh. The red fluid on my jacket was oily and not like blood but was perhaps hydraulic fluid from the turret.

Behind me now I could hear men shouting, not far from my hiding place. They were using strange words. Now those words seemed to be directed at me. Either the brush had not hidden me or someone had seen me crawling into it. "Raus, raus [out, out]!" they were shouting.

Backing out, I stood up, raising my hands over my head. There were no guns in sight, but the farm tools they were waving about were enough to intimidate me. I knew just what to say now, and I could say it in their own language. I remembered it from my dime novels about the flying aces of World War I. When they were unlucky enough to be shot down on the wrong side of the trenches they would raise their hands and say, "Kamerad!"

I raised my hands over my head and said, "Kamerad!"

As they encircled me, one asked, "Haben Sie eine Pistole?"

That needed no interpretation. "No, no. No gun. No pistol." We had been issued Colt .45 pistols and shoulder holsters before leaving the United States but were recently ordered not to take them along on missions. If we were lucky enough to be on the ground and alive, then we weren't expected to carry on a hopeless shooting war as individuals.

Asked if I was an Änglander I said, "American."

This didn't seem to register until one of them said, "New York?"

When I said, "Yes, yes, New York," he smiled and said, "Ah, New York. Verstanden, Verstanden." These men who were making me their prisoner looked very old to me. I was only two months beyond my nineteenth birthday.

Motioned and prodded into the roadway, I was joined by Cran and two others on their way up the hill toward the village. My thoughts were that we had just torn up their farmland and ripped out some trees and they might be angry about that. They probably were not aware that we'd just blown up one of their aircraft factories.

Some of the women and children who came out to see us seemed to be angry and threatening in their words and gestures. This village nestled in the hills with its red tiled roofs and neat buildings and narrow streets reminded me of the one pictured in an old storybook, the fairy tale "The Pied Piper of Hamelin."

It was late in the afternoon as we captives stood, then later sat on the ground surrounded by the German villagers. The square was really just an open area where two streets joined. Under better circumstances it would be a pleasant spot to sit down, chat with friends, and enjoy the view. I could look out over the rooftops to the hill where our airplane sat.

Two were taken back out there, returning with a first-aid kit and some of the flying gear that we'd abandoned in the field. Aside from a kick and a little shoving around there was no physical abuse. Those standing guard appeared to be protecting us from a few more hostile villagers as well as preventing our escape.

Some young children crept up close to see what enemy soldiers looked like. As they stared, Bill Hamilton found a package of chewing gum in his pocket. Thinking he might get the happy reaction he had gotten back in England, he offered a stick to a young boy. Instead Bill was hit on the arm by one of the guards while the boy got a swat on the seat of his lederhosen.

The only serious wounds seemed to be those suffered by Ed Kolber. Each of us took a close look at his arm wound, lifting the cloth that now covered it. The flesh between elbow and shoulder was badly torn, and it seemed to me he might lose the arm.

Another wound on the back of his neck looked like a burn, as though a hot poker had been laid across it. There wasn't much blood showing from either wound, and we talked about what else might be done with the first-aid kit that had been brought up from the airplane. One of the items in it was a tube of morphine with attached needle. Since it was obvious that Ed was having some pain, we decided to use it. Air crews were taught how to do the injection. It was Ed's friend Cran Blaylock who actually jabbed in the needle, and the soothing effect on Kolber was almost immediate.

Other wounds among us appeared to be superficial. The metal fragments in my hands and neck were covered with caked-on dirt. All four of us were terribly thirsty, with mouths so dry and dusty that we could hardly talk.

Now a man appeared who seemed to have some authority. He talked with the village men, looked us over carefully, and pointed at Bill, asking, "Sprechen Sie Deutsch?" The meaning of the question was obvious, although none of us did speak German.

As we were shaking our heads I thought that it might be the time to try two of the few words I can recall from the novels, other than that word *Kamerad*. "Wasser, bitte?"

The response was encouraging. A woman walked to a nearby house and came back with a small pail of water. In spite of some protesting words from others, she motioned for us to go ahead and drink. We needed little urging to wet our mouths and wash down some of the heavy dust that had been choking us ever since the landing. As the Germans talked with one another a word that sounded like "soldier" was mentioned several times. This was not bad news to us. We were in no position or condition to escape, and we had all heard stories about what sometimes happened to flyers captured by angry civilians.

After sunset we were urged to our feet and moved down between the buildings and into a stone barn. Hamilton exchanged glances with me and, putting a finger to his forehead, made a clicking sound with his mouth. He was suggesting that maybe a firing squad was waiting for us, which might explain the mention of the soldiers. I shook my head. I didn't think so.

Inside the barn lay much of the flying gear. The parachutes

were still in their packs except for one that was open and spread on the floor. I wondered if one of the jumpers has been captured or his chute discovered where he had gotten out of it. Maybe one of the Germans had inadvertently pulled a rip cord.

By hand motions we were told to take off our clothes. This was worrisome; however, when only the items considered to be flight clothing were on the floor we were allowed to keep the rest. This was my chance to take off the felt flying boots and put on my leather GI shoes. As I did, one of the men took the boots and tossed them over into a pile of hay. Now I was left wearing a regulation OD shirt and pants over long underwear, with two neck scarfs. The others wore different uniform clothing—suntan shirts, sweaters, or field jackets.

As the sun was setting, I felt the chill of evening and wished we'd been allowed to keep our flight jackets.

Soon we were prodded back up to the square. There was a line of dust along the roadway down the hill, and at its point was a car. As it got closer, I could see a smoking stovepipe sticking up from a box on the back. There seemed to be an engine mounted where the trunk ought to be, and as it climbed the hill it was leaving a trail of white smoke puffs behind it.

It stopped near us and a large man wriggled out of the driver's seat. He wore a handsome green-trimmed jacket and knickers. The hat, with a little brush on it, was just what I might expect to see in these surroundings. He wore an armband of some sort. If not the *Burgermeister* of a nearby town, then he must be some other government or party official.

Holding out paper and pencil, he motioned for each of us to write. We took it one at a time and put down name, rank, and serial number, the only information that prisoners of war are supposed to be required to give, according to the "Rules of Warfare." Someone wrote Ed Kolber's information down for him. As the official took back the paper, from his tone of voice it was my guess that he was asking for the identity of the other flyers who were on the airplane with us.

No one offered anything further. Hamilton and I couldn't, even if we wanted to. We were only now getting acquainted with some of the men of the crew for the first time. All there had been, early this morning, was a quick introduction as we got ready for the mission.

The official climbed back into his car and puffed down the hill again. When he returned he had with him a few more items of U.S. Air Corps equipment from the B-17. I noticed a few packages of field rations and some Clark candy bars that must have come from someone's B-10 bag.

Now we were ordered to get up and get into the car. Cran helped Kolber get in back with the pile of flying gear, while Hamilton and I squeezed into the front with the driver.

The ride that followed seemed to be at high speed, but probably we never went faster than thirty miles an hour. The road was narrow and curving, and the headlights were narrowed to a slit, as headlights were back home for the nightly blackout. But continual use of the horn helped to clear the road in front of us.

18

"Die Einwohner erinnern sich"

(Translated from *Die Fliegende Festung bei Bubach*)

The four American fliers were marched off the Buberg and up the road into the town. Leading them was the local leader of farmers, Adam Harth, the only man who had a gun. As they halted near the *Burgermeister*'s house they were surrounded by villagers. Young and old, men and women, all were watching the foreign soldiers with much curiosity.

Certainly there were some of the Bubach people making angry remarks and one or two demanding that the airmen be shot, but they were restrained by the more level-headed people.

Adam Schneider, road attendant, had no better idea than to be out for the wounded turret gunner (Ed Kolber), still in shock from his wounds. Schneider gave him a "kick up the backsides" when he did not respond to his agitated comments.

This soldier was only able to stay on his feet for a few minutes without assistance but was conscious of what was going on around him. It was the older flyer (Cran Blaylock) who did most to look after him, doing an injection of something for the pain of his injured arm.

They were permitted to sit down and while resting there one of the prisoners (Ed McKenzie) made motions of drinking and asked, "Wasser?" Some would not have permitted them to drink anything; however, Bertha Harth, niece of the *Burgermeister*, resolutely went into her uncle's house and brought out a container of water. She put it in front of the men and being very thirsty, dusty and exhausted they drank eagerly.

*   *   *

As Cran and I stand in the same little square in Bubach where we stood as prisoners all those years ago, he began to remember a few details of the crash and the capture.

"Isn't that the house where the woman went to get us some water?" he wanted to know.

Our young historian knew the whole story. "Yes," Klaus said. "That is the one. It was Bertha Harth, the *Burgermeister*'s niece, who got water for you. Some did not want her to do it."

There was a large stone-faced building next door, and I pointed it out to Cran. He remembers being marched inside, where we were ordered to take off our clothes.

"Bill Hamilton told me they were going to stand us against that wall and shoot us," I told Cran. Good old Bill!

Now, as we looked out over the red roofs to the hill where our plane had crashed, I asked Cran if he remembered any of those last minutes as we were coming down. "Didn't you go up front to check on Ed Kolber after we were hit?"

Cran said Dick Anthony ordered him forward to see if he could man the top turret, in case one of the German fighters decided to make sure we were really finished. When he found Kolber under the turret with his upper arm torn open, the thought went through his mind that he might have to throw Ed out of the plane. It had been done before when a badly wounded mate had little chance of surviving a crash or staying alive until reaching medical help in England.

"But Kolber didn't seem to be bleeding very bad," Cran said, "and those of us still in the plane were going to be on the ground soon anyway." Cran remembers there was enough damage to the turret so it couldn't be used and he leaned in to yell the message to the pilot.

"But then you went back through the bomb bay," I said.

"Yeah. Dick was trying to stretch our flight, and I went back to help throw stuff overboard. My crash position was back there, too, and I had noticed that you were having some problem with your ball turret."

He was right about that. Thinking that I might be the only one left in the plane and working on my escape procedures, you could say I was having a problem. When finally I worked the turret into position with the crank and opened the hatch, there stood Cran. He reached down and helped me unhook my wires and hoses before lifting the flap on my helmet and yelling in my ear.

I don't recall that we ever spoke about it during the next twelve months we spent together at the stalag. It just never came up.

"Do you know how much like a guardian angel you looked right at that time?" I asked him now, fifty-two years later. He just grinned.

After getting the hatch open I had the plan firmly fixed in my mind. In one smooth set of moves I would scoop up my parachute, snap it on while taking the few steps to the waist hatch, and then do a rolling dive out into the slipstream with the rip cord in my hand. After the experience a week or two earlier I was able to set myself on "fully automatic" for those moves, without hesitation.

"But we were pretty low by that time, Ed," Cran said. "I don't think your chute would've had time to open."

The thought had crossed my mind. "Thanks for stopping me, Cran. Of course if you had spoken more clearly I wouldn't have snapped on my chute. It almost broke my nose when we hit the hill."

I told him I wasn't sure whether he had said, "Come on, we're going to ditch!" or "Get out of this sonovabitch!" and I was going to be ready for either one. The others wondered what Cran and I were laughing about as we stood in the village of Bubach.

19

Back to Bubach . . . as Friends

Now we were standing in the same little square in Bubach where we stood as prisoners all those years ago. There was a light rain falling, and we'd each been given an umbrella by our hosts. It wasn't like this in 1944. The sun had been shining and it was warm, at least until the chill of evening sat in.

Today as we looked out over the red rooftops to the hill where our plane had sat, I could tell by Cran's face that he, too, was reliving those awful hours we spent on this very spot fifty-two years and twenty-two days ago. Others were speaking to us, but we didn't hear them.

Dan was taking it all in. He had had a picture of this village in his mind ever since I described it for him many years ago.

It was a relief when we got back in the car and drove away. Bubach was a beautiful town, and its people today were warm and friendly. But the memories were too vivid.

Even climbing into Dr. Keller's late-model BMW car was too strong a reminder of the 1944 Bubach experience, that of leaving the little village for all the hardships that would follow.

20

Handed Over to the Police

Huddled inside the little wood-burner car, we four arrived in Kusel, capital of the district. As we were driven through the gate of a fancy iron fence I could just make out the high entrance to an impressive stone-faced building in the darkness. A few men held dim flashlights as they motioned us out and toward some stone stairs. A door at the top opened, and I could see a human figure profiled against the light inside.

Our flying gear was dumped on the ground, and two uniformed policemen pushed us into some sort of alignment. Bill Hamilton seemed unimpressed with the pushing, and when he was shoved off-balance he cocked his fist at the pusher. I had seen that expression on Bill's face before when he was about to get into one of his combative positions. This was not good.

Before he could make another move, Bill was knocked to the ground by a blow to his stomach, by a fist, club, or the butt of a gun, I couldn't tell which. Immediately we other three were threatened and we raised our hands in the air. When Bill was on his feet again I whispered, "What in the hell is *wrong* with you?"

As his breath came back he said, "Don't know. Couldn't help it." I hoped he had now learned a lesson in "helping it," because he could get us all killed.

We were marched up the stairs and into what seemed to be an official meeting room. Behind a table sat three men looking very important. As they talked to each other they shuffled some papers, perhaps the ones that had come along with us. They didn't appear to be soldiers or police. However, half a dozen uniformed men were lined up behind us now. Gradually it became very quiet and all attention was focused on us.

Now began a shouting confrontation that was to go on and on for what seemed like hours but was perhaps only half an hour. I prayed for something to happen to interrupt it before my knees buckled and my abdomen exploded. We were being questioned and the authorities seemed to get more angry and red-faced each time we shook our heads and looked dumb instead of answering. They perceived it to be stubbornness and seemed to feel that if they could just shout loudly enough then we would respond. I was sure the subject must be the number and identification of our missing crew members.

The more puzzled we looked and the more we shook our heads, the angrier the voices seemed and the closer to our faces came theirs. I was trying very hard not to look hostile but to keep a calm expression. Occasionally one of the questioners would take out his frustration with a shove or a poke. When one such poke hit my lower abdomen I doubled over with pain. My problem had to get some attention soon, or I was going to collapse.

I was totally incapable of urinating in my pants and would have died first. A long, long time had passed since the morning coffee back in England. There was a moment in my gun turret when I had considered whether some connection might be made between the appropriate part of my anatomy and one of the open link chutes beside my thighs. The threat of frostbite was too real, even if there had been the possibility of overcoming the heavy clothing and cramped position.

Now I was in crisis. There could be no further wait. With gestures and words I thought might have some meaning I tried to explain the problem. The first try with a *p* word made them think I was talking about a pistol, and that got a whole lot of attention.

But then I tried words such as *urine* and finally *pissin'*. With the last one I seemed to have struck a word that crossed the language barrier.

There were grins, nods, and looks of comprehension. An order was given and I was edged toward a doorway behind the table. An armed guard pushed me in, crowded in behind me, and closed the door. The open toilet "bench" there was a welcome sight. In spite of my anxiety about the man crowded in behind me, relief came at last.

Back in line a few minutes later, I became more aware of the injuries to my hands. The wounds were not deep, but fragments that were imbedded under the skin were a problem when I tried to close my fingers. My hands were so dirty that I could see only bloody spots where the fragments were located.

Watching as each of the others was given a turn in the back room, I thought about our orders to always be alert for chances to escape. It appeared to me that right now there wasn't even the shadow of a hope. But I would keep it in the back of my mind.

An hour passed. People came in and looked at our papers and then at us, and conferences were held at the table. Suddenly a German military officer stepped into the room and all became quiet. He was addressed as Herr Hauptmann, and the blue uniform he wore meant that the Luftwaffe was now involved in our captivity.

"Hello, English soldiers," he said, smiling. "For you the war is over." His accent was strong, but we understood him easily. Over the next several days we would many times hear that comment about the war being over for us. We had been called *Änglanders* and New Yorkers by others, but hearing it stated in English was a relief, and our expressions must have shown it. The captain told us that up to now we had been in the hands of dummkopfs, but that now we would be treated as fellow aviators who had been outfought.

"You are now in the good hands of the Luftwaffe," he said.

The pose he struck would also become a familiar one whenever we were confronted by a German officer, it seemed, with one hand slid in the blouse and the other crossed behind the back. Then he gave us our first instruction in speaking the German language.

"When you do not understand something, then you say, 'Ich verstehe nicht.' And when you mean 'yes' you say, 'yeah,' 'Ja,' the same as in your language. For 'no' say 'nein'."

The captain turned and had a discussion with the officials. Papers were picked up and examined, additional entries were made, and then we were marched out the door, down the steps, into the darkness and I stumbled into the pile of flight gear. Following the little flashlight ahead, and with the policemen around us, we went out through the iron gate.

It was a short walk to where some stairs led down under a building. In the darkness, a heavy door was opened and we four were thrust inside. It was suddenly quiet, and I could hear faint sounds of moaning and heavy breathing. As I sat down, it felt like a dirt floor under us, with perhaps some straw thrown about. We four made voice and hand contact with each other and whispered some guesses about who might be in there with us.

I asked, in a voice that came out louder than intended, "Who else is in here?" No one answered. But we continued to hear the low sounds of someone in distress. It was eerie, but it didn't prevent me from dropping off into brief periods of sleep.

After a while I began to feel around on the floor to get an idea of the size of our dungeon. It wasn't very large. Once my hand touched warm, slippery flesh and it startled me. Near the door I felt a metal bucket, and from its smell I knew what it was for.

After a while I could see a line of light at the door. Someone was coming for us. The door was kicked open and men with flashlights urged us up and out using words that sounded like: "Out, out," actually, "Raus, raus." Now we could see who our cellmates had been. They looked as bad as we no doubt did, covered with dirt and caked blood and some of their clothing torn.

We had "blackouts" back in the USA and in England, and now I became aware that the Germans also endured them, no doubt because of the nightly raids of the RAF. Perhaps we were in a target area, and I thought, *For us maybe the war is not over, after all.*

Lined up back in the courtyard, police or soldiers moved about and papers were exchanged and orders given. We settled down to a seated position, and no one protested.

Eventually a truck drove up to the gate and we were urged up and into the back. Our parachutes and other flight gear were no longer with us, and a soldier holding a machine gun sat at the tail end on each side. It seemed like more than an hour of bouncing up and down on the hard bench before we came to a stop and the canvas flap was thrown open.

When we had been pushed into alignment, a bucket of water and a dipper were set out in front of us. I was still terribly thirsty, as the others must have been, and we quickly passed the dipper around to one another.

We were inside a Wehrmacht training base called Baumholder, and we were about to be housed in its prison, or "guardhouse," as it would be called on a U.S. army base (as Baumholder was fated to become).

21

Imprisoned at Baumholder

The German army base was very active. Many soldiers in gray uniforms with black belts were moving about, some wearing field caps and others with the coal-scuttle steel helmets. A few groups were marching in columns of four and were counting cadence with strange-sounding words. There were white-painted stones lining some of the walkways, just as I'd seen on several American military bases.

Midway along the length of a barrackslike building, we were directed down a short flight of stairs and into a corridor. There were slatted doors along either side, and through their slats I could see iron bars. Partway down the corridor sat a soldier at a small table with a bare lightbulb shining over his head.

As we stepped up to him, he checked our names on his paper, assigning each of us to a cell. Mine was easy to remember: "Fear!" Actually I learned that it was "Vier," or number four. Anyway, the word sounded appropriate. The top turret gunner with the wounded arm also drew number four, to be my sole companion.

As we moved into the cell, we got a helping shove, nearly knocking both of us to the floor. The barred door and then the wooden door slammed, and I saw what looked like two tables, one on each side of the narrow room. Nothing else. A little light filtered in through the slatted door, and I could see a barred window high on the back wall. As the sounds in the corridor died away, I became aware that the two items of furniture were not tables but beds. There was nothing else in the cell. I helped Ed up onto the one to the left of the door, then crawled up on the other one. It was hard and it was cold.

As I lay there shivering I became aware of aches and pains all over my body. Maybe it was from the shake-up of the crash, along with the cold and hunger. But maybe it also was the growing sense of foreboding I felt about our future. Exhaustion made me fall asleep for a while, but then I became aware that my cellmate was moaning. In the bit of light from the door I could see him lying flat on his back, head tipped far backward on the hard bench. His arm had been held against his chest with a scarf, but now it was twisted and down at his side. When I stepped over to adjust it I could tell he had a high fever. The shot of morphine that Cran had given him must have worn off by this time.

The cloth bandage was stuck solidly to his wound. Once I had lifted and straightened the arm and pulled his shirt collar up over the groove on his neck there was little else to be done. Something to hold his head up would have helped, but there was nothing at all here in the cell with us.

As I crawled back onto my bench, wishing with all my might that some blankets would appear from someplace, it occurred to me that we might help each other. Crowding onto his bench, I let his head rest on my arm. That made his breathing easier, and it also let me share some of the heat from his fever. I had no concept of whether only four or twenty-four hours passed that way, but eventually I moved him onto his good side, went back and curled into a ball on my own bench, and hallucinated about warm campfires and hot sunshine.

A patch of light on the wall told me that it must now be daytime. Unable to get any response from Kolber, I knew that something had to be done. Some of his agony was probably due to a need for water. Shaking the bars and rattling the wooden door a bit, I tried to make just enough noise to get attention but not enough to give the impression I was being aggressive. In the mildest shout I could muster I said, "Guard! Hello, Guard! Can you please help us in here?"

No response. But after I did it another time or two there were sounds of footsteps in the corridor. Our outside door was opened, and a guard motioned me back against the wall. When he opened the inner bars I pointed to my companion and said some words that probably sounded like, "*Doktor* . . . can he have *Doktor* und *Wasser*? He is *krank*." I wondered if my "dime novel" German would be of any help at all.

Keeping one eye on me, the guard leaned over and put his

hand on Kolber's forehead, glanced at the arm, listened to his breathing for a minute, then backed out and slammed the doors. It was only a few minutes before I heard more sounds of footsteps. As two men entered the cell, I tried to put on my most courteous manner, hoping that they would understand that there really was a problem and that I was not just a troublemaker. Helping Kolber down off his bench and carefully avoiding jarring the arm, they moved him outside the cell, then slammed the two doors. Their sounds died away down the corridor, and I could imagine Kolber was being taken to get medical help. Most of us believed that the average German soldier was no less human than the American soldier, at least at our level of rank. They would care for him.

It was the last time I ever saw Sgt. Ed Kolber, top turret gunner and engineer of the *Toonerville Trolley*.

By standing on one of the "beds" I could see through the barred window. There were German soldiers walking around out there between the buildings. It could have been an American base except for those uniforms with the strange markings and the short leggings or boots the men wore. A platoon marched by singing in cadence. They kept perfect step and looked far too strong and healthy. One of the wilder thoughts crossing my mind was that soon they would be surrendering and we could all go home. Now I began to have serious doubts as to whether or not I was even on the winning side.

Probably, I imagined, they were marching to the mess hall, where they would sit down to a hearty meal. They might even ask the prisoners to join them. But considering that I had just been involved in a bombing raid that could have set back their cause quite a lot, maybe that breakfast back in England was the last one for me, ever.

Being alone in the cell with no sign that there were other Americans nearby was very depressing. I tried to think of people back home to convince myself that someone was probably concerned about me right at this very moment. Still a "romantic" about the war in the air, I thought about my heroes in their Spads, Camels, and Jenneys during that earlier air war over Europe. After all, some of *them* had been shot down and captured and came out of it alive and well.

I thought about some songs that were popular back home and sang several of them in a fairly loud voice. "That Old Black Magic" had a nice echo to it in the bare cell: "...that icy tingle that I feel inside, then that elevator starts its slide, and down and down I go, like a leaf that's caught in the tide."

Bill Hamilton said to me later, "I heard someone singing and said, 'It's gotta be that crazy McKenzie.' But it sure was good to hear an American voice singing an American song."

I tried doing some "side-straddle hops" to get warm but just could not keep it up. My joints and muscles ached too much, and I was getting weak and shaky.

It seemed like several hours before the silence of the corridor was broken by the sounds of heavy boots. The doors were opened, and a soldier holding a rifle made a motion for me to come out. My comrades were being moved out, too, and we were herded along into a side room where there was a long sheet metal sink under a row of small faucets, a welcome sight. First we held our mouths under the streams; then we splashed water on our faces. Off came layers of dirt and blood, and I began to feel as though I was part of the human race after all.

The next stop was at a row of toilet stools; then up the steps we went with calls of "Schnell! Schnell machen! [Quick! Be quick!]" The sun was warm outside and we absorbed all we could. Several other Americans had now joined us. Lining up, we were counted, had names checked against a list, then were counted again. It was becoming possible to respond to commands given in German. The similarity of their words to ours made it easy to understand *halt, marsch*, and *achtung* (halt, march, and attention).

An "underofficial" stood in front of us shouting something that I could not understand. He must have just eaten, and he stood so close I could see bits of food in his teeth. I thought, *Wouldn't it be terrible if he is asking if we are hungry and want to eat and we are just standing here like dummies?*

After a while we were left alone and we sat down on the cobblestones. A few men still had cigarettes with them and lighted up. One found a pack of gum, and he shared it with us.

A truck came rumbling into the area, and all of us were

prodded up over the high tailboard into the canvas-sided body. Two guards with machine guns got in last, taking seats on the ends of the benches. They dropped the back flap, and the truck slowly rolled out.

22

Baumholder Revisited: "It's Ours, Now"

It was now fifty-two years later, and in a late-model BMW sedan we were driven through the gate of Baumholder, a huge U.S. military base. There was a coffee reception with a colonel who was in command while most of the forces were deployed in Bosnia. We each made brief comments to the assembled staff and historians and were given souvenirs of the 222d Base Support Battalion. Then the colonel asked a smiling soldier to bring around her van and give us a tour of the base, but especially the "old quarter" where the German guardhouses used to be.

Cran and I were a little overwhelmed remembering our earlier visit with Hamilton and Kolber, and also with all the interest now shown by our German hosts, particularly Dr. Keller, Klaus Zimmer, and, of course, the one man who was responsible for our incarceration fifty-two years ago, ex–Luftwaffe fighter pilot Hans Berger.

After one or two false leads, I was able to point out for them what I believed was the long barrackslike building. It was ancient, now, apparently used only for storage. There were the steps leading down to the cell blocks, half below ground level, and there were the barred windows I recalled seeing from the inside. The troops I watched as they marched by my window must have passed over this very spot where we were standing. All of them were now old men, as we were, or perhaps more likely had been killed in the war.

Pictures were taken, questions were answered, and the rain was beginning again. I could tell that Cran was as depressed by it as I was, and we were not unhappy to climb back into the van to continue with the tour of Baumholder.

During our tour Cran and I talked with Klaus about what had happened to Ed Kolber after he was taken from my cell. In 1995 Klaus Zimmer found Ed living in Arizona, learning that he survived and had not lost the arm, as we feared might happen. Ed had visited with his old pilot boss, Dick Anthony, in Colorado. I exchanged a few letters with Ed to learn more of the details.

Hans Berger joined in the discussion about Ed, with Cran Blaylock, Klaus Zimmer, and me. Hans's was the most recent contact, as he had reached Ed by phone from Munich only a few weeks earlier. Here then is the story of the top turret gunner whom I had last seen being half-carried from my cell at Baumholder about April 27, 1944:

> I was taken to some sort of a medical building there at Baumholder. A nurse came in and with hand signals, pointing and wrinkling up her face, she asked me if I was having pain.
>
> I shook my head, to tell her that I wasn't feeling any pain from the wound.
>
> When she made a signal for me to try and move the fingers on my injured arm I showed her that I could and she responded, "Ah, gut!"
>
> Another attendant plucked some blue threads from the wound with a pair of tweezers. They must have come from the electrically heated flying suit. He sprinkled some surgical powder on the wound, made provisions for draining with some special cloths or wicks, then bandaged the arm.
>
> Then they moved me out, taking me to an orthopedic hospital, or *Lazarett*, as it was called, located in Obermassfeld.

Klaus Zimmer in 1996 found that this facility was located in the region of Thuringia, nine kilometers south of the city of Meiningen. The main building was a large three-story stone structure built after World War I for use as a boys' school. The Hitler Youth movement had taken it over for a while before it was converted to a hospital. Wooden tarpapered barracks were put up in the courtyard to house internal medicine cases and to be used as an isolation ward.

Klaus explained that before the invasion of 1944 the patients were nearly all British and American airmen shot down on raids over German-occupied Europe. After the Normandy invasion some ground troops began to show up there for treatment. It was mostly staffed by British POW medical personnel, as most of the early flyers shot down had been Britons.

According to a U.S. report in 1945, the German rations of food, supplemented by the Red Cross parcels, provided the prisoners with a sufficient diet. All three countries, England, the United States, and France, were sending parcels at that time.

Most of the airman patients had very serious wounds, and there were many amputations and infected flak or gunfire wounds. As the patients convalesced they were transferred to the Meiningen Reserve Lazarett, where their orthopedic treatment was under supervision of a British specialist, aided by various physical therapists.

Ed Kolber's story continues:

> The RAF bombed the city while I was there and it was not at all enjoyable to hear the antiaircraft shrapnel bouncing off the slate roof, even though it didn't seem to bother the Germans at all.
>
> My next move was to a town called Schlitz, in Hessia, where there was a facility for British, Canadian, and American wounded airmen. There were some English doctors there who were taken prisoner as they were trying to evacuate Dunkirk when the Germans had taken Belgium and Holland. They took care of the infirmary and it was one of these doctors who removed a 20mm shell nosecap from my arm where it had been lodged close to a nerve. They used a local anesthetic while three men held me down.
>
> It really didn't hurt that much, but I was trying to see what the doctor was doing as he carried on an explanation to the medics. He gave me that piece of the Focke Wulf's cannon shell to take home for a souvenir.

When able to get out of bed, Ed was sent to Stalag Luft IV, located at Kiefheide, near Belgard, in eastern Pomerania, now a part of Poland.

23

Meanwhile, Back at Bomber Station 109

Ninety-second Bomb Group, 326th Squadron, Activities Journal, Monday, April 24, 1944

Mission was to Oberpfaffenhofen. A rough way to start the week. Crews taking part were those of Lt. Makowski, Capt. Belongia, Lt. Ledyard, Lt. Rosenfeld, Lt. Mahone and Lt. Anthony. The latter was assigned the *Toonerville Trolley*.

Target was the Dornier aircraft assembly and repair complex about fifteen miles south of Munich. It was exceptionally well defended. Bombing altitude was 21,000 feet and good accuracy was recorded.

The Anthony and Rosenfeld crews did not return and were listed as "missing." Also, three of the 407th Squadron Forts went down.

There were three major fighter attacks reported during the long flight and heavy flak was encountered at the target area. Some of the fighters were silver ME 109s attacking out of the sun. Most were massed head-on FW 190 attacks. Estimated one hundred fifty enemy fighters were involved in the separate attacks.

Gunners made fewer claims of German fighters shot down, perhaps not able to identify them fast enough. Also the cunning tactics of the Jerrys was something else to be reckoned with.

Crews going down today were said to have been under some control and chances are that Rosenfeld was able to make it into Switzerland. [He did.] Two of his engines were shot out so he was lucky not to have met more fighters.

Lt. Anthony plane reported last seen with engine fires, no chutes observed and not seen to crash. They may be residents of Stalag Luft.

During the bombing one Ninety-second Group Fortress was

damaged when two 500-pound bombs dropped from a bomber above hit it. They had apparently not fallen far enough for the propellers to spin off and activate the fuses before hitting, thus did not explode. In the *Toonerville Trolley* some of the crew wondered about the strange movements being made by the plane but had not seen the bomb that the pilot was trying desperately to get rid of. He did succeed and made it back for an emergency landing in England.

In Roger Freeman's book *The Mighty Eighth,* he explains that there were fifty-seven aircraft in the two groups making up our bombing wing and that we ran into the heaviest fighter defenses of all the many heavy bombers over Germany that day.

It was learned that as the bombers passed Munich on the homeward leg at least two German fighter groups, with more than two hundred ME 109s and FW 190s drove home attacks, most from straight out in front of the bombers.

Losses by the Eighth Air Force for the whole effort on April 24 were 40 bombers and 17 fighters. Of the 400 airmen in those planes only 11 were known killed; the remainder would remain classified as "missing" until more information concerning parachute sightings, explosions, prisoner notifications, or evadee recovery was available. Families were not notified of "missing" status until after thirty days.

On the day following the 326th Squadron's Oberpfaffenhofen mission, Lt. William Sage, statistical officer, completed a missing air crew report for each unaccounted-for crew. From the postmission debriefing records he obtained information reported by accompanying crews. For Lt. Richard Anthony and the *Toonerville Trolley* he entered: "The plane had been last seen in clear and smooth weather with two engines on fire at 1507 near Kaiserslautern. Loss was the result of enemy aircraft fire."

The missing air crew report showed name, rank, serial number, and function of each of the ten man crew, as well as the serial numbers of each of the thirteen Browning fifty-caliber machine guns mounted on board.

Fifteen days later, on May 9, 1944, a telegram was received by each next-of-kin from the secretary of war stating that the subject had been missing in action since April 24, 1944.

Seven days later a letter was received explaining that "attempts will continue to make further determination, and should a different status be revealed then that information will be forwarded to you."

Information was sent to hometown newspapers, and an article appeared on the front page of the *Haverhill Gazette* stating that "Sergeant McKenzie was the first casualty of the one hundred forty-one service men and women of the town of Plaistow, New Hampshire. He had been overseas only sixty days and in action less than thirty days."

One month after the MIA telegram, on June 9, 1994, another telegram was received by Choate E. McKenzie announcing: "It has been learned through the International Red Cross that your son is a prisoner of war of the German government."

Those of us taken prisoner at Bubach did not know what had happened to our two pilots, nor to the three who parachuted while we were diving with engines burning. It was the Oster Valley historians who, half a century later learned the details of how they came into captivity. This was what they learned. It is titled: "Gefangennahme der anderen Besatzungsmitglieder (meaning "Capturing the Others Who Were Not Yet Found").

Three more crew members were as yet unaccounted for in the vicinity of the airplane. One was the first parachutist who was seen descending near Pfeffelbach. He had drifted past Kusel, then finally came down near the quarry in the vicinity of Haschbach am Remigiusberg (assumed to be navigator/bombardier DePaoli).

He was taken captive and brought to Kusel to be locked in a *Keller* [cellar] which had been converted to a prison cell, and would be joined by the pilots in this prison early the next day.

The *Keller* was dug into a hillside, located on the left side of the road leading from Kusel market square down into the town center *Landschaftsstrasse*.

In 1996, it was still there. Cran and I were shown inside, while carefully watching to see that no one closed the door. A reporter from *Stars and Stripes* took our picture in the cell, and it appeared with a feature story in the next issue of the worldwide newspaper.

One parachutist seen descending over Herchweiler landed near the country lane leading from the fountain in Herchweiler to Selchenbach, about 250 meters above the last houses there. Immediately people crowded around him and made hostile remarks. He was taken into custody and later removed to the local fire station before a later move to Baumholder Military Base.

(This chutist was believed to be nose gunner Fields. He was ultimately moved by train to the *Dulag Luft* at Frankfurt, where he rejoined his crewmates.)

Fred Seyler became involved as he was riding home on a bicycle from Selchenbach to Frohnhofen. When passing the Krottelbacher Loch forest he heard shouting in English.

(This could have been Sergeants Blank and Wildman, who were not yet accounted for.)

It was near Krottelbach where they were eventually arrested in a field called Hoch Stubb, which borders on the Krottelbacher Loch forest, situated only a few kilometers from the crash site.

When the men were sighted, farmers began to chase them with forks and other implements, finally overtaking them. One of these men was Rudolf Wagner of Niederselchenbach, and he transported the two prisoners to Herschweiler-Pettersheim in his cart. There they were locked up in the *Keller* of the village hall. Many people came to look at the captured Americans.

In a few hours party leader Jakob Gerlach of Konken picked them up in his DKW type car. He sat one of the Americans next to him and in the rear placed a policeman with the other one. The two prisoners wore sandy brown khaki uniforms.

Later the car came to a stop in front of the Gerlach Inn and the party leader went inside. In back the prisoner and the policeman studied a map spread out on their knees, perhaps the map from one of the American escape kits. Walter Blohn and Karl Muller, two teenage boys, approached the car and said something in English. Karl had been in college and was showing off some of the language he had learned there.

The prisoner in the front seat responded, "Junge, sprich nur Deutsch [boy, simply speak German]." The two Americans seemed to give no impression that they were concerned but seemed relaxed. Finally the car was driven off in the direction of Kusel.

In an area near the field where the two had been captured, the villagers discovered a parachute. They later used its material for making clothing, it was claimed.

The pilots, Anthony and Raney, had got away. Maybe they had evaded capture and possibly even got back to England.

Or so we let ourselves believe for more than a year afterward. Their freedom lasted only overnight, however. Dick Anthony tells what happened to them:

We saw some of our crew heading down through the field and toward some woods below, so Ray Raney and I took another direction. As we made it into the cover of the trees we could hear sounds of people approaching and also what we thought were the sounds of motorcycles somewhere nearby.

Hurrying our pace and staying in the cover of the trees we half-ran and half-walked. We were guessing that our course was taking us in a westerly direction. Several hours later, as it began to get dark, we were totally exhausted and could go no farther. Dropping to the ground where the woods were a little thicker, we tried to rest. Talking in low voices we discussed the chances of getting over the border into France, where we might connect with members of the French Resistance. The odds were very high against it, we knew, but we planned how we might approach someone and even how we may be able to make our way to the coast and find a way to get across the Channel to England. After all, we had heard of a few men who had done it.

When the dawn came and it was light enough to see, we again began walking. By this time we were not only exhausted but thirsty and hungry almost beyond endurance. To try and determine where we might be we decided to leave the cover of the woods and head out across an open field to where a farmer was working with an ox cart.

That was a mistake. When we asked if he was French he became agitated. He was a big strong man and he rushed up and grabbed us by the arms, shouting for others nearby to come and help him.

Then the two of us were escorted, by guards armed with farm tools, to a nearby farmhouse. While being held there we were

101

given some water to drink, while the man who had apprehended us proceeded to shave and change his clothes. We imagined he must be planning to meet someone important to whom he could turn over his prisoners.

By the time our host was finally ready we had gotten some badly needed rest. We were marched ahead of the men to a nearby village and were placed under guard of other civilians. We knew that some officials had been told of our capture and they would be coming for us.

It was a Luftwaffe officer who eventually arrived and officially relieved the farmers of their prisoners.

Courtesy Edward McKenzie

Courtesy Hans Berger

Sgt. Edward McKenzie (B-17 Gunner) and Lt. Hans Berger (FW 190 Pilot). Adversaries in 1944, friends in 1996.

Sgt. John Cran Blaylock in 1943.

Blaylock with Klaus Zimmer in 1996. (Courtesy D. McKenzie.)

The vapor trails from our engines were long, white arrows pointing out our positions to guns on the ground and in the air. They could also screen Luftwaffe fighters attacking from the rear.

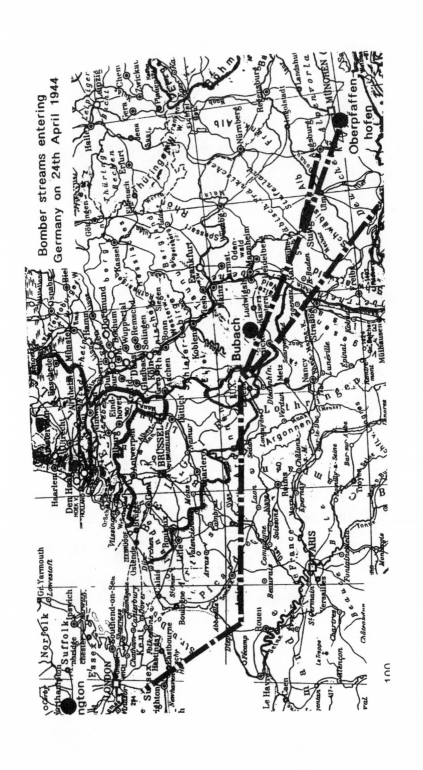

Bomber streams entering
Germany on 24th April 1944

100

Start of the Eighth Air Force bombing attack on the Dornier aircraft works, on April 24, 1944. Smoke trails of marker bombs can
be seen.

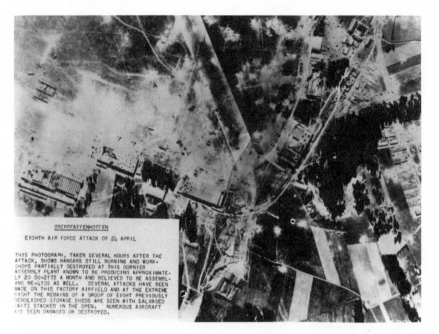

OBERPFAFFENHOFFEN

EIGHTH AIR FORCE ATTACK OF 24 APRIL

THIS PHOTOGRAPH, TAKEN SEVERAL HOURS AFTER THE
ATTACK, SHOWS HANGARS STILL BURNING AND WORK-
SHOPS PARTIALLY DESTROYED AT THIS DORNIER
ASSEMBLY PLANT KNOWN TO BE PRODUCING APPROXIMATE-
LY 20 DO-217S A MONTH AND BELIEVED TO BE ASSEMBL-
ING ME-410S AS WELL.   SEVERAL ATTACKS HAVE BEEN
MADE ON THIS FACTORY AIRFIELD AND AT THE EXTREME
RIGHT THE REMAINS OF A GROUP OF EIGHT PREVIOUSLY
DEMOLISHED STORAGE SHEDS ARE SEEN WITH SALVAGED
PARTS STACKED IN THE OPEN.   NUMEROUS AIRCRAFT
ARE SEEN DAMAGED OR DESTROYED.

Several hours after the attack, hangers are still burning and work-
shops are partially destroyed. Evidence of a previous attack is at
extreme right where remains of demolished storage sheds are seen
with salvaged parts stacked in the open. A number of aircraft are
seen damaged or destroyed. (Friedrichshafen, Dornier, press
photo.)

"Sometimes we sit here on alert all day long, but today it will be only a few hours" (Lt. Hans Berger, Luftwaffe, JG/1). (Courtesy Hans Berger.)

"This is the FW 190 I flew that day," says Hans Berger, pointing out the cannons in the wings. Then he says, "Ed, it is a gift that I made for you." He has written on it "In memory of our first encounter on April 24, 1944." (Courtesy D. McKenzie.)

Luftwaffe fighter pilot Berger had a close call a month earlier in a duel with a Flying Fortress. The rudder was nearly destroyed on his Focke Wulf 190. His mechanic (left) poses with him at the tail. (Courtesy Hans Berger.)

TOONERVILLE FOLKS
Fontaine Fox (1884-1964)
"The Toonerville Trolley
That Meets All Trains"
began its run as a part of
the colorful landscape of
Toonerville in Fox's panel
cartoons around 1910. The
Skipper and his out-of-con-
trol car inspired toys,
games, and movies. The
panel ran 1910-1955.

The USPS recently saluted many old cartoon characters by issu-
ance of a sheet of 32-cent stamps. One showed the trolley that was
represented on the nose of our Flying Fortress. (Stamp Design ©
1995 U.S. Postal Service. Reproduced with permission. All rights reserved.)

Hans Berger watches (right center) as Maj.Schnoor offers congratu-
lations to *Oberfeldwebel* Rudi Piffer for his latest victory over a B-17
"Viermot" Fortress. Another fellow pilot and good friend Lt. Gottfried
Just is in photo (center left). Both Piffer and Just were shot down and
killed before the year ended. (*Courtesy Hans Berger and Eric
Mombeek.*)

A b s c h r i f t !

Der Reichsminister der Luftfahrt
und Oberbefehlshaber der Wehrmacht
Ausz. u. Diszipl. (V.)
Az. 29 Nr. 374 / 44.

Berlin, den 31. 7. 1944

An 1. / J. G. 1

Der 1. / J. G. 1 wird der Abschuss eines amerika=
nischen Kampfflugzeuges vom Typ Boeing "Fortress II" am 24.4.44
15.12 Uhr durch Lt. Hans B e r g e r als sechzehnter (16) Luft
sieg der Staffel anerkannt.

I. A.

gez. Unterschrift.

Für die Richtigkeit der Abschrift:

U., den 24. 10. 1944.

Leutnant und Staffelführer. /Kö.

(Translation)

The Minister of Aviation
and Supreme Commander of the Wehrmacht

Berlin, 31st July, 1944

To: 1./JG 1 (1st Squadron/Fighter Regiment 1)

The 1./JG 1 is acknowledged the downing of an American combat plane of type Boeing "Fortress II" on 24th April 1944 at 15.12 hrs by Lt. Hans B e r g e r as the sixteenth (16) air victory of the squadron.

Hans Berger's documentation of the shootdown or *Abschuss* of the American bomber. It was verified from Berlin three months after the "kill," on July 31, 1944. "Boeing Fortress II" indicates it to have been the newer Model G, featuring the nose, or chin turret. (Courtesy Hans Berger.)

Soon after the second catastrophic Schweinfurt mission in October, 1943, Reichsmarschall Hermann Goering visited Schnoor's No.1 Gruppe of Jagdgeschwader One to recognize several victories over Flying Fortresses of the Eighth Air Force. While an *Unteroffizier* is receiving the Iron Cross First Class and a handshake for his score, Karl Demuth, then an Oberfeldwebel, stands ready to accept his Iron Cross Second Class. Facing the camera, Hauptmann Schnoor introduces his pilots to Goering. (Courtesy Karl Demuth.)

Young Ewald Neu watched the bomber descending toward the hill, while working in the forest with his grandfather. He later drew this sketch, providing it to local historians when the full story of the *"Fliegende Festung bei Bubach"* was published.

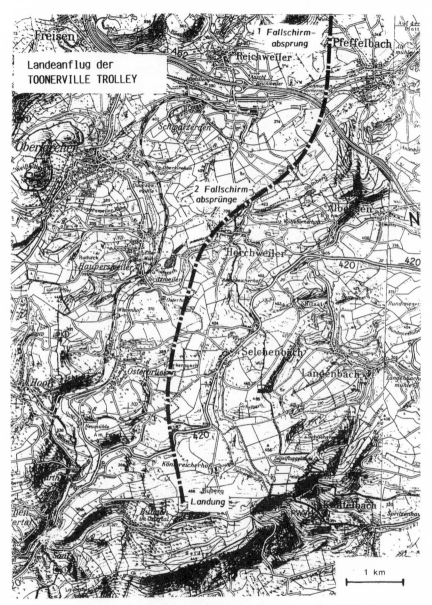

Reports by ground witnesses resulted in this map of the "landing flight of the Toonerville Trolley," showing where parachutist jumpers *(Fallschirmabsprunge)* were seen, (Courtesy Klaus Zimmer.)

"That cherry tree stuck in my left wing acted like an anchor, steering us away from disaster in the woods below." (Pilot Dick Anthony.) (Courtesy Hilda Schneider.)

In a 1944 family photo, Gernot Spengler is held in his grandmother's arms. All came to see the great American airplane at
Bubach. In 1996 Gernot Spengler was the church organist for
special services at Niederkirchen, afterward providing a tour of
the ancient structure for the two men of the Toonerville Trolley
and the fighter pilot who shot them down. The lifesaving cherry tree is shown, firmly lodged in the wing root. (Courtesy
Gernot Spengler.)

Pilots Ray Raney and Dick Anthony (standing) "fight to feather the props, dive to blow out the fires and pray a landing site will appear."

Engineer Ed Kolber (at left), was "hit by cannon fire, nearly losing an arm....wasn't sure he'd be able to jump."

Nose Gunner Charles Fields snapped on his chute and dove out the nose hatch. The navigator was right behind him.

Waist Gunner Irving Blank saw the flaming engines and opted to jump out the waist door. (Crew picture 1943.)

Three boys discovered the missing No. 4 propeller. Only the one in the center was still alive in 1996 to meet crew members of the B-17 who had lost the propeller. (Courtesy Werner Weisgerber.)

Ewald Schenkel arrived at the scene early and removed a few souvenirs from inside the B-17 with his bike wrench. Fifty-two years later he presented one souvenir to each of the three flyers, beautifully mounted and inscribed. (Courtesy Zimmer.)

24

All Flyers Routed through the *Dulag*

On their way to the *Dulag* the pilots went to the temporary Luftwaffe facility some miles north of Frankfurt in Oberursel known as the Auswertestelle. It was a special camp for evaluating captured flyers "out of the West." After interrogation the two were sent to the *Oflag*, a transient camp near Berlin, before being shipped to a permanent stalag, the one called Luft Three.

Shortly after the *Toonerville Trolley* men had departed, the facility was destroyed in a bombing raid, and a new one was developed farther out beyond Frankfurt, at Wetzlar.

The five days of intermittent solitary confinement and interrogation experienced by the two pilots may have been more intense than ours, since it was assumed they probably knew more about their organization and equipment than did we enlisted members of the crew.

As a rule, all that the prisoners got for sustenance was the sour black bread and a bit of soup during this period. There were instances when an ace fighter pilot or high-ranking officer might be taken out for a special meal or a social visit, but they were rare.

Our two pilots talked with each other about what may have happened to the men of their crew. Their bombardier parachutist would not catch up with them until they reached the permanent camp in Silesia.

It would be more than a year after the end of the war before they learned that all the men of the crew had survived and had returned safely home.

Parachutist De Paoli had been lucky, it turned out, as were the two gunners, Irving Blank and Charles Fields. Their jumps had been successful, and they were not physically abused when captured.

Dick Anthony knew that some of his men had jumped and

some rode the bomber down with him. At least five stayed in the plane, he guessed, having talked with the wounded Kolber and seen at least three others running from the crash site. He and Raney talked very carefully about it with one another, suspecting there might be listening devices placed where they were allowed to be together. They could hope that some may have evaded capture and reached the underground.

After their interrogations the officers of the B-17 *Toonerville Trolley* were placed in boxcar shipments to go to Stalag Luft Three, in Silesia. This would be their address for the next eight months.

The map of Germany at that time was shaped like a wolf's head, with Czechoslovakia between the jaws. Using that simile, Luft Three was in the upper jaw, while the five noncommissioned officers of the crew were in the lower jaw, at Stalag Seventeen B, between the towns of Krems and Gneixendorf, on the Danube River, in German-occupied Austria.

25

Recycling of a Slightly Used Fortress

The *Toonerville Trolley* would never fly again. It lay on its crushed belly near the bottom of the Buberg. A large cherry tree was imbedded solidly in the left wing, between engine and cockpit. A propeller, hub and all, had been torn from its mounting on number four engine.

Here is how witnesses at Bubach described it in in the book *Die Fliegende Festung bei Bubach in Ostertal. 24 April 1944:*

For a few hours people were not prevented from approaching, even going inside the fuselage. One man claimed to have pulled a switch, out of curiosity, turning on a light in the edge of one wing. Some things were taken from inside the plane, perhaps as souvenirs, before there could be any restrictions.

Before dark, after the word had spread, people came in droves to have a close look at the bomber and admire the unusual vehicle. This could be done without any restriction for about three hours. Some who were especially crafty showed up with barrels and tubes, hoping to tap off some of the badly needed fuel. Children were climbing on and in the aircraft, which was not without some danger. Edmund Kaiser of Konken, for example, was messing around with the top turret and started it turning.

Then some men of the Bubach Landwatch arrived led by Wilhelm Harth, who wore a white armband and had a gun slung over his shoulder. They cordoned off the area within a radius of fifty meters, using two parallel wires fixed on wooden posts.

The Kusel County leadership of the Nazi Party had a very special idea. Before the day was over they would organize a coach to cart people from Kusel and surrounding villages to the Buberg hill. On their way, at Konken, they picked up more passengers. Among these "bomber tourists" was county leadership member Dr. Krebs, a dentist in Kusel. By 6:00 P.M. the bus arrived at the site of the crash, and all were given a lesson in the vulnerability of the American machines they had seen so often flying overhead at a great distance.

One of the huge three-bladed propellers from the Flying Fortress was discovered in the "broom" and also became an object of curiosity. Werner Weisgerber and two other young boys from Saint Wendel sat on it and had their picture taken.

Several families came to take pictures of the huge airplane. Little Gernot Spengler, with his brothers Dieter and Ingo, posed with their mother and grandmother so that the cherry tree and the words *Toonerville Trolley* could be seen in the picture.

On the next day soldiers arrived and removed armament from the plane, such as any machine guns that were left or had not been destroyed in the landing. It is claimed that the belts of fifty-caliber bullets remaining were "fired off" by the military, since they would not fit any weapon used by the Wehrmacht or Luftwaffe.

The restricted area around the B-17 existed for three days, the aircraft being guarded by the Landwatch from surrounding villages day and night until the Luftwaffe experts came to remove technical material and ammunition.

The silvery metal of the airplane glittered in the sun and was visible from as far away as Werschweiler. When an "air mine" was thrown in the vicinity, people interpreted this as an attempt of the Americans to destroy the aircraft to prevent it from falling into enemy hands.

According to the Oster Valley historians, after the Flying Fortress had lain on the hillside for nearly two weeks, guarded by the Landwatch, a regiment of Luftwaffe *Techniker* arrived and began taking it apart. Hundreds of gallons of valuable high-octane gasoline were pumped out of the wing tanks; then engines and instruments were removed before the major wing, tail, and fuselage sections were dismantled. All was loaded onto trucks, hauled to the railroad facility in Niederkirchen, and stacked there. The sun continued to reflect off the bright silvery surfaces, causing some displeasure among the people who feared that enemy bombers might be attracted to it and use it for a target.

At the end of June, three empty freight cars arrived and all the material was put on board. By six o'clock one evening they were all loaded and connected to a train going in the direction of Ottweiler. The last car held the barrels of fuel taken from the *Toonerville Trolley*'s tanks.

A technical army unit, the First Squadron of Combat Regiment 200 (1/KG 200) specialized in rebuilding enemy aircraft and putting them back in service for the Luftwaffe. Several B-17s were known to be in the hands of the Germans, one nearby in Bavaria used for testing and decoy. It is doubtful, however, that the bomber from Bubach could have been reassembled. Most likely the aluminum was delivered to a foundry for recycling into Luftwaffe fighter planes.

While doing historic research on our Toonerville Trolley and the fate of its crew, Klaus Zimmer learned about another Flying Fortress shot down in this region. The name on the nose was *Bombo*. It broke up in the air after having been hit, and all were able to bail out except the top turret gunner. Two of the parachutists fell into the wrong hands and were executed.

The tail gunner was successful in leaving the plane and opening his parachute, but as he was descending one of the wings that had broken from the bomber smashed into him. His chute and clothing were stripped from his body as he fell, and the silken canopy was seen taking several minutes to flutter to earth by itself.

Over fifty years later, after many letters and phone calls, Klaus Zimmer located the brother of this tail gunner, living in North Carolina and learned that the family had been told only that the boy had parachuted and was killed. A regional newspaper picked up the story, telling of the brother's gratitude in finally learning how the death had occurred and that there could have been no opportunity for pain and suffering.

26

Standing Together as Friends

Fifty-two years had passed. It was almost incomprehensible.

Of all of the traumatic moments of the war, for me those brief ones on that German hillside in Bubach may have been the worst. When I slid down off the fuselage of the crumpled B-17 and stood in the field I had little idea where I was. But I knew we were deep inside enemy territory and in really bad trouble.

From a great distance I could hear the rumble of our squadron's surviving bombers going home without us. Our bomb group's base at Podington, England, no longer existed for us. The odds against our ever seeing it again just went up to a million to one.

That was on April 24, 1944.

But today, in 1996, as I stood on that same exact spot, the German and American flags were flying side by side. For one quick moment I pictured the red flag with a black swastika in a white circle that had flown here then.

Now, as our two national anthems went echoing down the valley, we were all comrades, at peace, and all was well. The three of us flyers, ex–tail gunner Cran Blaylock, and ex–Luft-waffe pilot Hans Berger, who had brought us to the ground, reached out to hold hands together. We did not need to see each other's faces to know we were deeply moved. We could feel it through our clasped hands.

We turned to enjoy the spectacle out beyond the flags where the balloon ascension was about to happen. A number of American schoolchildren from Baumholder were standing within the marked profile of our bomber, each holding a handful of colored balloons. On signal, or actually just before the signal, catching many photographers off-guard, the colored balloons were released. They streamed up into the cloudy sky as Dr. Keller said they represented the disappearance of our bomber, and our enmity, forever. Today was the German religious holiday Christi Himmelfahrt, Ascension Day, and the symbolism was doubly important to those watching in the fields.

Our clasping of hands was a spontaneous move, intended only for the moment, but many people with cameras and camcorders insisted we hold the pose for them. This would be the picture chosen for the newspapers and for the evening TV news programs.

Hans turned his head and whispered, "One of the most moving moments of my life." Cran and I could only nod agreement.

Col. Roger Hansen, deputy commander of Ramstein Air Force Base, came to the speaker stand and courageously read his speech in German. Dr. Keller seemed to feel that it was understood and made no move to translate it. When my turn came I spoke for the American crewmen who parachuted or came down with the plane and give a quick description of my feelings as we leaped from the plane, right where we now stood half a century later. Dr. Keller stepped to the microphone and inadvertently began to translate my remarks into English. I reached over and tugged at his sleeve, reminding him that the people might like to hear them in German. This took a little of the somberness out of the ceremony, and all laughed together.

There was a brief pause in the speech making as a NATO jet fighter did a fly-over. The cloud cover was low and we agreed with Hans that the pilot was wise to stay above it. "One *Notlandung* on the Buberg in our lifetime is enough," he said.

Hans wore a blue cap just like the white one I wore. The "Gray Eagles" emblem on it showed the USAF "star and bar" and above it a flying eagle, very much like the one on Luftwaffe pilot wings. We three had decided on the caps to symbolize the bond between the nations' flyers but chose blue for Germans and white for Americans to help people in the distinction as they spoke with us in one language or the other.

Cran forgot to bring his. He was interviewed by a *Stars and Stripes* reporter as he stood at his tail position within the B-17 outline, while other reporters talked with Hans Berger and me. We both marveled at the skill, and luck, of course, that pilot Dick Anthony had shared with us that day. My quiet remark to Cran was meant to get a grin out of him, but it didn't. "We may owe

Dick our lives, but Hans owes us for the 'First Class' he got added to his Iron Cross."

A number of people were getting our signatures, or *Autograms*, on their copies of the book *Die Fliegende Festung bei Bubach,* and many were asking us to pose for one more picture. Klaus Zimmer was having difficulty moving us up the hill to where we were to plant the cherry tree, and I could tell by his high level of anxiety that we were running late. His name was mentioned several times during our speeches, giving him credit for all of this, but he simply stood back in the crowd and smiled.

Forty bombers and seventeen fighters were lost by the Eighth Air Force on that April day in 1944. Wartime statistics show that we were in the lucky fraction who made it to the ground and lived to tell about it.

The Americans claimed that eighty-six German fighters were shot down on that day. As was usually the case, that number was reduced somewhat after the verification processes and cross-checking for multiple claims. Some of the German flyers shot down survived their parachute jump or *Notlandung* and went back up to fight again, as Hans Berger had done on at least two occasions. There was no limit to the number of sorties they had to fly. They were in for as long as they were able to fly or until the war was over.

Neither JG/1 (the Oesau *Geschwader*) nor JG/26 (the Abbeyville Kids) reported any losses on April 24. This meant that other units involved in the attacks on our Forty-first Wing did suffer losses, since German fighters were going down, observed both from the air and from the ground.

One of the *Toonerville Trolley* crew made a positive sighting of a brown parachute. As far as we knew, all chutes used by Americans were white. More than once I saw aircraft debris fly past my turret, and I had thought some was from Luftwaffe planes. However, it all could very well have been marked:BOEING, USA.

The black crosses on the wings of one German fighter were clearly visible to me as he pulled up sharply from a shallow dive. What I believed to be his cockpit canopy went flying off before I spun away to try to put another attacker in my gun sight. It was possible that he brought his plane down for a landing with no canopy from the high altitude at which we were flying. He may also have made a successful bailout. He would be of much higher value to the Luftwaffe than his airplane.

When Hans Berger made his presentation to the German people and American guests assembled on the hill at Bubach, he said that he was trying to knock down an American bomber, not to kill men.

"What a good feeling it was to learn from Klaus Zimmer, after all those years," he said, "that all ten men of this B-17 called the *Toonerville Trolley* had survived both the shooting and the crash of their airplane right here where we stand today."

All reacted with applause, the German people, the Americans, the French officers, the schoolchildren, and especially Cran Blaylock and I.

It took over three months for official Luftwaffe records to acknowledge Hans Berger's "kill." Certification of an *Abschuss*, an enemy plane shot down, could come only from the minister of aviation and supreme commander of the Wehrmacht. Included with illustrations is a copy of the Hans Berger certificate datelined Berlin, July 31, 1944.

Awards of the Iron Cross and Knight's Cross were based on certified kills. With the high casualty rate of Luftwaffe fighter pilots during 1944 and 1945, many such awards were posthumous.

27

A Time for Gemütlichkeit!

Delayed by the many people shaking our hands and thrusting copies of the *Fliegende Festung* book toward us for *Autograms*, we three former enemies and now friends were almost the last to leave the hilltop site of the "Peace Tree" planting.

"Please hurry," said Klaus. "People are waiting at the giant marquee which is set up down toward the village." Then he rushed on ahead to make sure all was in readiness.

Ex–Luftwaffe pilot Berger invited Cran, Dan and me to ride down with him in his BMW sedan, but first we sat and got the chill out of our bones, talking about the emotions we had just experienced while standing in front of our two nations' flags.

As we wound down the narrow roadway we saw a number of cars parked along the shoulders. The former fighter pilot expertly worked his way in between two of them. As we got out and hurried toward the colorful tents, a group of happy people surged toward us with words of greeting. We shook hands all around, and bottles of Pilsener were thrust toward us.

"This is great!" Dan said, getting into the spirit of things. One of the men quieted the crowd and, in halting English, said, "We are so glad you are taking time from your busy program to come and visit with us, and we hereby present you with honorary membership in our association." With that, he gave to each of us a lapel pin shaped like a boot and imprinted: WANDER-UND NATURFREUNDE.

"This is strange," said Hans. "They have just made us members of a hiking club, and this is their annual outing."

Before we could learn more, one of our historian hosts ran up, all out of breath. "You are in the wrong place," he said. "Our group is farther on, and they are all waiting your arrival."

Our festival was just down the hill a bit. There was plenty of room for parking and for the huge marquee, as well as some small tents from which beer and sausage were being dispensed. It had been cold and windy on the *Buberg*, and at this point a cup of hot coffee would have been more welcome than anything. But when I asked at one of the kiosks for such a *Getrank* the fraulein seemed to be telling me that she had "kein Eis," or "no ice." Dan reminded me once again to strike that word *heiss* from my German vocabulary. "They think you are speaking English and saying 'ice,'" he reminded me. "Just ask for *Kaffee*. It will be hot."

At a table in one corner, our hosts, the Cultural and Historical Association, were selling copies of the book *Die Fliegende Festung bei Bubach*. They were well into their second thousand, and for the next few hours it seemed that Cran, Hans, and I were all asked to *autogram*, or sign, the cover of every copy. Although hard on my cold hands, it did wonderful things for my ego. If these German people, young and old, were not genuinely glad to have us with them for this occasion, then they had us fooled.

Klaus Zimmer introduced Cran and me to a man named Ewald Neu of Pfeffelbach. I recognized the name right away. It was the signature on the drawing of the *Toonerville Trolley* made by a young boy who had witnessed the descent while working in the woods with his grandfather.

Now an artist of some note in the region, Ewald Neu asked Klaus to tell us he would be presenting each with a drawing he had made especially for us. What a strange feeling to be shaking the hand of someone who actually had watched our airplane during its final moment of flight fifty-two years ago.

Ewald described, and Klaus interpreted for us, what he remembered about the event. "People said that your bomber seemed to be gliding down into our valley. It flew first over Herchweiler, then Bruckerbusch Wood close to Osterbrucken and the Klingelberg hill. When it approached the hill called Buberg, near Bubach, we watched it and were certain it would hit the ground."

Another introduction was made: "Ed and Cran, here to meet you is Werner Weisgerber. He was the boy sitting on the hub of the propeller you lost. The two who were sitting with him are both dead." I quickly flipped open one of our books to the picture, and he smiled, nodding his head when I pointed at his picture. Werner was now sixty-four. He got our signatures in his book.

131

One newspaper story on the next day described it this way: "All three of the flyers were much wanted people to talk to, had constantly to answer questions and to give autographs all the time. They all fulfilled the many wishes indefatigably and with friendliness."

At the far end of the marquee was a stage, and on it was a band. The members were in Bavarian costume and playing honest-to-goodness "oompah" German band music, the kind that will not allow the feet to remain still. They were listed in the program as the "Musical Association Saal/Hoof." Saal and Hoof were two villages in the Saint Wendel district. As we pressed our way toward the table held open for us near the bandstand, a little girl of three or four stood in front of me, doing spins and bows, seeming to be saying, "Come and dance with me."

In the newspaper it was reported: "Spontaneously, McKenzie took a little girl by the arms and danced with her through the marquee."

Her mother and father and Dr. Keller smiled and clapped encouragement. "Berger and Blaylock," the article went on, "seemed to enjoy all the publicity. McKenzie's brother was deeply moved, with tears in his eyes."

On reading this, Dan commented, "Maybe my sore throat and inability to talk had something to do with those tears in my eyes."

A young boy named Schenkel had heard about the bomber crash on the Buberg, and he rode his bicycle over from his village, arriving before guards were posted around the airplane.

He wanted to get some souvenirs to take home, but having only his bicycle wrench for a tool, there was little that he could dismantle. He climbed into the waist and a few minutes later rode away with some items in his pockets.

For over fifty years those items were among the tools on his workbench, and when he heard about the community's plans for our visit he got an idea. He would give back to the Americans a part of their airplane and give one also to the Luftwaffe pilot as a souvenir of his victory that day.

When Herr Schenkel was given the microphone, he made a

long presentation speech, getting many laughs from all the people gathered in the marquee. Dan was now so hoarse that he was unable to explain what was being said, and by the time Dr. Keller gave a formal interpretation the humor seemed to have been lost.

Nevertheless, each of the three of us would take home a piece of the *Toonerville Trolley*, beautifully mounted on an oak panel with an explanatory inscription on a brass plaque. My own treasured memento of the *Trolley* is a hose clamp from the oxygen system, probably removed from a waist gun position by the young Mr. Schenkel on that day so long ago.

Another regional newspaper, the *St. Wendeler Zeitung*, reported on May 14, 1996:

> Fritz Jung of Saal handed back an oxygen control device from the bomber. Ewald Schenkel of Marth presented them with three pipe clamps he had taken off the bomber as a youth, which were now fastened to boards with an inscribed dedication of commemoration.
>
> The Bubach Horticultural Association has taken over the responsibility for the planted cherry tree. Armin Lensch gave to each of the flyers a jar of honey collected by his bees in the area of the plane's crash landing.

When Hans Berger and I were each asked to describe briefly for the crowd what our recollections were of that day, April 24, 1944, it became very quiet. Although I had what I wanted to say clearly in my mind, it was not an easy thing to do. It helped somewhat to be able to pause so that Dr. Keller could translate my remarks into German. I felt an obligation to conclude by telling them that considering the cruelties and killings that were almost commonplace in Europe in those days, Cran, the two other crewmen, and I were treated with firmness but compassion by the people of Bubach. "We thank them for our lives," I said.

Hans's description of his day was a summary of what he has provided for this book. When he told of his flying career with his *Staffel* and of the many friends and comrades killed during the war there were tears in his eyes, and when he told of their brave actions in attacking into the guns of hundreds of bombers, all in defense of their country, there were tears in most eyes in the crowd.

Their pride in him and his flying comrades was clearly evident and had nothing to do with governments, politics, or policies.

When we returned to our seats I heard Dan say to Hans, "What a wonderful thing you have just done for the morale of all these people. I watched them as you spoke. Young and old, they were bursting with pride in you and your comrades. Maybe it was pride that some were unwilling or unable to express in the years right after the war."

There are no words to describe the experience of being saluted by an Alpine horn quartet playing "Amazing Grace," a hymn that had been popular with the Eighth Air Force flyers. The versatile Walter Harth, whose grandfather had marched us into the village with a weapon at our backs, played the lead horn. When the long instruments were laid aside, Walter gathered his *Hausmusikgruppe* for their program. It began with "Am Loch Lomond" and was dedicated "to the Scotsman Ed McKenzie."

Near the end, Hans and I moved out to where we could sit with the audience to join them in singing a song that not only was popular with German soldiers but had been picked up by English and American soldiers as well. I was familiar with the German version and sang, in harmony with Hans, "Wie einst, Lily Marlene; wie einst, Lily Marlene," as the program concluded.

PART II

28

The Dreaded Interrogation

We had all been instructed how to act if taken as a prisoner of war, whether or not we would remember it when the chips were down.

The "Code of Conduct" for members of the armed forces included these pledges. Emphasis is on interrogation by the enemy:

If captured I will continue to resist by all means available. I will make every effort to escape and will aid others to escape. I will accept neither parole nor special favors from the enemy.

If I become a prisoner of war I will keep faith with my fellow prisoners. I WILL GIVE NO INFORMATION nor take part in any action which might be harmful to my comrades.

I will obey the lawful orders of those appointed over me and will back them up in every way.

WHEN QUESTIONED, should I become prisoner of war, I AM BOUND TO GIVE ONLY NAME, RANK AND SERVICE NUMBER AND DATE OF BIRTH. [Many did not realize that their birthdate was not a military secret.]

I WILL EVADE ANSWERING FURTHER QUESTIONS to the utmost of my ability. I will make no oral or written statements disloyal to my country or its allies or harmful to their cause.

I will never forget that I am an American fighting man, responsible for my actions and dedicated to the principles which made my country free.

I will trust in my God and in the United States of America.

Now, half a century later, we three ex–prisoners of war, one German and two Americans, sat and talked together about the experience, as our tour was held up for a while. There was some hope that the squalls would end soon.

Whether German, American, or English, soldiers were

sworn to obey a "Code of Conduct." These countries had signed the articles of agreement we refer to now as the Geneva Convention.

All members of the German armed forces had to swear an oath to support their Fuhrer, Adolf Hitler, beyond their Code of Conduct.

When Hans Berger was captured late in the war, his situation was somewhat different from ours. When he and Karl Demuth were made prisoners by the British, there was little, if anything, to be gained by their questioners that might affect the outcome of the war. Their technical knowledge of the Heinkel jets? The Allies had gotten everything, airplanes, tools, blueprints, tech manuals, and no doubt many of the engineers who had designed them.

But we American flyers had found ourselves in the interrogator's office at the *Dulag* when the Luftwaffe was still building its intelligence files about people, locations, techniques, and equipment of the Eighth Air Force. The questioners had acquired plenty of experience. Thousands of flyers had sat in those cells and on those stools, and file drawers were loaded with data.

The *Trolley* crew added to those files when a photograph of our B-17 arrived at the *Dulag* with us. The markings on the tail actually meant more to the Germans than they did to me. I did not know that the triangle on our tail meant we were in the First Division, nor did I know that the series of numbers below was the Boeing company's identification of that particular airplane. Our interrogators had new information to add to their files.

There were differing ideas among the flyers, whether in the fighter pilot or bomber crew sections of the *Dulag*: (A) If you were kept there very long, then it might be suspected back home that you were being cooperative and giving information to the enemy, or (B) if you were shipped out to a permanent camp right away, then you must have been very cooperative with the enemy. The Germans knew about this and sometimes made use of it in determining whether to extend one's stay or speed him on his way to the stalag.

The Luftwaffe's master interrogator, Hanns Scharff, commented on this in the book by Raymond Toliver. Scharff suggested that he might reinforce the beliefs of flyers that a long stay at the *Dulag* might mean they could be subject to court-martial after the war. It became a tool to use in breaking down a prisoner's will. Just by hearing, "Well, I guess we'll keep you here for another few weeks," a prisoner might be influenced to start talking.

Many prisoners were surprised to learn that brutality was not used at the *Dulag*. The Germans had become experts at getting information without resorting to torture. This does not mean that the POWs were without hardships and suffering. A great many who experienced the *Dulag* have unpleasant memories of solitary confinement in tiny, cold, and/or overheated cells while on a diet of black bread and water.

Arriving at the Frankfurt interrogation center, we *Toonerville Trolley* crew members were marched into a building and up before a long table where a German soldier sat, pencil in hand. There was a sign-in procedure; then I was asked to empty my pockets, remove anything that was not clothing, and place it on the table.

I was still in possession of my wristwatch and wallet and little else. The escape kit had long ago been removed from inside my shirt. I was asked to raise my arms, and a soldier went through my pockets. The tiny compass was still in the button-hem of my shirt and the magnetized needle in one of the belt loops of my pants. *If they find them will they consider me a spy?* I wondered.

To my surprise, I was quickly motioned to pick up my things from the table and go along outside.

Waiting there was an English-speaking *Unteroffizier*. When all in my group had come out, he ordered us into a line, called "Attention!" then proceeded, in a loud voice, to read some warnings and instructions.

"You must make no attempt to escape," he said, "and even by accident you must not touch or approach that single strand of barbed wire that encircles the area."

He pointed to a small sign hanging from the wire strand. It read: WARNING. IF YOU TOUCH OR CROSS THIS WIRE YOU WILL BE FIRED UPON WITHOUT WARNING.

"If you get too close to it," he went on, "the guards in those towers," he pointed upward, "are ordered to shoot you. Is that very clear?"

As we looked up at the machine gun pointed directly at us it seemed very clear indeed. We were dismissed from the formation.

At long last there came an order to assemble at one of the buildings for *essen*. I now knew the German word for "eat." Two Americans were approaching with what looked like a large wooden tub, a *Kebo*, suspended from the pole on their shoulders. It was steaming and from it came the strong odor of turnips, a smell I would learn to love and hate over the coming weeks.

Behind the *Kebo* men were two others with a gray blanket slung between them. From the blanket they dumped onto the floor a heap of black disks, each about the size of a washbasin. These disks were soon hacked up with bayonets, and a chunk was handed to each man in line. Those bread loaves had hit the floor like stones and appeared to have been rolled in the dirt of the yard. However, none of us were in a mood to be critical at this point.

One of the American POWs came along the line, giving to each a bowl and a tablespoon. As we approached the tub of soup, it appeared to be very thin and I assumed that the pale yellow cubes in it were turnip. There were also many specks that may or may not have been spices. I found that the warm fluid was necessary to the process of chewing the sour black bread so it could be swallowed.

As the sun was setting we talked together, trying to think of anything but what lay ahead. The interrogation that we dreaded had to be something terrible. My only consoling thought was, *How much can a kid like me know about things that might be helpful to the Germans? Why will they go to any trouble to pump me for knowledge that I couldn't possibly have?*

Not only was I ignorant of the name of my commanding officer and location of my air base, but I didn't even know the name of the pilot with whom I had just been flying or the tail gunner who had helped me out of my turret. If I was forced to talk, then I might have to make up some stuff in an awful hurry. I didn't know what my reaction would be to torture or beating, but I

140

would hold out as long as I could and just see what happened. We all assumed, wrongly, that there would be some physical abuse connected with the interrogation.

There was agreement that one must simply respond with his name, rank, and serial number to whatever question was asked. One man later said that when handed a paper to fill out with information he simply made a big *X* on it and threw it back. I found that hard to believe. Who would respond in that way to the courteous, pleasant comments and casual questions of a Luftwaffe officer giving every appearance of being anxious to just finish off his check sheet with a smile and send you on your way? Most would not try to antagonize him. Well, my turn was coming and I would find out.

We talked only light subjects with one another, having been warned that German agents would have been placed in with us to gather information. Our conversations were kept on things like how hungry or cold we were or the conditions around us. There were some stories told about how we had each gotten into this fix, things we supposed would give nothing to German intelligence people. I heard many strange tales about airplanes being shot out of the sky and flyers surviving all sorts of flames, explosions, and falls from miles above the earth.

There were some who had no recollection at all of what had happened to them. One moment they were involved in an air battle; then they found themselves out in the air hanging from their shroud lines or even in a tree or on the ground. Some had to overcome several "G" forces to push themselves out of their spinning planes. Two B-26 gunners had been blown out when their plane exploded.

We were ready to laugh at almost anything. There was a Louisiana tail gunner with an accent that made him barely understandable, and he loved to tell stories. He had parachuted from his B-17 just seconds before it exploded. He claimed to have crashed through the tile roof of a large country home, ending up sprawled on top of a grand piano. When he came out of his daze the family members were standing around him, staring at him, while calling for a servant to come and take him into custody.

"Can y'all 'magin' thet?" he said. "Ah s'rended to a gawdam *butlah!*"

We thought up lines he might have used in that situation, like: "Hope you folks don't mind my dropping in this way" or "Is there anything by Beethoven you'd like me to play?" It seemed hilariously funny.

One of the men said this was his fourth day at the *Dulag* and told us what we might expect next. He said, "You'll be taken in and put in a cell to wait your turn. The waiting may last only a few hours, but it could last many days and nights." He had heard about prisoners questioned and returned to their cells over and over again for a long time. It could depend on what one might reveal, what they thought one might be able to reveal, or maybe even the mood of the Luftwaffe officer on that particular day. It would also depend, we learned, on the volume of flyers who had to be processed. There were large numbers being shot down over Germany these days. Few of the survivors managed to avoid capture for very long. There was lots of company with me at the *Dulag*, and another truckload was arriving even as we talked.

When it was dark we were ordered inside, finding sleeping places on or under the triple-tiered bunk structures. There was no bedding of any kind. As I lay there shivering, I thought of the heavy wool overcoat I had been issued and how I wished it were here and not back there in my barracks bag in England.

Sometime during the night air-raid sirens sounded from very nearby. It was a terrifying sound, but when it stopped then came the "thud-boom" sounds of antiaircraft guns. Then I heard the rumble of RAF bombers passing high overhead, but no bomb bursts. The noises died away and an "all clear" was sounded. Somehow I was able to sleep for a few hours.

At dawn the stomping of steel-clad boots and shouts of, "Appell! Appell! [Roll call! Roll call!]" had everyone up and moving toward the cold mist in the compound. Now there seemed to be about a hundred of us, and the guards pushed and shouted us into ranks. As one of them walked down the rows, he would poke a finger at the chest of each man as the signal for him to shout out "Name und Vorname." This caused confusion among some GIs who had never fully comprehended "last name first, first name last" during basic training. The German guards' wild pronunciations of names added to the confusion, but eventually the clipboard was lowered and we seemed to be all accounted for.

We were held in ranks while there began a calling out of names in groups of four. I stepped out with three others and was prodded along into another section of the camp. The building we entered had steel bars at the windows, and entry was through a heavy door. We went up a flight of stairs and along a corridor past several doors; then I was halted.

As a door was pulled open, I saw a peephole and a small trapdoor before it was slammed behind me. In the light from the bare bulb overhead I saw I was in a small cubicle, perhaps five or six feet square. The only thing in there with me was an electric radiant heater mounted on the base of the rear wall. There was no window. Sitting down with my back against the door, I let the heat soak into my cold, aching bones. It seemed that maybe more than hunger was keeping me weak and shaky and that the grippe or flu might be involved. I had forgotten whether the old saying was "stuff a cold and starve a fever" or vice versa. That heat felt so good that I didn't think there was any fever to be concerned with. Unable to lie straight out in the small space, I turned like a roast on a spit for several hours and finally got relief from the chills.

The lightbulb never turned off, nor did the heater. It was probably a hundred degrees in the cell, and now it was becoming oppressive. In my naiveté I thought, *Gee, the Germans must be having a problem with their heating controls. They shouldn't be wasting electricity this way.*

Later, when I stood and read some of the graffiti scratched into the wall by other POWs, I began to suspect that maybe the discomfort was intentional. One had printed out, cyclorama fashion: "Don't give up hope. God is with you." Another had written: "They can kill your body but not your soul." Here I was, supposedly a Christian, with a Bible back in my footlocker, yet I hadn't given a thought to religion until now. If those words had been meant to bring comfort, they didn't seem to be working for me. I considered taking off my belt buckle and inscribing my own message but had to conclude that I really had no advice to give to anyone who might later be confined here.

There were a dozen or so names on the wall, and I realized that this had not been just a brief interlude for some of them and that the guards might already have forgotten I was here. The cell gave just enough space for my almost six-foot body, but it meant that either head or feet had to be too close to that heater. The best position seemed to be the one I was used to in the ball turret, back against the door and knees drawn up.

It seemed an eternity before I heard the trap being lifted. A bucket, obviously for body waste, was passed in. While I stared at it a hand came through the trap bearing a pan of soup and I very carefully took it, upending the bucket to use for a dining table. I sipped slowly on the soup, saving the few chunks of vegetable matter for last.

Later I used the bucket for its intended purpose. The heat soon made it an unwelcome companion. Eventually the trap opened and a hand motioned for me to pass out both my utensils.

Although it seemed longer, it probably was not more than twenty-four hours before I was pulled from the cell. I imagined how terrible it must have been for those forced to spend many days there.

Even though it was now the dreaded "interrogation time," I was glad to be out. My final hours had been spent in trying to avoid staring at the lightbulb, turning my body for even exposure to the radiant heat, and reciting any poetry that I could recall. I was glad that I had been forced to memorize a few verses of Whittier's "Snowbound" and all of "Abu ben Adam." Then there were a few limericks about a young man from Nantucket and an old lady from Worcester (rhyming with *rooster* and *used to*). I had learned all of Poe's "The Raven" during evenings in the barracks, and the word, "Nevermore," echoed ominously in my cell as I said it aloud. This all helped me to fight down the panicky claustrophobic feelings that continually nibbled at the edges of my mind.

It was now, too, that I had my first real thoughts about the world outside. Was it really only a few days ago that I had left England and written that letter to my sister? I imagined that my name already had been removed from the status board and my 201 file sent back to the States. Someone had already removed my name tag from the bicycle and put his own on it. The personal items from my footlocker had been picked over, some of them shipped back home to my family (as it turned out, even the dirty socks and underwear).

Some of my original crew might still survive back there. We had developed a close relationship, and I pictured their concern when they had seen us peeling away from them with two engines burning. In the old movie *Dawn Patrol* the buddies would have gathered in the pub and raised a toast to the guys who didn't make it back. But I had always imagined myself being one of those doing the toasting.

As the guard pushed me along down the corridor my legs kept folding under me, from having been bent at the knees for so long in the cell. This, along with the curious habit of the guards of shoving rather than simply pointing the way, caused me to stumble as I stepped into the room.

It may have been intentional, perhaps to humiliate or intimidate me, because here I was on my knees before a little table, behind which sat a smiling Luftwaffe officer. As I stood, I was holding my clenched hands up near my face, not as an act of hostility but just a reaction to having the little pieces of metal driven deeper into my hands as I hit the floor.

I unclenched and gave a military salute, which he returned while motioning me toward a chair opposite him. It felt good to sit down and be over the chills and fever that had bothered me since that night in the *Baumholder* cell with Ed Kolber. I was not shaking now, and I felt calm.

"Well, Sergeant McKenzie, I hope you are being treated all right?" Then he introduced himself and poised his pen over a paper on the table. "Give me your full name, rank, serial number and birthdate so we can get that out of the way," he said. While I was pondering that last item, birthdate, he surprised me with the next comment, which sounded quite logical to me. He said that it was his duty, as agreed to under rules of the Geneva Convention governing the treatment of war prisoners, to send certain information to the International Red Cross. "Your government and your family must be notified," he said, "that you were not killed and are a prisoner of war."

The form seemed official, all right, and there were lines there for "next of kin" and "home address." But there was also something about "most recent military unit assignment."

While I was considering the implications of refusal and

seeking a way to do it without hurting his feelings, he read my hesitation as uncertainty about orders and motioned me to go ahead and write. No doubt this had been successful with many, understandably. But I had psyched myself to stick with the basics only. He offered me a cigarette and a light from a Zippo lighter. Even though I really didn't want it, I accepted it. No need of being more negative than I had to be, so I took a puff, then began to say, "I'm sorry, sir, but I am not allowed—"

"*Ja, ja,* I know. Why is it that a few of you Americans are so suspicious when we are only trying to do what is required of us and what is best for you?"

As I said, "I don't know how it's done, sir; I was just given simple instructions," the thought came to me: *Oh boy. Here you are violating one of the rules of those simple instructions: do not let your interrogator get you into a discussion.*

"Perhaps you would like to have your parents or your wife spend the next several years not knowing if you are dead or alive? Is that it, Sergeant?" he asked, seeming to be disgusted. "Of what possible use could such personal information be to the German government?"

It sounded quite rational. "I don't know anything about that, sir. I can only give my name, rank, and —"

He cut me off, "*Ja, ja,* I know," in a harsher tone now. "You insist on using up my valuable time to your own disadvantage. This hurts only you and your family."

(I would learn many years later that some U.S. flyers' dog tags showed the name and address of next of kin.)

Now he reached into a pile and pulled out a folder. "We do have you clearly identified with your airplane. I have the photo right here, so please simply acknowledge what we already know to be facts and we can be finished."

He held up a picture showing the huge tail of our Flying Fortress standing out sharply against the hillside, and clearly readable was the big letter *B* inside a triangle. Just below was a series of numbers.

"Now you can save me the bother of looking it up in our Eighth Air Force records. What was your base and commanding officer's name?"

I couldn't have given him that even if I had decided to confess all. I had no idea what my CO's name was, and I knew little about the Ninety-second Bomb Group location, other than East Anglia. I had an idea that the triangle B tied us to the air division and group. Other markings were a mystery to me, but I guessed that the Luftwaffe could figure them out. "I don't know," I said.

"Well, Sergeant McKenzie, this *is* a picture of your airplane, isn't it?" he asked impatiently, and I nodded my head.

Damn! I had done it again. The nodding of my head had told him something beyond my name, rank, and serial number. This was not as easy as it had sounded at briefings. I was determined not to make any more mistakes.

After a few more comments and questions, during which I kept my mouth closed and my head still, the officer's voice seemed to become louder and he leaned across the table, nearly bumping heads with me as he stood up. Then he shouted, "Posten. Schnell!" It was an instant before I realized that he was not addressing me but the guard outside the door. To me he said, "Stand up and be at attention."

As I leaped to obey, I heard the guard step up behind me and his rifle butt hit the floor. I braced to take some kind of a blow. He stood quietly, however, since the shouting was now at him and not at me. Not understanding the words, I figured they concerned my immediate welfare. Like waiting for the dentist who had picked up his drill, I was preparing myself for the next phase of interrogation, which was bound to involve pain.

But it didn't happen. In a calm and quiet voice the *Leutnant* said, "Sergeant, I gave you this opportunity to act like a good soldier to help me with these simple questions. They are not military secrets; don't you know that?" He gave a quick laugh, motioned to the guard, and gave an order that I hoped meant "get him out of here!"

Going back down the corridor, I felt almost elated that perhaps the dreaded interrogation was over, that I still had a relatively intact body and had not drawn out the secret plans for the Norden bomb sight or the coming invasion of the Continent. Nevertheless, there had been a parting hint that I might be given another chance.

It was a different "hotbox" cell this time, but like the last.

The heat was now unwelcome. I sat once again in solitary, fighting down claustrophobia while trying not to stare at the lightbulb overhead. I lapped sweat from the backs of my hands to moisten my lips and tongue. Still, I did feel better than before. The fever and chills had ended, and now the sickening concern about interrogation was over.

In a few hours it was soup and bucket time and I tried to extend the few minutes of relative pleasure, but the guard's insistent hands motioned at the door slot for return of his utensils.

Then there was plenty of time for me to examine graffiti. There seemed to be a lot of references to God. Should I be asking for His help? I had always been too analytical in my religion and wasn't sure just how God decided which individual He was going to help when two opposing sides were presented to Him. I had surely been "hoping and wishing" for things to turn out OK for me and for my buddies, and perhaps that would be taken as "prayer" when the final judgment was made.

After an eternity, which may have been less than twenty-four hours, the door opened and I was ordered to "komm mit" down the stairs and out into the compound.

There was little to do but await the daily wooden tub of soup and the "wheels" of black bread and fall in for regular roll calls by the Luftwaffe guard staff. It was hard to find walking space in the small compound area, and those signs hanging from the single strand of wire inside the fence were quite intimidating.

29

Pilots Evade Capture

Lieutenants Anthony and Raney had gotten away. Maybe they had evaded capture and possibly even got back to England. Or so we let ourselves believe for more than a year afterward. Their freedom lasted only overnight, however.

It was not long before the two pilots were captured and delivered to control of the Luftwaffe, as we had been at Kusel. The farmers were officially, although somewhat reluctantly Dick thought, relieved of their American prisoners.

Parachutist De Paoli had survived the jump, as had the two gunners, Irving Blank and Charles Fields. After hitting the ground they were quickly captured by civilians who turned them over to police or soldiers before SS or Nazi party officials could get to them.

Dick Anthony knew that some of his men had jumped and he wondered about their fates as he sat with his copilot in the cold cell before being removed and marched to the railroad station to await a train for Frankfurt.

Arriving at the *Dulag*, the two pilots talked very carefully, suspecting there might be listening devices placed where they were allowed to be with each other.

Over fifty years later Klaus Zimmer was able to find a report listing men of the Anthony crew who had been turned over to the *Dulag* authorities. One officer and five NCOs were shown.

It is interesting to speculate on why only six men of the *Toonerville Trolley* were put on this report.

Official German Report

Dulag Luft; 20 May 1944—Report number KU 1620

This report covers the *Abschuss* of a Fortress type 2 at 1530 on 24 April 1944. The following American flyers were taken prisoner:

Abschussort: Kaiserslautern
Meldende Dienststelle: Baumholder

Besatzung:

Name und Vornamen. Geburtstag und -ort	Dienst- grad	Erk. Marke:	Gef.: Tot:	Verbleib: Welches Lager
De Paoli William John	2.Lt.	0-746993	gef.	Dulag-Luft
Kolber Edward John 7.1.22 Albany, N.Y.	S/Sgt.	12170907	gef.	Dulag-Luft
Blaylock John Cran	Sgt.	39272772	gef.	Dulag-Luft
Fields Charles Robt.	Sgt.	34625789	gef.	Dulag-Luft
Wildman Chalmer DeW.	S/Sgt.	35742552	gef.	Dulag-Luft
Blank Irving 27.3.23 New York City	Sgt.	12156262	gef.	Dulag-Luft

Bemerkungen: Dulag-Luft, den 20.5.44

The two pilots were not associated with the crew, on this report nor were the two non–regular crew members, McKenzie and Hamilton.

Birthdates and home addresses were imprinted on the dog tags of Kolber and Blank, even though U.S. soldiers were instructed to provide only name, rank, and serial number to the enemy.

A separate Luftwaffe prison facility some miles north of Frankfurt in Oberursel was known as the *Auswertestelle*. It was a special camp for evaluating captured flyers "out of the West." After their experience there, the two *Trolley* pilots were designated for a stop at the *Oflag,* a transient camp near Berlin, before being shipped to Luft III.

There was a Gestapo commando unit stationed next door to the *Oflag,* and the Luftwaffe was aware of being under its gaze much of the time.

Shortly after the *Toonerville Trolley* men had departed from the *Dulag,* the facility was destroyed in a bombing raid. A new one was developed farther out beyond Frankfurt, at Wetzlar.

The five days of intermittent solitary confinement and interrogation experienced by the two pilots may have been more intense, since it was assumed that probably they knew more about their organization and equipment than the enlisted members of the crew did.

30

Destination for Officers: Stalag Luft Three

Within ten days after the crash in Bubach, Dick, his copilot, and his bombardier were squeezed into boxcars headed for the permanent prison camp designated Stalag Luft Three. It had been principally for British officers until American arrivals in ever-increasing numbers after the Eighth Air Force became heavily active in 1943.

Located at Sagan in Nether Silesia, this huge prisoner-of-war camp lay some sixty miles southeast of Berlin, in the easternmost part of Germany. The *Toonerville Trolley* men were marched into the newly opened West Compound, an expansion area built for a capacity of 2,500 prisoners but already holding many more than that. There the newly arriving officers got a new perspective on the war. While flying missions they were aware of three categories of American airmen: "active duty," "missing in action," and "killed in action." Of course, some of the "missings" might eventually turn up as POWs, but the accumulated numbers were staggering. Here in this one camp were thousands who had somehow survived shellfire, explosions, crashes, and bail-outs.

They reminded themselves that German prisoners numbering in the hundreds of thousands were being held in the United States, taking some comfort from the "hostage exchange" situation that existed between the two countries.

Segregation by rank was the rule in German camps, as in British and American camps. The commissioned officers had their camps, and the noncommissioned officers had theirs. Officers of any rank were not required to work outside the barbed-wire enclosures, under provisions of the Geneva Convention, and nearly all Air Corps prisoners held the rank of Sergeant or above. Rank was attained as technical training was achieved for flying crew members.

This created a problem, in that there were few privates for assignment as officers' orderlies, another provision of the Geneva international conference. Enlisted men who volunteered for orderly duties protested when it came to emptying slop buckets and performing other menial tasks. However, under the enlightened leadership at Luft Three, democracy eventually prevailed, at least among the Americans, and each man did his own dirty work. The Army Air Corps in World War II put up with a more liberal attitude among flying personnel and often between flyers and the men on the line who supported them and their aircraft.

Prisoners at Luft Three were consoled by the thought that there were approximately two thousand German soldiers required to keep them secured. The Germans were successful in this, but with a few major exceptions. Just before arrival of the *Toonerville Trolley* men the famous "Great Escape" took place. Eighty prisoners crawled out through one of the well-engineered and strongly built tunnels (named Tom, Dick, and Harry) before the Germans found out what was happening. Nearly all were English, Australian, or Canadian officers. Four of the escapees were quickly caught, but the rest managed to get away from the camp, creating one of the largest man hunts the Reich had ever experienced. Fifty of the men recaptured were shot and killed.

The camp where five other *Toonerville Trolley* men were held was featured in a play and then Academy Award–winning movie named *Stalag Seventeen*. Nearly everyone who watches TV is familiar with that camp or the plot carried over into the Stalag Thirteen of the *Hogan's Heroes* series. Luft Three also got major postwar exposure in an award-winning movie called *The Great Escape*, named for the March 1944 event.

Conditions became much harsher after that escape. Just as the three *Trolley* men arrived, a new *Commandant,* Oberst Braun, arrived to replace the one who was sacked and court-martialed for having allowed such an occurrence.

Several top U.S. and British fighter pilots became POWs here as their luck ran out, including ace "Gabby" Gabreski. John Dunn, a U.S. Navy flyer, was the earliest American to be a resident, but Col. Albert "Red" Clark was only three months behind him, possibly the very first U.S. Army Air Corps pilot out of England to be shot down. He had arrived in England early in the war and had barely unpacked before joining an RAF Spitfire attack on the Abbeyville aerodrome. During a classic battle with Focke Wulfs of the famous Richthofen Geschwader his plane was badly hit. Although he was able to nurse his "Spit" out to the Channel, it was not the British who rescued him. The Germans were no doubt puzzled by the arrival of a U.S. colonel in dress uniform.

One of Hitler's principal aides, Rudolph Hess, had earlier flown a fighter to England, then parachuted. Might they have wondered if Colonel Clark was bringing some special message from the Allied high command? He was not, however, but just unlucky in his christening battle with some of the Abbeyville Kids, in his borrowed Spitfire.

Before arrival of Col. Charles Goodrich, a more senior officer, Al Clark, was the American camp leader of Luft Three. He would, after the war, become superintendent of the Air Force Academy at Colorado Springs, and in the limited society of Men of Confidence, POW camp leaders, he would become friendly with one K. J. Kurtenbach of Stalag Seventeen. Each had held similar levels of responsibility, one as a colonel, the other as a staff sergeant.

During an Eighth Air Force reunion in 1992, in New Orleans "the shot-down experience" was the subject of a symposium. English author and air-war historian Roger Freeman moderated a panel of five of us ex-POWs. We represented inmates of several of the larger German prison camps during the war years. As a part of the program, Roger Freeman solicited recollections from Albert Clark, Donald Jones, Don Wassner, Herb Schlicker, and me about our experiences being shot down, and then of life in captivity.

We five represented Luft Three at Sagan, Luft Four in Pomerania, Luft One at Barth, Luft Seven A near Munich, and Luft Seventeen B near Krems, Austria. The program was video-recorded for the society's archives.

Although most ended up in Luft Three, during their capture and interrogation nearly all fighter pilots were treated differently from other flyers. For one thing, the location of their base and organization generally was known, just as we knew which

Luftwaffe groups attacked us. But further, fighter planes carried gun cameras. The films from those gun cameras provided important information to interrogators, particularly if they were seeking out pilots who may have been guilty of strafing civilian targets. The Germans were serious about that.

It seemed to be accepted that a bomber could hit a school or a hospital while aiming at a factory, in spite of claims for the computing bomb sight and skill of bombardiers. "Dropping a bomb into a pickle barrel" was only a fantasy that had been dreamed up by our own propaganda systems.

However, a fighter pilot's gun camera film would show just what he had been aiming at when he fired his guns.

31

Noncoms Move Out to the Stalags

After groups of noncommissioned officers were processed through the *Dulag* interrogation center, they were lined up, warned about the consequences of any escape attempt, then marched out through the city streets to the railroad yards.

American veterans of World War I called the boxcars used on French and German railroads "forty and eights." They were still labeled "40/8" during this period, meaning that the load limit was either forty men or eight horses, but not both. Numbers of war prisoners or "undesirables" en route to concentration camps would often reach 100 to one car, however.

In our case there were about fifty of us occupying one end of the car while three German guards occupied the other, separated by a rope stretched across.

Small window openings at each end of the boxcar were laced with barbed wire. Some POWs have told of having hay for bedding and a toilet pail, but ours had neither. The guards had control of a water pail at their end. No food was provided on our trip, which lasted about twenty-four hours or perhaps longer. There were many delays while higher-priority traffic used the rails, when an air raid was in progress or when there was bomb damage to be repaired.

A single toilet stop was allowed on our trip from the *Dulag* into Austria. We jumped down in groups of ten, doing our toilet functions while trying to ignore track workers of both sexes who watched in idle curiosity. It was too crowded in the car for any but the seriously sick or injured to lie down, so much of my time was spent standing or sitting with knees drawn up.

Pushing to the side of the car as we got in, I could use the wall for back support, while cracks in the wall gave me plenty of cold fresh air. Once I fell asleep and awoke in a panic with no feelings in my legs, which had stretched out and been buried by others. The weight had shut off blood circulation.

No doubt each of us was contributing in some way to the awful smells inside the car. It didn't seem to bother the guards. I looked over at them once and saw them chatting in the light of their oil lantern, boots kicked off, chewing on bread and cheese.

When it seemed that things had gotten far beyond "unbearable," at last the train creaked to a stop. From outside I could hear the shouting of commands, then the sounds of the heavy lock being hammered open. As the door rolled back, we spilled out onto the tracks of a fairly large marshaling yard area. A sign on the nearby railroad station building read: KREMS/STEIN.

With shouts and shoves we were moved into lines, counted several times, then prodded out onto the main street of Krems, moving toward the east across the Krems River bridge before turning northward, up a long hill on a gravel road, past a group of farm buildings.

Many of the men were worse off than I, but even with my GI shoes the stones of the roadway caused some stumbling. John Gray, later assigned to my group and a friend after the war, had damaged both ankles and knees when his parachute collapsed during his descent. He was hobbling along with a makeshift crutch and the help of one of his crewmates.

As we finally crested the large hill we had been climbing, there spread before us down the eastern slope lay a complex pattern of barbed-wire fences with guard towers on every corner and rows of ugly barracks buildings. Sentries opened the wide double main gate for us, and we proceeded along through barbed-wire-enclosed lanes into a receiving area called the *Vorlager*.

We could not have known that we were following a procedure similar to that used in delivering Jews and other "undesirables" to their executions in gas chambers. Had we been aware of it, only God knows what we might have done at this point.

But the thought of undressing and taking a shower seemed awfully good to me. "Leave your clothing. It will be deloused and ready for you when you finish," we were told. The water was cold and the small chunks of yellow soap were incapable of making a lather, but it was a welcome experience.

Then we each sat on a stool while French or Serb laborers,

using shears that must have last been used on a flock of sheep, removed all the hair from our heads. A few long strands remained, but hundreds of bumps and hollows that none of us knew existed on our skulls came into view. What a frightening and hilarious sight!

Suddenly we were all strangers again. The simple act of removing our hair had changed our appearance so that we were unrecognizable to one another and had to get reacquainted.

As had been promised, the clothing awaited us, and we blotted ourselves dry with it as we dressed.

Marched through an interior set of gates, we proceeded along a lane enclosed by barbed wire, with rows of strange-looking men watching from beyond. As we proceeded they began to shout out greetings and seemed actually happy to see us.

Standing starkly in the middle of the bare brown earth of the northeast compound stood four long shacks. Behind them was a latrine building, or forty-holer, open-bench outhouse. We were entering what would be our living space through the next summer and winter seasons.

"Welcome to Stalag Seventeen," cheerily announced the compound chief, directing us toward the more formal greeting to come.

32

Welcome to Stalag Seventeen

The arrival in Stalag Seventeen B of the "April '44" group was an important event for all those men already imprisoned there. They must have had mixed feelings as they watched. We were relatively healthy-looking and were bringing news of the world from which they had been cut off, some for a year or more. And yet our coming meant more men to share meager German rations and occasional Red Cross food parcels. The guards dismissed us into the compound; then a man who may have been Camp Leader Kurtenbach, or one of his compound chiefs, invited us to follow him up the hill to one of the older barracks.

To our amazement, there were hundreds of men forming a corridor for us and they were all cheering and applauding. They began to pass us tiny sandwiches made of black bread and oleomargarine, while pouring real coffee into our tin containers. They knew that our stomachs and spirits both needed help and were getting obvious pleasure from providing a little for each.

Although still in a mood to suspect that German spies might be among them, I began to respond more freely to questions while listening to some of their experiences. They were eager to get news about the home front, after many months of German news stories about how Americans were suffering from starvation, union strikes, and public actions close to civil war. Although they suspected none of this was true, they were glad of our confirmation that "things are just fine back home. . . . We have their full support."

"When will the invasion come?" they wanted to know.

It was actually only a month away, but none of us had any knowledge of that. We encouraged them to believe it would be soon.

A few of the men came over and peered into my face and into the faces of other new arrivals. They were looking for someone from their group or squadron or perhaps looking for missing buddies who had bailed out with them, then disappeared. In spite of the distortion of appearance caused by the shaved heads, some reunions were made.

A number of these men had been prisoners for longer than a year. A few were survivors of the disastrous Ploesti oil field raid that took place while I was taking basic training. The B-24 Liberators from Africa had lost fifty airplanes on that one. Air crew survivors were few, they said, due to the attack "at almost zero altitude" and the warning the Germans had due to a navigational screw-up, "not by a navigator," they said, "but by some general."

I talked with some of the survivors of a big Schweinfurt raid in October 1943. The Eighth Air Force lost sixty B-17s on that one, and that translated into 600 men.

In 1996, as Cran Blaylock, brother Dan and I sat and talked about this I reminded them that we had a personal relationship now not only with one of the German fighter pilots who helped knock down those sixty B-17s, but also with the American navigator who had directed the bomber forces toward their target and then on to Africa. It was Harry Crosby of the 100th Bomb Group, whose recent book, *Wing and a Prayer*, has provided a new perspective of the air war. He lives only a few miles from me, and we are good friends.

When I told Hans Berger about Harry, Hans said that perhaps he will remember that the Luftwaffe called it the *Grosser Tag*. Record numbers of Iron Crosses were earned during that one day when both Schweinfurt and Regensburg were targets. Berlin thought that the Eighth would not be back for any more daytime bomb attacks after that, but the pause was only a brief one. Then they were back in even greater numbers.

"But," Hans said, "remember that a great toll was taken from our ranks, too, even though we were declared heavy winners that day and we all received special commendation from Marshal Goering."

Historians say that it did cause the American top brass to pause and consider whether daylight bombing raids were really all that wise, penetrating deep into Germany without fighter escorts.

While in the prison camp I never got my fill of stories from the bomber crew men. No two were just alike and many would have been declared unbelievable, had we not known better. With the experiences these men had suffered, what could they have possibly benefited by exaggerating? There are hundreds of ways in which a flyer can get from an airplane at high altitude down onto the ground, and someone there had experienced every one of them, wounded or without a scratch.

"How do you remember so much about a time fifty-two years ago?" asked Cran. "All I can remember is my first letter from home and how hungry I was all the time."

"Some memories trigger others, I guess, Cran. For instance, that small green blanket I was issued. It had an orange stripe on it and a Polish name sewn into a corner. Do you remember yours?"

He did, now that I mentioned it. Also, the U.S. Army field jacket and knit cap he was given to help him exist through the coming winter. I had forgotten about those items.

"Some of the men pulled those stocking hats down over their ears in November and never took 'em off 'til spring," I said, recalling one of the old jokes about those hats: "You couldn't take it off once your hair started to grow into the weave. It could only be removed by a barber."

The clogs we were issued are remembered now. They were pieces of wood shaped like feet, with a canvas strap nailed to each one, worn in place of shoes. It was very hazardous to move quickly while wearing them, and walking in mud or slush was almost impossible without losing one or both.

"Remember the noise," Cran said, "when a hundred men all jumped down from their bunks and slipped into those clogs to go out for a roll call?" It sounded like a kettle drummers' convention.

33

Cruising on the Rhine, Remembering the Stalag

It was a beautiful sunny day and we were relaxing on the bow deck of a Rhine River tour boat. When a group of French teenagers took chairs in front of us, lighting cigarettes and providing us with "inhales" we had all forsaken many years ago, we moved upwind of them.

The cool, drizzly weather had finally ended, and our German hosts brought their families along, renting a van for the ride from Hassel so we could all be together. There were many bilingual conversations during the two-hour ride. As we three Americans enjoyed the beautiful scenery, we listened to Hans Kirsch and Klaus Zimmer discussing, in German, how we came to be on the wrong highway and how likely it was that our delay meant we had probably missed the boat. Dan interpreted for us so we could all share in the rising anxiety level.

On arrival we saw the boat still at the dock, but we were urged to hurry to the ticket kiosk before the gangplank was drawn in. The imperturbable former fighter pilot Hans Berger went on ahead, motioning for us to relax and take our time.

"Don't worry," he said. "I will take care of getting the tickets and will meet you at the boat."

Again our ex-Luftwaffe enemy-now-friend had earned our gratitude. But when the boat captain saw how many there were in our group, he appeared happy to delay his departure until we were all on board. The summer tourist season was still a month away, and our fares would surely help pay the costs of running the large boat.

Ahead of our cruise boat on the Rhine there was a famous rock, called the Lorelei. Dan had rejoined us now, and he related the story of this rock standing in the narrowest part of the great

Rhine River, under the high cliffs. We were at Goarshausen, about halfway between Bingen and Koblenz. As he told us the story, the Wagnerian opera about a gold ring and some Rhine maidens came to mind.

Fairies stood on that rock in ancient times, it is said, tempting sailors toward disaster while the fairies guarded the treasure hidden below. Dan put special emphasis, and a bit of innuendo, on the "treasure hidden below" and the sailors who would love to get their hands on it. Was that what Wagner had in mind?

The boat trip was a great day off not only for Hans Berger, Cran, Dan, and me, but also for our hosts and their families. The Zimmers, Kirschs, Geigers, and Morgensterns and Walter Harth were all enjoying it immensely. My brother and I have often talked about the beauty of the Rhine Valley and its ancient castles and made vague plans of someday taking the long journey over to Germany for just such a tour. Now we were absorbing all we could of it, and a trip ashore at Saint Goar was an extra-special treat.

The men of the party all had lunch together at an outdoor café in the warm spring sunshine. I sat next to Walter Harth. We each knew just enough of the other's language to communicate, and I learned about his wide range of talents, especially how he had not only learned to play an Alpenhorn but also organized a harmony quartette of the huge, long instruments so often associated with the Bavarian region. The accordion, however, was his principal instrument.

Having time to talk with my old tail gunner friend Cran Blaylock was a bonus. It was a chance to speak about some memories only meaningful to someone who had shared them.

There were a few we did not want to talk about at all, like the column of Jews who were leaving a trail of their dead along the roadside, or the sights, sounds, and smells of the Mauthausen death camp as we passed through that area.

But we talked about the boys we knew in the barracks, some great guys and some oddballs, laughing as we each triggered remembrances. "Ah, those were the —"

"Don't finish that, Ed," Cran interrupted. "Those were in *no* way the good old days."

Of course they weren't. But we were both able to find a few good memories to help offset the bad ones. I told Cran that Camp Leader Kurt Kurtenbach eventually got to our lines safely, taking along with him the sick and wounded who had been left behind, and how they were able to avoid being "liberated" by the Russian troops and what happened to our two *Toonerville Trolley* men we had left behind with Kurt.

Under way, we moved past ancient castles perched high above the river, hearing them described over the address system first in German, then French, then English—a good way to learn the languages, if one listened to all three.

Relaxed in our deck chairs, we drank it all in. Ever sensitive to the level of our enjoyment, Klaus Zimmer pointed out what was missed by the announcer, supplementing the narrative with his knowledge of regional history. After a while, the others gathered to focus attention on some specific structures that stood high on the bluffs, leaving Cran and me alone to talk.

"Tell me something, Ed," he said. "Did anyone ever escape out of our camp? There were always rumors and wild stories, but only a few POWs ever got directly involved in the tunneling and other stuff dealing with escapes."

He reminded me about the German "ferrets" who used to be constantly searching for tunnels. Cran claimed one of them told him we all must have been Pennsylvania coal miners back home, we were so good at tunneling.

I never learned of anyone actually escaping through the tunnels. Some of them served a good purpose, though, as hiding places for men who were not supposed to be in the camp. Also, they kept a number of German soldiers busy, soldiers who might otherwise have been fighting.

"And what about the big SS general who was supposed to have come in to talk with our leader? Did you ever find out what that was all about?" Cran went on.

I did indeed find out but it was not until many years after the war. Cran added another question before I could answer the first.

"What the hell was the story on that guy Harry Vozic? Remember him? Remember the rumors that he wasn't really an

American flyer POW at all? He disappeared sometime during the summer and we never saw him again."

Cran would be amazed when he got explanations for all of this later. But there was one "escape" I wanted to tell him about now. It was a tragic failure.

"Cran, one guy did get out, and he got back home long before we did."

"You mean Shorty Gordon," Cran said, "but he didn't get out of Stalag Seventeen. That was the other camp."

"No, not him. It was Ralph Lavoie, and you wouldn't want to go through what he did to get back to the States before the war ended. I'm going to be seeing him next month, and I'll say, 'Hello,' for you. He lives near me in New Hampshire."

Cran looked at me in disbelief. "OK, the whole story later," he laughed.

"But just to whet your appetite, Kurt's visitor was Sepp Dietrich. He was a *Panzergeneral Oberst* of the Waffen SS. One of Hitler's favorites, at least earlier in the war, he was. And Harry Vozic? The rumors were right. He was neither an American nor a shot-down gunner, but he was one of the 'good guys' and he went home with Ralph."

34

A Military Democracy

"When thousands of American airman noncommissioned officers, all sergeants, were crowded together in a camp far removed from any other American authority, how could they possibly organize and govern themselves under the eyes and gun muzzles of the enemy?" Many have wondered about this.

The German government segregated war prisoners by rank, as did the U.S. and British governments. It was, perhaps, a holdover from the ancient feudal system. Officers could not be mingled with enlisted men, in spite of later portrayals on TV shows such as *Hogan's Heroes*. It had been agreed that noncommissioned officers could not be made to work outside the camp, and the Germans tried to bring together all Air Corps men wearing from three to six stripes.

They referred to camps for commissioned officers as *Oflags*, and leadership was established by rank and date of rank. Although there was a preponderance of lieutenants, then fewer captains, majors, and colonels, date of rank would determine the level of authority of highest-ranking officers.

Col. Albert "Al" Clark was placed in charge of Americans at Luft Three until another colonel, with earlier date of rank, was shot down and brought in. Then Al, predesignated by Americans as "Man of Confidence," became the rapidly expanding camp's "Big S," or security officer.

Also a Man of Confidence, Sgt. Kenneth Joseph "Kurt" Kurtenbach rose to the leadership position at Stalag Seven A in Moosburg, and when the airmen prisoners were moved to a separate camp in Krems, Austria, in October 1943 he maintained the top position of responsibility. In April of 1945, when most of the men were evacuated from the camp, he placed the marchers under leadership of his assistant, Sgt. Charles Belmer.

Sergeant Kurtenbach wore the same number of stripes on

his arm as did hundreds of others at Moosburg. But he had some other things going for him. He had good ability with the German language and knowledge of the rules governing treatment of war prisoners, rules agreed to by Germany and the Allied powers. Most had heard of the Geneva Convention but knew little about what was resolved there.

Army chaplain Eugene L. Daniel was captured in February 1943 in North Africa by Rommel's forces. It was during the Tunisian campaign, when the Americans suffered a major defeat. Major Daniel got to know Sergeant Kurtenbach very well. In Daniel's book, *In the Hands of Mine Enemies*, this is what he had to say about Kurt:

> After I had been back at Stalag 7-A for a few weeks a group of several hundred American Air Force Sergeants arrived. They were transient, but their final camp was not yet ready. Ultimately they went to Stalag 17-B at Krems, Austria, but while at 7-A they brought new life, revolution and much besides. These boys were high-spirited gunners and engineers from bombers shot down over occupied Europe in the past year.
>
> Since they outnumbered the ground force soldiers in camp and since they had outstanding leaders in their group, they soon took over the American group. Sergeant Kurtenbach, a German speaking American with superior personality, power, judgement and just plain guts, became their leader. He knew how to work with the Germans and when necessary he could be very rough with them, citing the Geneva Convention and demanding his boys' rights.

Dr. Daniel died in 1995 at age eighty-four.

In correspondence nearly fifty years after the war, I learned from Kurt about the move from Moosburg to the camp at Krems and the long trip in boxcars the men made, just as we did six months later. He told me that when the number of air casualties continued to grow and many were taken prisoner the Germans vacated several barracks of a Russian prison camp in the Krems-Gneixendorf area and shipped the American noncommissioned officers there in October of 1943.

"Our first challenge was to make the decrepit and vermin-ridden buildings sanitary and tight enough so that we might hope to survive the coming winter," Kurt added.

Under his direction, compound chiefs and barracks chiefs were chosen, with everyone participating. Then within each barracks there were group leaders elected, each responsible for about twenty men. All authority was delegated through this structure, and regular staff meetings were held so that Kurt could exchange requests, complaints, and orders with the German leaders, Oberst Kuhn and Major Eigl.

He went on to describe the camp: "It was really an old one, built around 1937 or 1938. I learned that while visiting Krems many years after the war, talking with an old Austrian war veteran who had been there for training.

"Although the German camp staff and the facility were supposedly adequate for about sixty-five thousand prisoners there were usually only about ten thousand Russians or French there at any one time. The rest would be in satellite work camps scattered throughout the region. There were initially eighteen barracks in the sector set off for the Americans. A washroom was in the middle of each of the long buildings.

"The capacity was to have been limited to a hundred fifty in each end, three hundred for the building. The Americans were segregated from the other nationalities by double eight-foot barbed-wire fences and our compounds separated from one another by single fences, with four barracks in each compound.

"We were at the far eastern end of the camp, isolated by the fences and guard towers with mounted machine guns and searchlights. Guards with rifles patrolled regularly between the double fences.

"By evening of our first day I knew we had a severe problem. The Russians had just been moved out. The bunk units, built to hold twelve men per unit, were infested with lice and fleas. We had not yet been given any of the straw and burlap palliasses which were to be our mattresses.

"On the second day I persuaded the Luftwaffe officers who were to be over us to allow some of our men outside the fence, under guard, to cut willow branches and make brooms. Then they granted my request for some strong lye soap. Our men began to knock every bunk apart, clean, and then reassemble them. Within a few days the danger of a 'flak typhus' epidemic

168

was reduced, though it was never eliminated. [Typhus scars looked similar to healed flak wounds.]

"It was important to become organized as quickly as possible. Many of the men had already formed themselves into small groups for sharing their food and looking out for one another, and we simply built on that concept. The first order of business was to select a barracks chief for each end of the buildings. With assistants, they would be responsible for discipline, allotment of food and blankets, and communications to and from me so that I could try and resolve problems as they rose.

"It was a democratic process and the men made excellent choices of barracks chiefs and then of group leaders, each of whom would take responsibility for fifteen to twenty men. In most instances the chiefs were selected from the longer-term prisoners and they were, to a man, capable and tough when they had to be, yet also compassionate. They generally displayed true leadership qualities throughout their terms," Kurt concluded.

"What about the food supplies, preparation, and distribution?" I asked him. "That must have been the toughest responsibility."

"It's true, of course," Kurt said, "that food is always uppermost in the minds of hungry people. I felt that the most important men in camp were the head cook and his staff. With very limited facilities they were charged with making palatable the various vegetables that were supplied to us for making soup.

"Their instructions were to plan one meal each day, to make it as nourishing as possible under the circumstances. There should be as few weevils showing on the surface as they could control. They were also to see that the *Kebos*, wooden tubs used to distribute the soup, were measured exactly and delivered to appropriate barracks."

I remembered that the heavy, round black bread loaves were carried to my barracks by men we would dispatch each day. In good times the ration was eight men to a loaf. No one was ever so carefully watched or subjected to such critical comment as the group leader when he measured the loaves for carving. Since he was last to take his portion, then any perceived inequities were all sorted out, leaving what may have appeared to be the smallest for him.

Kebos of hot water were generally carried to the barracks after morning roll call. If it had some chicory in it, then we called it "coffee." If not, we might drink some and shave with some of it.

Kurt said that in other stalags it was the potato, a staple of the Germans, that was the prisoners' principal diet. However, they were being provided from Italy, and after the September 1943 Allied landing occurred the supply was cut off. Soup quality suffered after that.

How well I remember the continuous flow of soup made from rutabaga turnips during the spring of 1944. Later on the carrot crop came in and carrot soup was the staple.

It was easy for me to give up cigarettes, but there were many who seemed to need the nicotine more than they needed food. The four packs in each Red Cross parcel were very valuable for bartering with other POWs, with Russians across the fences, or with the guards. German cigarettes seemed highly perfumed, and each one had only half the amount of tobacco in it that an American one would have.

On one occasion it was announced that a ration of meat would be included on a certain day. When the day arrived we all gathered round the small pail that was brought in. On top was a hand-lettered sign reading: HORSEMEAT, OK. It was a tiny portion, but no hamburger ever tasted better than that "shredded stallion."

Once during the fall of 1944 *Wurst* was to be on the menu. Each man dreamed of a nice, fat sausage dropping into his eating can. As it turned out only one sausage was allotted to each group of twenty men.

Another time a pail of some sort of sweet brown jamlike substance arrived along with the bread ration. There was much speculation about what could have been processed to have created such a rare delicacy, but the source has never, to my knowledge, been revealed.

35

Escape Plan Has Tragic Ending

Two men, Sgts. Ralph Lavoie and Jim Proakis, were not going to take it anymore. They got word of a wire-cutting escape attempt just before Christmas and decided they wanted in on it. Guards shot both men repeatedly, and Jim was killed. Ralph was assumed killed, also. Half a century later, he is a good friend of the author and can recall the details clearly, up until he lost consciousness.

How he came to be a POW in the first place is part of the story. It began on the morning of June 25, 1943.

His Flying Fortress named *Yankee Powerhouse* took off with the 384th Bomb Group from its base in England and headed for Hamburg, Germany. Ralph was in the ball turret. Flak and fighter opposition were very heavy, and three of the group's bombers were shot down, including the *Yankee Powerhouse*.

During a fighter attack a shell exploded in the cockpit, killing the copilot. The pilot was also hit and was left with only one hand to try to keep control of the plane. He dived out of the formation to avoid collision with other B-17s.

One of a fighter's shells had exploded in the power unit of the ball turret. Although Ralph could unlock the double latches of his escape door, he could not roll the turret to bring that door up inside the fuselage. Meanwhile, the mortally wounded pilot pulled out of the dive and ordered "bail-out."

As the plane leveled, the weight of the ammunition in Ralph's turret shifted and, without power, rolled into position so that the door swung open inside the fuselage and not out into open space. Ralph climbed out, clamped on his chute, helped two of his crewmates out, and then dived through the waist hatch himself.

Worried that he was still well above ten thousand feet and without oxygen, he delayed opening his chute as long as he

171

dared, falling several thousand feet before pulling the ripcord.

As he floated down, a German fighter circled him, perhaps to point out the jumper's location to people on the ground so they could be waiting to take him prisoner. When he hit the ground, it was a farmer with a pitchfork who made the capture.

Many years after the war ended, Ralph was approached by an ex-POW of Stalag Seventeen B one day.

During their discussion the man related "the facts about the double killing" that had occurred that December in 1943. Ralph broke in to correct the story, explaining that one man had been killed, but the other had survived and was still very much alive today. The man with the "facts" wasn't buying any of it.

"Don't tell me what happened," he stormed. "I was there!"

The healthy and active survivor, Ralph Lavoie, gave up, unable to convince this witness that he, too, was there and really ought to be recognized as an authority on the subject.

The six months following the shooting were difficult ones for Ralph in the *Lazarette*. Although he says that the staff people went far out of their way to help him, their facilities and medications were limited and recovery from all of the effects of the shooting meant many days and nights of pain and suffering.

He remembers regaining consciousness at one point and finding a tube stuck in his arm, the other end in someone else's arm. It was one of the POW staff, giving a transfusion of his own blood, since there was no other source of Ralph's type immediately available.

It was in August 1944 when Ralph was brought before the Medical Repatriation Board by Sergeant Kurtenbach. After the doctors' examinations he was declared totally unfit and disabled. With several others, including amputees, blind, and severely crippled or sick prisoners, he was carried down to the Krems railroad station. Kurt was permitted to go along with the group to see that they all got on board safely and to wish them Godspeed as they headed for Sweden.

At Stockholm they were put on board the Swedish hospital ship *Gripsholm*, which steamed to Liverpool, England, for their first stop.

Although Ralph was unaware of it at the time, one "medic"

who had helped carry him to the *Lazarette*, Harry Vozic, was on board, too. While docked at Liverpool many were puzzled as a colonel from the U.S. Secret Service came aboard looking for one particular man, a man who was interviewed at great length and in depth. That man was a noted Canadian surgeon, Dr. Reuben Rabinowitz, alias Sgt. Harry Vozic. When the questioning was over he was escorted to a big black sedan and was taken to Supreme Allied Headquarters to meet an old acquaintance, Gen. Dwight D. Eisenhower. But that is another story, to be told later.

Another man on the *Gripsholm* was a B-17 ball turret gunner from Ralph's 384th Bomb Group of the Eighth Air Force. Luther Earl Smith, half a century later, is a good friend of both Ralph Lavoie and the author. "Smitty" lost his right hand when hit by a German fighter cannon shell but somehow was able to bail out.

Ralph Lavoie's recovery was to take place at a U.S. hospital and at home. It was years later when I caught up with him. We were both at the Veterans Administration hospital in Manchester, New Hampshire, and I was undergoing a so-called "protocol" physical and mental exam that all ex-POWs were asked to undergo.

I did not read Ralph's medical report, but outside of noticing just a slight limp, I saw a happy and healthy husband, father, grandfather, and very active member of society. The review board at Stalag Seventeen had been quite wrong in its assessment, as had the ex-POW who had declared Ralph "dead."

Was the tragic escape attempt a total failure for Ralph? Well, he did get back to the United States nine months before the rest of us, and that has to be taken into consideration.

In all of its various forms, the story is a part of the lore of the stalag, but the real story is even more astounding than any of its variations.

Official War Crimes Office Report

TO: WAR CRIMES OFFICE: concerning shootings on December 2, 1943, at Stalag XVIIB in Krems, Austria, re attempted escape of Sergeant James Proakis and Sergeant Ralph Lavoie.

Prisoners were crawling from their barracks toward a fence when their presence was discovered and they were fired on by German camp guards. Sergeant Proakis stood up and ran toward a slit trench (in mid-compound) but was cut down by machine gun or rifle fire. Two guards approached and fired bullets into his body. Sergeant Lavoie, although wounded, stood up when the guards approached. One of the guards showed intent to shoot him and Lavoie lunged forward to protect himself and was shot through the right shoulder. Then he was shot again through the neck and he lost consciousness.

Inside a barracks, Sergeant Binnebose, while sleeping in his bunk, was seriously wounded by a bullet fired in the indiscriminate shooting by the German prison guards.

The two men outside had surrendered when shot, according to an eyewitness and one of the victims.

Evidence given that firing continued not only after surrender, well within the fence, but even after incapacitation. This was "unlawful wounding," violating the Law of War, Geneva Prisoner of War Convention of 1929.

It is noted that in the war crimes report concerning the shooting of Lavoie and Proakis there was testimony taken from POW medic Harry Robert Vosic, staff sergeant.

No entry is shown against "Serial No. or Organization"; however, our Dr. Rabinowitz now had an alias middle name.

One witness testified that as Ralph lay on the ground, Camp Leader Kurt Kurtenbach ran up, protesting to the German officer using the pistol, insisting that he cease firing and demanding that his men be allowed to carry the two victims to the *Lazarette*.

A few eyewitnesses declared both men dead, having seen them lying on the ground, and subjected to further gunshots. Adding to the certainty that neither man had survived, one witness went on record with this statement:

Two Americans were murdered and a third shot during an escape attempt at this camp. One was shot and killed apparently while escaping, but still within the fence. The second, Lavois [sic], was running from the fence to the barracks, and was at least 75 feet from the fence when he was knocked down by a bullet. While [he] lay on the ground calling "Kamerad" a guard shot him several times in the head. The third was in the barracks but was hit when a German deliberately turned a machine gun on the barracks.

The real story, in the words of Ralph Lavoie himself, is this:

Jim Proakis had already tried an escape once, climbing on the undercarriage of a garbage wagon that was leaving the camp. He was spotted by the guards. He and I learned of a plan being organized, involving one of the guards who had agreed to a bribe of a big sum of money after the end of the war.

The guard's part was to make a cut in the outer fence while a group of POWs cut their way through the inner fence and the coils between. Jim and I decided we would follow the group through the fences and to freedom.

The bribe offer, however, was reported to the German staff and the organizers were warned not to proceed.

Word of that did not get to us and we crawled out to the proposed location of the fence-cut as scheduled. It was cold and snowy and we thought that the guards would be less alert. We crossed the single-strand warning wire back of Barracks #36 and crawled toward the high inner fence on our stomachs. We were almost immediately caught in the beam of the corner guard tower's spotlight.

As we quickly turned to crawl back, the tower guard began shooting and I heard the bullets whizzing overhead. Over my protest, Jim leaped up to run toward a nearby air raid trench. He was immediately cut down by machine gun fire. I kept crawling until a bullet hit my left leg. The force of it knocked me over onto my back.

The shooting continued, later estimated by some POWs to have been more than a hundred shots. My only injury up to now, however, was the leg wound.

As I lay there on my back the firing stopped and I saw, against the tower lights, the silhouettes of two men approaching. One was a guard with a rifle, the other was an officer with his pistol drawn.

I was not unduly concerned that they had their weapons ready. After all, it was wartime and I was a prisoner who had tried to escape. But what came next was totally unexpected. The officer, seeing that I was still alive, aimed his pistol directly at me and fired. He was standing right over me and trying to murder me. "No, no, don't shoot!" I pleaded with him, but he took a step back and got ready to fire again.

Using my good leg I tried to roll back and forth so as not to be such an easy target. He fired and missed. Telling the guard to hold me down with the butt of his rifle against my chest, he began firing again.

One bullet went through my right shoulder, others through my neck, left side, off my ribs and one actually went through my cheek and out my mouth, which was open wide as I yelled at the shooter. He fired about five shots, which, I think, emptied his pistol. I suddenly went very weak and thought the end had come.

The same officer had used one shot to fire into the head of Jim Proakis as he lay there, perhaps already dead, I was later told.

Camp Leader Kurtenbach recalls that he, with a few other POWs, ran out demanding they be allowed to reach the two who had been shot. Finally permission was given. Finding that Ralph Lavoie showed signs of life, they loaded him onto a stretcher that J. J. Katuzney had brought out, then rushed Ralph to the camp's first-aid station. As they went, Ralph's belt was used to tie a tourniquet on his shattered leg. Both the lower femur and upper knee joint had been smashed by the bullets.

Half a century later, Ralph Lavoie remembers and says, "I owed my life to those men who had the guts to get involved and who got me to the surgeon in time. When the Germans had a grave dug for my friend Jim Proakis they also prepared one for me and for Binnebose, the fellow hit while in his bunk. We were expected to be soon dead."

"Bill" Binnebose Jr. had been injured when shot down over Belgium in 1943. Being shot while in his bunk earned Bill a second Purple Heart medal. He died in 1996, at age seventy-two, survived by two children and five grandchildren.

When Ralph learned about my return to Germany fifty-two years after the event to meet with the fighter pilot who shot down our plane, he wrote a letter to me in which he commented about his own brush with a Luftwaffe fighter pilot:

It certainly must have been a thrill to meet your German "enemy," and I use the word in the kindest way possible. Here is something I shall always remember about my experience with a fighter pilot, perhaps the one who shot down my plane.

After I had bailed out and eventually pulled the rip cord opening the chute, he made a pass at me. Then he made a tight turn and made another pass. Each time the belly of his plane was toward me and his slipstream was causing a partial collapse of my parachute, dropping me for fifty feet or more before it refilled.

On his third pass his cockpit was toward me and as he went by he gave a big smile and a snappy salute before peeling off and disappearing. I had thought that he was going to kill me but, thank God, that turned out not to have been his intent.

Although Ralph and I had both heard stories about men being shot while descending in their chutes, Americans, British, and Germans, we had no knowledge of anyone who had experienced it or observed such an event. It was a general rule that a man in a parachute had, in effect, given up the fight and surrendered.

36

Inside the Stalag . . . the War Was Not Over

Stalag Seventeen was spread across the southeast slope of a large hill a mile northeast of the ancient Wachau Valley town of Krems, now the Austrian part of Germany. It seemed romantic to me somehow to be near the region of the "Vienna Wood" made famous by the Straus waltz Father loved to play on our piano. High on a hilltop not far away was a castle where Richard the Lion-hearted had once been imprisoned and held for ransom. How fantastic it was, I thought, to be held prisoner within sight of the place where a character from the tales of Robin Hood had been held. To us, our armies and the folks on the home front were our "Robin Hood and his merry men." They would pay no ransom but would come to our rescue.

Broad fields spread out toward the horizon. During the growing seasons there were diminutive figures of peasants with horse-drawn wagons out there tending rows of cabbage or turnip. Before the war the Wachau Valley's principal crop had been grapes and the region was famous for its wine. Now it was a market basket for the Reich.

The workers wore long, dark skirts, but no clue as to their gender was needed. The men knew instinctively that they were women. As they worked bent from the waist out there, all day long, some horny POWs would stand and stare at the profiles of their broad hips. A few even sent an occasional wolf whistle out toward them before returning their thoughts once more to food and freedom.

When Brother Dan drove through the Krems area five years after the war, many vineyards were being redeveloped. A scattering of artifacts showed that some large camp had once been here. It was thirty years after his visit when I came, and the vineyards covered the landscape, except for a small aircraft landing strip. I saw no evidence that Stalag Luft Seventeen B had ever existed there.

In 1944 the brown earth inside the warning wire of each compound was beat into concrete hardness by the thousands of feet marching over it every day. Rain would quickly change it to a sea of thin, slippery mud, and when tracked into the barracks it would grow to several inches in thickness. Our twig brooms were useless then, and wood slats from the bunks were used to dislodge the dirt so it could be thrown outside.

Those twig brooms issued to each barracks were said to be made by concentration camp prisoners "down the road" someplace. These brooms were about a yard long when new but were quickly reduced to a nub after a few days. When time for a cleanup, my assistant would say, "OK, men. Time to rearrange the turf." Ace could always get a laugh with his comment: "Gimme a gawdamn Missoura mule 'n' a plow and I'll grow ya a crop o' *tunnips* right heah!"

There never was a garbage disposal problem, since we had no garbage, but there was a serious problem cleaning our meager eating utensils. They could not be scoured or boiled clean, and the flies crawling over them seeking out minor food particles no doubt left their own particles behind them. Some of our illnesses were surely brought about by unclean eating utensils and the swarms of flies that traveled between latrines and barracks.

Lining up in the compound during wintertime, hundreds of men continually coughed and spit due to chronic colds. Some actually suffered from pneumonia and TB, we later learned. It was especially bad during mud season or after a light snowfall. Germans and POWs alike were revolted by all the expectorations, but there was little that could be done about it under the circumstances.

On sunny spring or autumn days there were many bared bodies spread out in the compounds and even on the roofs gathering the rays. There was believed to be some health-giving quality to be received from exposure to the sun, and everyone hungered for it.

The shortage next in importance to food and cleanliness was

the paper shortage. Of all the many uses for paper, one of the principal ones was for bathroom tissue. With no toilet paper available the word *discomfort* takes on a whole new meaning, especially when dysentery is causing frequent trips to the latrine. Cigarette packages were carefully unfolded and smoothed. The paper wrappings were almost as valuable as the cigarettes themselves. When we talked about the wonderful luxuries we had known back home I often described the tall, neat stacks of Richmond and Statler toilet paper on Father's grocery store shelves.

Most of us never gave up trying to keep clean. The small bar of Ivory or Lux soap in the Red Cross parcel was a blessing, and occasionally there would be an issue of German "GI soap," similar to that of our own army. Often there was laundered clothing hanging on the interior fences to dry, very closely guarded of course.

Sergeant Kurtenbach and his staff knew that it was important to keep us occupied as much as possible. They had begun early to develop programs of education, sports, and entertainment. The staff of volunteers alone was large enough to keep several hundred men occupied.

Many activities became oversubscribed. Some had to be abandoned as the numbers of prisoners kept on growing and space was just not available. One of the worst winters on record in Central Europe was a major obstacle and just too much for "normal" activities. Only survival counted.

Heading up an education department required some special talents. Kurt delegated Sgt. Alexander Haddon to this office, and he soon had classes organized on many subjects, even creating evening discussion groups. He found resources for a small library for a while. Many of us were stimulated to continue our education after the war because of the efforts of Sergeant Haddon and his large group of qualified volunteers.

With very limited equipment, acquired through neutral powers, and when climate allowed, there were all sorts of sports activities going on. Archie Cothren, from my bomb group at Podington, was badly wounded when shot down. He arrived at camp in bad condition, but when he was able to get up he immediately volunteered to begin organizing all sorts of sports activities. "I

180

can't play," he told Kurt, "but I'd sure like to become involved."

After the war, Kurt wrote up a special letter commending Archie Cothren for his contributions to the well-being of the 4,000 Americans at Stalag Seventeen.

At a reunion fifty-two years after liberation, Archie told me to "be sure and read our new bomb group history book, page sixty." Editor Bob Elliott had included the whole story, including Kurt's commendation.

Leader Kurtenbach overheard our remarks and later told me that Archie deserved plenty of credit. "Many of us remember very well those soccer, volleyball, and baseball games, and even a few boxing matches that came about only through his talents and hard work."

Nights ended abruptly at first light of dawn. A German staffer with a few words of English at his command would slam through the door, beating a stick on the bunk ends, shouting, "*Aus, aus,* everyone off der sacks. Rrroll call, rrrroll call, *alles aus* vor der rrroll call!" When all had grabbed clothing and filed out the door he would stay behind to check under bunks and in corners to be sure no one was left. There was no excuse for missing a roll call.

Out behind the latrine, when all were aligned in rows of five the guards would summon the German officer in charge. In our compound it was sometimes a tall, slender *Offizier* who marched stiffly out and called for the reports. He was said to have been a fighter pilot who had lost a leg in a fight with American bombers, which gave him high status with some of us. Each counter would then, usually, shout his report that all were present, confirming that nobody had departed since the last roll call.

Occasionally a higher officer, Major Eigl or even the camp *Kommandant,* Oberst Kuhn, might officiate at a roll call. Higher-ranking officers generally wore high polished black boots, jodhpurs with red stripes down the seams and in cold weather an overcoat that came right down to the ground. A peaked cap with swastika clutched in an eagle's claw seemed to rise a foot above the officer's forehead. Only the word "Jawohl" would be heard as he accepted the reports, returning the Heil Hitler salute of the subordinate officers.

A roll call could be a simple count of the lines times five, or it could be a man-by-man dog tag and photo check. There were two roll calls each day, and if there were any suspicions that something might be amiss then special ones were called. Although we were usually dismissed within an hour, some might last many hours. On one occasion we stood all day long and into the night. Soldiers with dogs tore through the barracks looking for a missing POW while tags were compared with records over and over again.

After he was satisfied with a count, the German officer would about-face and march out of the compound while the *Unteroffiziers* returned control of the men to their barracks chiefs for dismissal.

After morning roll call we all poured back into the building to begin the rituals of finding water for personal hygiene and awaiting the *Kebo* of hot water from the cookhouse to make the morning "brew." Sometimes it was flavored with chicory, or we might spare a pinch of instant coffee and powdered milk from a Red Cross parcel.

Long roll calls often meant a breakdown of discipline, and men would be turning, talking with one another, or even sitting down on the ground. It took many loud shouts and threatening gestures to get us all up and into alignment once more.

Some frustrated POW from deep in the ranks would be sure to shout out, "You damned Jerries are driving me *crazy!*" With chuckles and murmurs of agreement coming from everyone.

Fleas were troublesome, but the common house fly nearly drove me out of my mind. I never got accustomed to flies landing on me or on my food. The open pits of the latrine building in close proximity to us gave good reason for being concerned about what they carried.

Once a month or so a team of English POWs would come into the compound with a horse-drawn tank-cart, which of course was known as the "honey wagon." Although escape was once tried by clinging to the wagon's undercarriage, I knew of no one who had the courage to get inside. Through an access hole in the wall of the latrine the contents were pumped and bailed out of the trenches, then hauled to the fields. These English soldiers had supposedly told Swiss inspectors that they preferred this light duty assignment with the Americans to being sent to a work camp.

Our palliasses were filled with wood shavings, which soon became pulverized to a sawdustlike consistency. Fleas hid in it as they did in the seams of our clothing. Many men did not seem to be bothered by flea bites, but on me they raised red, itchy welts, especially around the belt line. Once I went up to see J. J. Katuzney, our first-aid "consultant," seeking relief, but I was soon convinced that the medical science he had available could do nothing for me. "Intensify the flea hunting," was his advice.

Typhus was rampant in the Russian compound, beyond the fence outside my barracks window. We believed that rats were carriers of typhus and there were rats migrating back and forth, unhindered by barbed-wire fences. How could I identify a bite as that of a crab louse, a body louse, or a rat flea? I watched the Russians carrying out the bodies of their comrades on many mornings, wrapped in paper and ready for burial. After joining in the salute to them I would look again at the coding on my dog tag. The impression "T-43" meant that my typhus shot would need renewal sometime during 1945. I could be dead from many other causes by then, which was somewhat comforting. We guessed all were protected, since there was no illness in the American compounds diagnosed as typhus.

Water was generally made available after roll calls and for an hour or so at other times of the day. It was pumped up from Krems, and the commandant had warned Kurt that we could be shut off anytime, since a lack of rain was causing a shortage. When we did have water we learned not to tie up a position at the sink but to draw off a can or two and hold it for later washing, shaving, or rinsing out socks and underwear.

Against one wall of the washroom was a waist-high structure of brick with a large iron tub set into it. In theory, a fire could be built in the opening below so as to provide hot water or perhaps cook soup. In practice, however, there was no provision for filling the tub with anything and no fuel with which to build the fire. As an alternative use in one barracks, at least until discovered by the Germans, the tub became the cover for a tunnel entrance.

Many of the casement windows in our barracks were broken out, and sometimes even the frame had disappeared, most often into the stove. Also into the stove sometimes went the RC parcel cardboard box material, which had been so carefully salvaged and cut to fit in the opening to keep out the winter wind.

The window near my group's bunk location looked out into the warning zone and across the double fence into the Russian compound. The area between the building and fence had intentionally been spread with the tin cans we had emptied. The idea was to make it more difficult for anyone to try to cross from warning wire to fence without being detected.

When the cans could be heard rattling sometimes during the night then it was a fair certainty that either the rats were out foraging or the "ferrets" were out seeking signs of tunnels.

Soon after sunset the German staff made a final check inside and outside the barracks and shouted out the curfew order. There would be several POWs scurrying for a final chance at the latrine, knowing it could be a long wait until dawn if intestinal cramps started in the night. Later on, some who preferred the risk of being shot to that of fouling themselves, dodged the searchlight beams, running the hundred feet of open area to the building with its long row of outhouse holes. Either they were very good at it or the guards took pity on them. None were ever shot while unbuckling pants and dashing for the latrine.

A few lightbulbs were turned on inside for an hour or two as the searchlights in the towers began to probe each foot of fence, every window and doorway.

Then came time for intense discussions about food, religion, food, politics, food, the war, and sometimes sex. Stories of home and families were told and retold. Hand-crafted playing cards were brought out into the tables or bunks, and games of bridge, red dog, whist, or poker began. A handmade chess or checkers set also might be brought out. Intensity of gambling games would depend on whether or not cigarettes were available. Bets might open for one cigarette, then go to greater numbers, and a pot might grow to a pack or more. When exhaustion ended the games, much of the tobacco had fallen out and only the paper tubes were left, from so much handling.

Bridge tournaments became so intense that they were threats to personal safety and mental health. Neil and I signed up for a month-long tournament but quit after a week. After many hours of concentration on the games, we found we were dreaming all night about drawing no-trump hands and making bids of seven spades. It was driving us both crazy.

Tin-can crafting was popular. Skilled and clever POWs created all sorts of useful utensils out of old Klim cans. Klim was the brand name of the powdered milk, *milk* spelled backwards. The small liver paté cans were useful, as was the little key that came on the corned beef can.

It was a long time after the dim lightbulbs went out before it became quiet. The talking and creaking of the bunk boards diminished, and the coughing and wind breaking gradually quieted but never stopped altogether. In cold weather I would pull my coat and blanket around me and curl up in a ball. In warm weather the coat and blanket went underneath, to add padding to the compressed straw palliasse. Although cigarettes were scarce, it seemed there was always the glow of a butt or two someplace in the barracks, regardless of the hour. Sometimes I heard the scurrying of tiny feet across the floor and someone might yell, "Get outa here, you Russky rat sonovabitch!"

Some claimed to have caught and eaten rats. Although I doubted their stories, I wouldn't have been reluctant to eat the meat, if it was well cooked.

Sometimes we heard a guard's challenge, "Halten! Wer ist?" out along the fence or from a tower, and all breathing stopped for a moment. Was someone making a try at freedom through the fence? Had a tunnel exit been discovered? Would gunfire be the next sound we heard?

In nearly all cases it was only a nervous guard.

37

News, Propaganda, and Rumors

Several little crystal radios were hidden somewhere in the camp, our windows on the outside world. The Germans knew we had them and continually searched for them.

With several hundred radio technicians in the stalag, I guessed that a radio could somehow be manufactured from Klim cans and barbed wire. Actually, a few crude receivers had been built using a piece of hard coal for a crystal, a fine wire as a "cat's whisker," and a length of antenna. An earphone would have been bartered with some guard for cigarettes, the international currency.

Sgt. Howard Adams, an "old-timer" in the barracks referred to as the White House, once got a parcel from home with plenty of cigarettes in it. He used some to barter with one of the guards for a radio crystal, and with a cat's whisker and a broken pair of earphones acquired in the same way he created his own radio set.

"I could only get a Vienna station," he said, "until I accidentally hit the antenna connection, and all of a sudden in came the British Broadcasting Company." Howard became one of the news readers whose notes were always ready to be chewed up and swallowed if detection was threatened.

The official source of our BBC news, however, was a battery-operated set that was clandestinely brought in early in the war, perhaps even from the camp at Moosburg, where many of our men originated. If a search was imminent, then it was hidden, I have since been told, in the false bottom of one of the slop pails or "night buckets." No person in his right mind would closely examine a filthy toilet bucket, and it was never discovered.

About once a week a "news courier" strolled into our barracks. He would find Barracks Chief Norius Crisan and whisper something to him. Chris then ordered security guards put at the doors and windows, and a stool was pulled to the center aisle.

Mounting the stool, the courier would yell, "At ease! At ease!" In military jargon that meant "shut up!"

The cry would be repeated down to both ends of the barracks. When all was quiet and the windows and doors were secure, the courier would begin to read, sounding like a news announcer on the radio. There was generally something on each of the major war zones, then a couple of minor items from the USA or England.

"Women are wearing skirts above the knee in New York this season." That would get a howl, and another cry for silence with more, "At ease!" calls.

"Latest on the Lucky Strike Hit Parade are 'I'll Walk Alone' and 'Don't Sit under the Apple Tree.'

"A Boston woman has invented a meatless meat pie."

When the courier stepped down off the stool and everyone was again acting normal, many little assemblies were held to analyze everything just heard.

Some of our war news got to the guards, and they came to depend on us as a more reliable source than *Die Zeitung*, where only Ministry of Propaganda material was printed. Most of what was in their papers was about the advances and victories of the Wehrmacht. "Then how is it," asked one guard, "that we are losing so much territory?"

Even we Americans were sometimes convinced that the Nazis had developed some fantastic secret weapons and they were about to be unleashed. This would force the Allies to plead for an armistice.

We, and most Americans, didn't know that Hitler had already unleashed thousands of jet and rocket bombs onto England. They were causing great damage and suffering, but that wouldn't be made known until after the war.

News of the Ardennes counterattack—we called it the Battle of the Bulge—was brought to us right away. At first we ignored it as strictly propaganda. It was surely something right out of Herr Goebbels's office.

The next BBC broadcast, however, was very sobering. Now we believed it.

A German staffer named "Joe" Schultz loved to hang around

and chat with us. Sometimes he would ask, "Vell, vat iss news today—anysing ve can be heppy about?" He would smile while reading news items to us from his newspaper, such as that of the British air raid we had watched destroying a nearby fighter base. His report told of the bombers being driven off with heavy losses and having caused little damage. We smiled, too, at that one.

How I longed for just an hour or two with the *Boston Post*, the *Haverhill Gazette*, even a copy of the *Saturday Evening Post* or a *Life Magazine*.

Rumors were our lifeblood. A greeting most often heard was, "Did y'hear the latest *Scheisshaus* rumor?"

Many of the stories bore little relation to reality. They were named for the latrine, because that unpleasant structure seemed to be the source of most of them. The dysentery that was common throughout the camp meant that the forty holes in each latrine were in constant use. Someone commented one day, after a crazy rumor was brought back to the barracks, "A lot of guys out there seem to have diarrhea at both ends." Leader Kurtenbach recalls believing that "Honest John" Morrison had been the instigator of a high percentage of wild tales, but a large number seemed to just rise up out of any hole left uncovered.

Rumors swept through the camp about the "capitulation" of the Italians, the Romanians, and the Hungarians. It seemed that someone was always capitulating or about to capitulate. It was, of course, wishful thinking.

We heard about the invasion of the Continent on almost every date except the one in June 1944 when it actually happened. The official news came right from Adolf Hitler himself: "The Normandy landing was only a feint. Like the foolish and disastrous attempt made at Dieppe, it also will fail."

Kurt learned about it officially at 6:00 A.M. when the news was picked up on the secret radio. The German guards did not seem too concerned as they got the invasion news, some predicting another Dunkirk. They were convinced that General Rommel's preparations were more than adequate to throw any invaders back into the sea.

Rumors sometimes spread concerning orders received from

Berlin by the commandant, some of which would affect our welfare. The story about the shooting of any escapee on sight turned out to be true and was confirmed by the posting of a notice to that effect.

Another that had a grain of truth to it was that the Allied POWs might be systematically executed as a warning that the bombing of German cities must stop. It never became an order, but we learned that it had been strongly recommended to Hitler by the fanatic minister of propaganda.

A great rumor was: "A freight car of Red Cross parcels is due in at the Krems station in the next few days." But it could be dashed with another one: "The RAF wiped out rail centers between here and Switzerland last night, and parcels are spread all over the countryside."

When a debating club was organized by someone with a few college credits in psychology, I was quick to join and learn about the art or science of logical argument. Having grown up with five brothers, I never dreamed that it was possible to have contrary positions and not be reduced to fistfights or wrestling matches. The lessons took well, and all these years later I can still construct a syllogism and draw a conclusion from two valid premises.

38

"Neutral Powers" Looking Out for Us

The neutral powers were Switzerland and Sweden, and although some questions have arisen about leanings one way or the other by the Swiss, both the United States and Germany recognized them as arbitrators of the so-called "rules of warfare" and the treatment of war prisoners.

The earliest inspection noted in the archives was when a Swiss delegation arrived a few months after Stalag Seventeen was occupied by the Americans. They arranged with the German command to march around the camp to check out the facilities and treatment, accompanied by our camp leader, Sergeant Kurtenbach, and the German officers.

They found severe problems with medical attention and sickness, reporting:

> Gunshot wounds arrive at the camp in poor conditions showing inflammations and lack of dressings. Diphtheria . . . in endemic form, still exists in the camp. Impetigo . . . more than 100 cases under treatment; due to lack of bathing facilities. Scabies . . . more than fifty cases under treatment. Presence of lice on men in several barracks and general de-lousing begun. Noted that the Russians formerly occupied these barracks.

A report on that visit reached the U.S. secretary of state within a few months, and Secretary Cordell Hull responded to the "Head of the German Government."

> [We remind you] . . . that German prisoners of war in the United States have consistently been provided with food, shelter, clothing and medical care which is equivalent to the very high level of those enjoyed by members of the American armed forces.
>
> In view of the obligation which the German government has

under the Geneva Prisoners of War Convention, the government of the United States vigorously protests the conditions which now exist at Stalag XVIIB and requests that immediate steps be taken necessary to grant the Americans held at the camp the same standards of treatment which are prescribed by the Convention, and to assure the American Government that such steps are taken without delay.

It was signed by Cordell Hull.

After an inspection in October 1944, a report by the American Legation in Switzerland ultimately reached the U.S. secretary of state. It told of unnecessarily harsh treatment being suffered, with a threat that things could get worse:

Inspector Denzler mentioned to the Camp Commandant the rather harsh orders enforced in the American section in regard to security. In reply [the German] stated that no regulations have been set up under which the Wehrkreis XVII office of commandant for POW's will receive his orders from the Viennese General of Police and SS Obergruppenfuhrer.

In this connection, the Commandant directed Denzler's attention to war operations in the southeast and Reich's security. IT IS ALSO HINTED THAT CAMP AUTHORITIES MAY EVENTUALLY BE REPLACED BY SCHUTZSTAFFEL (SS) personnel.

The German Army and German Air Force control POW's at this camp. The rivalry of these groups is disadvantageous to the prisoners. The Camp Commander relies a great deal on the orders given by the Camp Defense Officer.

The report goes on:

Spirits of the prisoners are now somewhat dampened by the possibility of camp evacuation and by the prospect of passing another winter with existing conditions at Krems.

During the summer of 1944 the American POW doctor Major Beaumont made this report:

On recommendation of the Protecting Power and the Red Cross the Germans have finally recognized that the care of the sick demands special consideration and have created a Revier Compound, by enclosing [the hospital building] in a fence, thus segregating it from the General camp.

The Revier [quarter or portion] compound and Revier buildings are for the exclusive use of the patients and staff, and are not to be used by anyone at any time for any other purpose.

No visitors are allowed in or about the Isolation Buildings at any time.

One report describing medical treatment described the infirmary as "not very well equipped. Isolation section for infectious diseases is without lights or water. Sterilization must be done on stoves. Complete lack of buckets, bed pans and urinals." However,

About half a mile from the camp is the Lazarette. All installations there are exemplary good and the American patients there stated that they receive fair treatment. Oberstabsarzt Dr. Weigler is in charge of the Lazarette, assisted by several doctors of various nationalities. Among them is an excellent French surgeon. The Delegate talked with all the American patients and was pleased to find them in good care.

Washing is done by the men themselves, but they have no hot water and no laundry facilities.

Since we were all noncommissioned officers, we could not be made to work outside the camp, according to rules of the Geneva Convention. Many thousands of German soldiers and airmen were being held as prisoners by the English and Americans, and that was believed to be one reason why the Nazis, noted for mass executions of prisoners, might want to keep us alive. They generally subscribed to the "Rules of Warfare" concerning prisoners from the Western nations, if not for prisoners from their own country or the Eastern nations. Their treatment of the Russian prisoners was about equal to the Russians' treatment of captured Germans.

Representatives of a "neutral power" were allowed into our camp from time to time to do basic surveys. Those visiting our stalag were from Switzerland. Their reports would be made through the International Red Cross and after many months might get to Washington. When the reports acknowledged such things as "vermin-infested barracks" or "extreme fuel shortage" and "calorie intake below subsistence level" we were not encouraged to expect any action to alleviate them.

Stalag Seventeen B was supposedly controlled by the Luftwaffe, but it was apparently also under control of an Abwehr officer. Kurt had to deal with this officer (whom he described as a "stiff, old Prussian army man") in addition to dealing with the Luftwaffe commandant.

39

Escape Attempts, Failures and Successes

Kurt provided some data to a researcher several years ago, sending a copy for use in this book. Commenting on the escape of the famous Lee "Shorty" Gordon, Kurt wrote:

> I am not privy to all the details of the escape of Sgt. Gordon, as I was not then camp leader at Moosburg, but it became necessary to cover his escape with someone else. An Australian soldier from North Africa volunteered and he remained under the alias of "Gordon" throughout his entire period of captivity. Shorty was the only American to make a successful exit from Moosburg all the way back to England.

By coincidence, while Kurt was corresponding with this researcher on this subject, Kurt and Shorty had a long-delayed reunion. Kurt said, "I had to fly up to Colorado and, during one evening got to see Shorty Gordon again. It was good to see the little rascal. He told me that it had been just fifty-three years to the day since I had given him some escape food so he could remain hidden when we shipped out to our stalag at Krems."

Kurt also related the story of some British POWs at Moosburg who tried to escape by dressing in Russian clothing. Then with a pail of whitewash they began to paint a white center line along the camp road and right out through the gate. They made it that far but then could not contain their enthusiasm. Dropping the paint, they ran, and were soon recaptured. Kurt said that he had not been an eyewitness to this alleged incident, but it sounded like one of the many ways in which Shorty had tried to escape.

Don Bevan wrote the "white line incident" into his play *Stalag Seventeen*, as though it had been some Americans at Krems who had made the attempt, and we all assumed it was pure fantasy.

Kurt said that he had been a witness to one attempt:

"A band of several prisoners, in some bartered Russian clothing, took a ladder, hammers and pieces of barbed wire and they worked for some time crossing and recrossing the barbed wire enclosure very carefully pretending to be repairing wire that had become loosened from the posts.

"They continued in these endeavors until close to roll-call time in the evening, at which point they were on the outside of the wire. The guards had seen them for such a long time that they no longer paid a great deal of attention to them. At a signal, they scampered off into the woods near the camp. However, they were returned to the camp over the next several days."

Kurt recalled another escape tale about an American GI wearing U.S. army shoes. He made his way carefully at night, resting during the days, until he was well south of Munich and very near the Swiss border. Then he began to walk during the daytime. He was dressed in civilian clothing made at the camp or perhaps acquired through trading. While crossing a stream over a wooden bridge he noticed that a child playing nearby was watching him. As Kurt heard the story,

"The child suddenly got up and ran from sight.

"Down the road the GI was halted by an armed constable. He was told that the child had run to his mother to tell her he had seen a man crossing the bridge and that his shoes had not made any noise. The mother knew at once that it was not a German, since they did not have rubber heels on their shoes. All rubber had been long gone for the war effort. The escapee was soon caught and returned to camp.

"In yet another escape tale, a group of three or four men had successfully made their way to the Swiss border. Seeing guards patrolling on the German side, they watched and waited, then sneaked past them when it became dark. They were concerned that Swiss residents in the area near the border might be German sympathizers, so they continued walking all night in order to get as far into Switzerland as possible.

"Next morning they entered the Gasthaus in a small town and, announcing that they were escaped American prisoners of war, asked to be interned in the neutral country of Switzerland. An old man who had been seated at a table got up and nodded at them, then walked down the street. Soon he was back with a contingent of German soldiers.

"When questioned by the Americans the German leader showed them a map and pointed out that they must have recrossed the border where Switzerland protrudes into the Bavarian part of Germany."

These escape stories came from Stalag Seven A, the original place where shot-down noncommissioned officers were kept before their October 1943 move to Stalag Seventeen B in Krems, Austria. Kurt explained that escape attempts there were by individual initiative, with little, if any, assistance from the leadership. In some cases they could assist by providing items that came into the camp through the constant flux of prisoners as various nationalities were shipped in and out of the camp. After the move to Krems, escape opportunities became severely limited, although there was never any reduction in desire or effort.

There were literally hundreds of escape attempts made at Stalag Luft Seventeen B. There were certain rules about coordination and group efforts that even today cannot be discussed. But there were always plans and schemes being developed by men who couldn't bear the thought of not knowing when, if ever, they would get out from behind the barbed wire.

In spite of the Germans' efforts to prevent the accumulation of materials vital to the success of any escape and the avoidance of recapture, of course there were some secret stores developed.

Conflict between attempts had to be avoided. The major shootings that occurred in December 1943 were due, in large part, to the lack of communication among groups. For resources we had a broad base of skills available among the Americans, including sewing, forgery, radio skills, tunnel digging, and abilities with languages and dialects.

Red Bryan claimed to have gotten out of each of three camps, up to and including Stalag Seventeen B, but only temporarily in each case. Sergeant Dietch of Barracks Thirty-six A was said to have whitewashed his clothing and tried to escape through the fence in the snow one dark night. A patrolling guard stumbled over the bag Dietch was taking along. He would spend the next thirty days in solitary confinement.

Tunnels were the most tried method of escape attempt. Some of the ones recalled by veterans of the stalag include a tunnel from Barracks Thirty-nine B to the cemetery grove outside the fence. The area of graves was referred to as "Barracks Forty-one."

Another tunnel led from Barracks Forty B "under the water tank," and a couple more must have been from Thirty-six A, since the men there were commonly known as "Groundhogs." The only instance that I knew about was an attempt from my Barracks, Twenty-nine A. We were next to the fence that separated compounds and the tunnel was to take us under the double eight-foot fence and into the Russian compound. From there, it was reasoned, we might go out with the "Russkis" on work parties and have some good escape opportunities.

My experience in a tunnel was a single shift on a single night. It was too much for me. The only continuing nightmare I experience about the prison camp deals with my being confined in a narrow space with damp, smelly earth around me, gagging on the smoke from a butter burner lamp and expecting at any moment to be buried alive by accidental collapse or by efforts of the German "ferrets" in their prevention efforts. If I ever got out of Stalag Seventeen B, I vowed, it would have be at the surface.

When our tunnel was discovered two of my men were drafted to go out into the "warning zone" to dig it up and backfill it—under protest, of course. My friend Vit Krushas still remembers that while he was working on it he spied a small rag-tied package lying among piles of tin cans. It was one that hadn't made it over both fences during one of the Russo-American exchanges. As Vit bent down as though to tie his shoe, casually reaching out to pick it up, the muzzle end of a rifle suddenly appeared next to his nose. He graciously permitted the guard to pick up and pocket what may have been a few cigarettes, an onion, or a potato.

Vit never forgot anything. Fifty years after the event, he told me one day the exact width of the high beam on which he tried to sleep one night during our long march when the Germans crowded hundreds of us into a small barn beside the road.

Kurt and Shorty Gordon have maintained a friendship, even though separated by the Pacific Ocean until recently. In some of his writings Shorty credits Kurt with assisting him in his escape attempts. After a career in the air force, Shorty went to Australia to live, becoming a successful stockbroker.

Shorty's first try was while being transported in a boxcar, in March 1943, with a couple of other men. They were soon recaptured. He did not get to Stalag Seven A until after Kurt and a hundred or so other men left for Stalag Three B with the infantry POWs; thus the two did not meet again until they were back in Seven A that summer.

On another attempt from that camp, Shorty was outfitted with a bicycle and a Hitler Youth uniform. Kurt says Shorty "rode off into the sunset, but before long was picked up and brought back," no doubt into solitary confinement.

Finally he was successful and made it all the way back to England.

"Shorty hid when the rest of us left Seven A to go to Seventeen B in Austria. The man we used for covering him was a young Aussie army kid named Frank Ferguson, supposedly a transvestite. I had Frank's photo transposed onto Shorty Gordon's German file through a bit of bribery."

Thus Sergeant Gordon never got to our Stalag Seventeen B, but would surprise everyone, including Gen. Curt LeMay, by showing up at his air base back in England. This is how the story is told by Kurt: "He left the camp after we had gone, out of either the French or Russian compound where controls were not so tight. Eventually he made contact with the underground and made it to the coast, to be picked up by a high-speed British boat." He told Kurt that the boat ride across the Channel was the most frightening experience of his fright-filled career.

Sergeant Gordon flew in the 305th Bomb Group, and in the book *USA the Hard Way*, Roger Armstrong says that he once talked with Curt LeMay about Shorty.

"I had to give him a medal [Silver Star]," said the general, commenting that it didn't do much to discourage Shorty's disrespect for authority. He would sometimes get busted to private until needed for another mission, then would go back to his ball turret as Sergeant Gordon once more.

Concerning Frank, the Aussie replacement, as a professional cross-dresser he became active in Don Bevan's show retinue at Stalag Seventeen B. He usually played the part of a beautiful woman, and effectively, too. Shorty has tried to find Frank in Australia since the war, but no luck. A couple of years ago it was said that Shorty spent several days with a Hollywood screenwriter and that the Fox Network was going to make a movie about his escape adventures. Michael Douglas was to finance the project. It was joked that they had an actor lined up for the part, but he would have to be cut off at the knees to be short enough for the role.

The general understanding was that a cover would be held, if possible, for up to three days to allow an escapee time to get far away from the camp. Then the trickery would end and the Germans would be allowed to discover the absence.

The cover was made easier by their practice of lining us up in rows five men deep. Then the count would be made by fives until the total number of men from each barracks was tallied.

By spreading out our alignment an extra foot or so, the fifth man of one of the first rows had space enough to bend down and scoot to the far end, to be counted twice. But if the guards had any uncertainty then they would call for a "dog tag check," where each individual was checked through a long line. There was no way that trickery could beat this one.

Kurt explained the problems that were created when a recapture occurred without his knowledge or that of his security people. He had made friends among the Frenchmen working in the *Vorlager* replacing Germans sent off to the front. They would get word to him that a man had been recaptured and was headed for or already in the "boob." Then the men would allow the Germans to "discover" the shortage and make an honest count. To supplement the bread-and-water diet and help keep him alive, the leaders would try to get food into the boob by bribing one of the *Gastarbeiters* (foreign workers) to smuggle it past the guards.

After Luft Three's "Great Escape" and the German high

command had posted its "Execution of Escapees" warning, it became a whole new ball game. Each man knew that if he should somehow be lucky enough to get outside the fence, there would be nothing at all that we could do for him from inside.

A few of the German staff were supposedly expert at finding tunnels. We called them ferrets or moles. They would poke around in and under the barracks, peering into every corner. They would check the floorboards and probe into the earth with steel rods. Once they brought in a heavy wagon and drove it back and forth over a suspected tunnel location.

There were telltale clues we were warned to avoid showing, such as especially dirty and broken fingernails, brown knee and elbow stains on clothing, and bloodshot eyes from lack of sleep and exposure to fumes from butter burners. A little pile of dirt of a different color from that nearby was sure to draw attention.

A ferret was easily recognized and the warning of his approach would go out like a wave as he proceeded into the compound. One ferret was sure he was onto something one day when he noticed a group of POWs standing in a circle facing outward with hands folded behind them. They whistled as they all rolled their eyes toward heaven, with an appearance of innocence that could only be an act. The ferret circled them several times, finally pausing to bend down and peer in between their legs.

Then he ordered them to move away, got down on his knees, and examined the ground where they had stood. Soon he walked away, muttering, "Verruckte Amerikaner! [Crazy Americans!]"

Three Russian prisoners had come along from Stalag Seven A to the camp at Krems, according to Camp Leader Kurtenbach. He describes them as follows: Sergei, the most aggressive one, was dark-complected, supposedly from the Caucasus Mountain region; Alex was a calm young man and seemed to be fairly well educated; and Paul was very quiet and not at all aggressive.

When Kurt learned that these Russians had been acquired to cover for two of our men left behind at the old camp, he was concerned about what to do with them. One suggestion was to cut the wire between compounds, next to Barracks Twenty-nine A where we "new" men had been put and move them over into the Russian compound, where they might have a slightly longer life expectancy.

Two men involved in a tunnel project volunteered to hide them in their holes. Meanwhile, since the German ferrets were always prowling around under the barracks nearest the fences, alternate tunnels were begun. The men were clever at hiding the tunnel mouths feeding air down into them. There were times when the Russians might be kept underground for up to twelve hours during a serious and sweeping search by the Germans. At other times they could walk around the compound, share rations with the men, and sleep in the barracks where they were known.

During a surprise search of the camp and the photo and dog-tag check that went with it, the Russians and their American conspirators would each take their places in the formation and would manage to avoid detection somehow.

One surprise search took place shortly before we were to be evacuated to the west, and the Russians were discovered. Guards concentrated on just one end of Barracks Seventeen. Kurt wasn't alerted until all three Russians were being taken away, and he was puzzled as to why the search had been localized right where the Russians happened to be sleeping that night. It had to be concluded that there was an informant, but there were no clues as to who and why.

When it was about all over and the Germans had left, early in May 1945, two of the three Russians who had come from Stalag Seven A approached Kurt with a confession of sorts. Sergei was the "snitch," according to Alex, not only about the men but also about the tunnel locations. The Russian said that when the Red Army arrived he would give them this information and he was sure that Sergei would be dealt with. It is possible that Sergei knew that they could never pass a photo check and head count and he decided to ingratiate himself with the Germans, who might just let him go to merge with his countrymen when they arrived.

There was one other "stowaway" in the camp, known to us as Sergeant Gray. The Germans had a charge against him for some crime committed before he had reached prison camp. Kurt was told that Gray would be removed from camp the next day and there was good reason to be concerned for his life.

The men who had been hiding the Russians agreed to take Gray into their custody, and he came to suffer the same hunted

201

existence they did. When guards came for him Kurt told them that he had apparently made an escape during the night and they would have to extend their search to the region around the stalag. For a few days there was a great hue and cry, but after a time it subsided.

40

The Anxiety and Boredom Factors

Life as a prisoner of war can only be described as fluid. Each day brings a new challenge to life itself. Few persons who have not experienced the mental duress of being a prisoner will understand. Most American lads I knew stood up to it well and in many ways I feel privileged to have been allowed to associate with them. They were as fine a group of combat soldiers as the world has ever seen.

Those comments were made by ex–camp leader Kurtenbach.

Although each of the long days was much the same for us, anxiety was always present. Sometimes it was right there at the end of a rifle barrel, but it might be also be in an official bulletin from the *Kommandant*. Always the anxiety about what lay ahead bubbled just beneath the surface. A violent change in the status quo was a real possibility at any moment of any day or night, in any season.

Just as deadly as the machine guns constantly aimed at us from the guard towers was the threatened withholding or withdrawal of food and water.

An announcement: "Beginning today the bread issue will be at the rate of one loaf for each ten men, instead of one for each eight men," was of tremendous importance to men already existing at a lower caloric intake than that required to sustain life over the long term.

Although we were coming to accept the idea that we had no control over what might happen to us from day to day, there was a rising awareness that each passing hour meant our physical condition was diminishing. Under the worsening situation inside Germany, and with their resources continually being reduced by Allied bombings, there was little hope for improvement.

Intimidation by heavily armed men, with power of life or death over us, could reach higher levels when a surprise alarm to abandon the barracks was shouted: "Take nothing with you. Fall into ranks in the open compound!" Weather and time of day were not considered.

The sudden appearance of Wehrmacht troops in the camp when we were used to seeing only Luftwaffe guards and staff could raise anxiety levels, as could the presence of soldiers with fixed bayonets and attack dogs on leashes. It was sort of a serious joke when someone would say, "That makes me lose my appetite!"

Boredom was the feeling that most often accompanied hunger and anxiety. There were twenty-four hours in each day to somehow be passed, and only a few of them could be spent in sleeping. Sleep could be most undependable, with all of the discomforts that were working to prevent it.

Sgt. Don Bevan was an important figure in the prison camp. If there was a medal for "boosting the morale of the troops" Kurt says that Don would have it with several oak leaf clusters. He was in charge of show business.

Sergeant Kurtenbach had recognized the need for such entertainment for the troops, and along with sports activities it got high priority under his administration. He appointed Don to head the activities committee for the whole camp of 4,000 men.

There was plenty of talent and ability among all of those airmen, and Don knew how to find and use it. Fifty men became involved, with regular assignments in acting and in running the theater. Almost overwhelming problems were confronted as to admittance and seating when all 4,000 men wanted to be in the opening-day show audience in the "Cardboard Playhouse" that seated only 200. The German camp staff couldn't be shut out but had to be accommodated, too.

Sergeant Bevan had been an artist with the 306th Bomb Group, painting nose art on airplanes and murals on the walls at the club, that sort of thing. The way he tells it, he happened to show that he understood the technique of "deflection shooting" one day when invited to go up and fire at a tow target. Next thing he knew he was a waist gunner on a bombing mission, credited with shooting down an enemy fighter plane.

His days of painting nose art and murals were numbered, and after a dozen or more missions, so were his days of flying combat with the 306th Bomb Group. His plane was shot down, and after hardships more difficult and extended than many we heard about he became a resident of a POW camp.

Don had earned a reputation as an artist while working with the New York *Daily News* before the war. His career of "show biz" for POWs began at Stalag Luft Three, with something different from the shows the British POWs had been producing. The camp leaders learned about it and invited him to do a presentation. He called his creation *Broadway after Dark*, and it was a smashing success.

Asked to do something special for the Americans at Stalag Three, he came up with a burlesque type show, strippers and all, naming this one *Hellzapoppin'*.

The German commandant "X-rated" it.

Later moved to Luft One, up on the Baltic, Don put on the same show and got the same result: another "X." The next move would put him with Kurt Kurtenbach and the Americans at Stalag Seven A, near Munich at Moosburg. This was just before their transfer to the camp near Krems in Austria.

After the move to Seventeen and establishment of a theater named for the Red Cross cartons from which the sets were created, back came *Hellzapoppin'* for another run. The American audience and Germans, too, gave rave revues. This time rated by a German command a bit more liberal, it was "acceptable".

Into Don's "office" one day walked a shot-down gunner named Ed Trzcinski. He wanted to get into show business. Don could see talent written all over Ed. They began the process of writing the script for what would eventually be the hit Broadway play *Stalag Seventeen,* produced and directed by Jose Ferrer. His performance in the film would win an Academy Award for actor William Holden. This came about neither suddenly nor easily. During its creation and production there were a few years of wild adventures that would make good material for yet another Broadway hit. When the show finally made the big time a *New York Post* review was typical of many. It read: *"Stalag 17* is altogether one of the best shows of the season. It captures an emotional appeal that an audience should find pretty irresistible."

When I asked Kurt whether Don Bevan had based some of his characters in the play on those we knew in the camp, he said that it could well be the case: "Don is a good friend and I know that many of his events in the play and movie were taken from stories and experiences he had heard about from many British soldiers. He was in Stalag Luft Three and two others before he got to Seventeen B."

Many Seventeen vets would have nominated a guy called "Honest John" Morrisson for the starring role in the play. One thing Kurt is sure of: if there was a slot for "best rumor starter" John would have won it hands down.

Don had evidently not authorized the takeoff from his play for the TV series on CBS, and it's rumored he got a "handsome" settlement several years ago after it became obvious that there was an awful lot of *Stalag Seventeen* in the production of *Hogan's Heroes*. I asked Kurt if he ever watched that TV series.

"I still do enjoy watching them," he said, "no matter how crazy they are. They had some great characters and many of their escapades were based on little real events that were carried to the ridiculous. I loved Colonel Klink, Sergeant Schultz, and the French lad, too. It made me wish that I could go back to that POW camp and try out some of their tricks. And if you believe that, then I have a bridge in Brooklyn I'd like to sell you!"

I didn't buy Kurt's bridge, but I did ask him about the young man who was so good at playing a female role. Many of our guys were convinced that someone had smuggled a girl into the camp. Everyone wanted to go to see "her" on the stage and everyone wanted to sit up front for as close a look as possible. Whatever happened to him?

Kurt said that this lad was not one of the American flyers but was an Australian. As a matter of fact, it was he who had taken on Lee "Shorty" Gordon's identity to cover for him after one of his escapes. Kurt referred to the Australian as a transvestite, but surely only in regard to his show business career. It would not have been possible for a real "cross-dresser" to exist in one of the crowded barracks of a POW camp.

Don Bevan once told about the Aussie's first presentation,

when the makeup people had created him as a stripper, even pasting on breasts to make him more convincing as a female. He really did fool the audience, in fact even some of the cast. It was only when one got behind him, Kurt recalled, that "it became apparent his paraphernalia had been cleverly relocated by use of adhesive tape, giving the appearance of a bad case of hemorrhoids."

During some of our few leisure hours of our return trip to Germany, after a fifty-year gap in time, Cran and I entertained Dan with our recollections of shows at the Cardboard Playhouse in Stalag Seventeen B. Dan was still recovering from his sore throat, thus had to listen more than he could talk, and we took advantage of this.

"Which of the shows did you get to see?" Cran asked.

"Actually only two shows. They were great, but for the life of me I can't recall today which ones they were, I heard so much about all of them. At the first one it just blew my mind that here I was sitting in an audience with hundreds of American POWs and a bunch of German officers and staffers and we're all laughing and applauding together. Tomorrow one of them might shoot me, but tonight we're all part of one big, happy group."

"Don't you remember the show I was in, Cran?"

He didn't, so I reminded him about the minstrel show. We put charcoal on our faces along with rouge and white paint and learned how to rattle some black "bones" between our fingers and to shake tambourines in time to Stephen Foster songs or others like "When That Midnight Choo-choo Leaves for Alabam'."

It was my impression that the Germans understood neither the makeup nor the jokes being told by the six end men and the interlocutor. Some of those jokes were pretty pointedly directed at specific Germans and it was probably just as well they were going over their heads, if that was the case. But maybe they were just being diplomatic.

Brother Dan had performed in a couple of minstrel shows himself, back in New Hampshire. They were put on by the American Legion boys in the days before television or even a local movie theater, and before black-face comedy became unacceptable to an enlightened society they were very popular. Dan knew every song and every joke told by the end men, and in spite of his present throat condition he performed a few for us: "Way down on the levee, in old Alabamy, there's Daddy and Mammy and Ephrium and Sammy . . ."

The one act from our show that I recall was a song created to salute one of the "Harry S." POW old-timers who thought he had devised a way to foil the head-shaving procedure. He rubbed a mixture of oleomargarine and sand in his hair on his way up to the *Vorlager* for the haircut.

It worked fine, jamming up a pair of clippers so they had to be taken apart and fixed. However, the hair was cut anyway and the guy spent the next week in solitary, in the "boob." The interlocutor introduced the parody with a salute to the POW who had gone to great lengths to save his precious hair, "even to the very boob itself."

Cran has a better recollection of the great swing-band concert that we all enjoyed. The musical instruments sent in through Switzerland by the Salvation Army were really put to good use and were almost as big a morale booster as the food parcels. There were some very talented musicians in Stalag Seventeen, and they were able to put together not only the big swing band but some smaller groups that could go out to the barracks and entertain.

"Didn't you get to play in one of those groups?" Cran asked.

"No, no. Not me," I protested, hoping Cran would not remember that my career as a clarinetist began and ended with just one rehearsal. The problem was I played by ear and when the score called for a solo by the clarinet and everyone turned toward me, I just sat there like an idiot, smiling back at them. I thought the number had ended. "Oh yeah, Cran. You're talking about my bass playing with the little hillbilly group. Right?"

With that bass fiddle I found success. Nobody has to read music for all those songs that have only C, F, and G chords, and I could do no wrong. There was only one such instrument in the 4,000-man camp, however, and our time was limited to only a few sessions.

I'm flattered Cran remembered the Baize-McKenzie duets.

My assistant, Neil, and I would sometimes entertain in our barracks harmonizing on some of the songs he recalled from his native hills of Kentucky and some I remembered as sung by Gene Autry or the Riders of the Purple Sage. They all seemed so terribly sad. Usually a sweetheart had died or a mother lay deep in her grave or a coffin of pine was being made for a loved one. They brought tears from some in our audience, presumably because of the sad lyrics and not the quality of the performance.

Neil remembered the time when, back home in Baizeville, Kentucky, his family all walked several miles down to a neighbor's home to hear something new called a "radio." They listened spellbound for a couple of hours, all but Grandpa, who kept yelling, "Why won't the damn thing play 'Maple on the Hill'?"

Before my arrival in 1944, many books had been sent into the camp through the efforts of some American agencies and cooperation of the neutral powers and the Germans. They were organized into a lending library and used for classes in technical subjects, languages, farming, and so on. Unfortunately, the books could not be broadly distributed without damage or disappearance. One reason for this was that people existing in a paperless environment will often go to extreme limits for a source of toilet paper when the need is great. Only letters from home were generally exempted from this use. As a vocation or pastime, writing was difficult due to this lack of paper, other than the rare letter form provided by the German government for outgoing mail.

Cigarette wrappers were a valuable resource not only for the toilet, but also for creating playing cards, writing notes, or sketching.

The waterproof cardboard cartons in which the Red Cross parcels were shipped served a variety of purposes. Our theater was constructed from them; thus it was named the Cardboard Playhouse. The carton material made good covers for the toilet holes. They could also be cut to fit the openings where window glass was missing.

Unfortunately, when the weather became cold then the need

209

for fuel often took priority over both the covering of open toilets and the blocking of window holes.

The principal physical exercise, and relief from boredom for many, was walking. When weather allowed, there was a continual mass of movement around the perimeters of the open compounds. The earth next to the warning wire was tramped down a few inches below the rest of the compound area hard-packed from the continual pounding of feet.

Commenting on this, long after the war, Kurt said, "Some of the prisoners became depressed with confinement and they would become increasingly withdrawn. They would walk incessantly about the perimeter as if contemplating escape by climbing the fences. That would, of course, mean almost certain death from the guns in the towers and outside the fence. [Many were] watched closely by friends who were prepared to try and stop them if it appeared this was about to happen."

One reason for all of the walking was exercise. We knew that if we were going to get out of this stalag for whatever reason, it would very likely involve a lot of leg power and physical stamina. This turned out to be true and could have been a factor in the high survival rate of those force-marched across Austria during April of 1945.

I enjoyed learning new things and took advantage of a group brought together to study psychology, led by one who had accumulated a few college credits before the war. Another course dealt with English and American literature and composition, but it was difficult without writing materials and appropriate textbooks.

Since some knowledge of the German language could be very useful in our situation, I accepted a friend's offer to teach me at least some key words and phrases. Karl Eckert and I had first become acquainted in the boxcar on the trip from Frankfurt. His German came out soft and clear, and his manner often seemed to have a calming effect on some of the more excitable guards. One of them asked him one day why he had been flying in an airplane made by Boeing instead of by Dornier or Heinkel. Karl explained that he was just an American boy whose mother wanted him to learn her father's native language.

Although there were physical games organized somewhere in the camp over its lifetime, I remember very little of it in the so-called "new compound" where we existed. The energy required for playing soccer, football, or baseball and the consequences of any injuries from "roughhousing" probably discouraged many of us from such participation.

Prisoner of War Richard
Anthony, 1944-1945

USAF pilot Anthony, Lt.
Col. USAF (Retired)

A friend sent Ed McKenzie his "mug shot" taken by the Germans many years before.

"This must have been right after the clothing search, and no time to redress. My white scarf was not considered 'flying gear' as were jackets, pants, and gloves. Cuts on my neck had been cleaned up. Steel slivers in my palms made it hard to hold onto the ID board for the picture," he remembers.

"Long underwear and a wool shirt had been a wise choice that morning. Boy, did I need a haircut, but not the 'baldy' one I was to get a few days later."

"The German officer saw that I was not dead, aimed his pistol directly at me, and fired. I asked him not to shoot, then pleaded with him as he took a step back and fired again." (Courtesy Ralph Lavoie.)

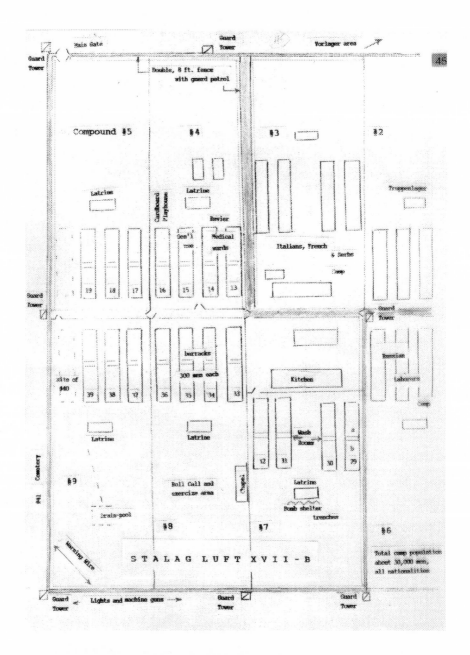

American portion of Stalag XVII B in Krems, Austria. 1943-1945.
(Sketch by McKenzie and Kurtenbach.)

Thanks to the cartoon "snapshots" done by a talented P.O.W., historians need not wonder what it was like in the barracks of one of Germany's stalags. A group leader serves up the daily ration of soup from a *kebo* under the watchful eyes of his men. (Courtesy Robert Noll.)

"Rrrroll call! Rrrroll call! Fall out, Schnell! Schnell!" (Courtesy Robert Noll.)

The barracks seemed warmer when we looked out the window to where a guard stood in a pair of straw "boots" to keep feet from freezing during his two hour shift. (Courtesy Cran Blaylock.)

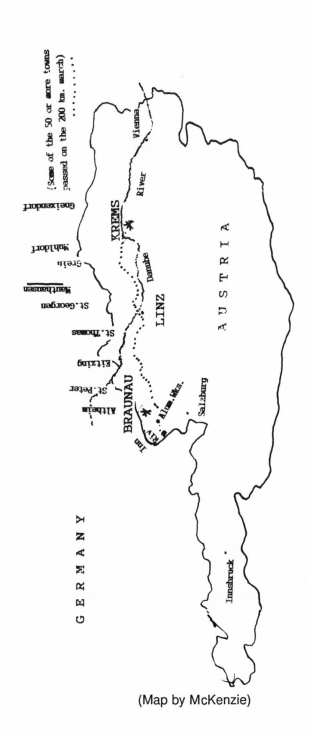

(Map by McKenzie)

POWs of the British Army, Hans Berger and Karl Demuth, play cards by their tent in a soccer field "stalag." (Courtesy Karl Demuth.)

Herr Doctor Professor Egon Keller from the Universität des Saarlandes, was ceremonial interpreter during the visit of the American flyers. "Call me Egon", he said, sharing bread and wine and telling the history of the cities and the castles visited during the week-long visit. (Courtesy D. McKenzie.)

One of the top fighter planes of WW II, a Focke Wulf 190-6/R11, with 66 gallon drop-tank and armed with 20mm Mauser cannons. (Courtesy Hans Berger.)

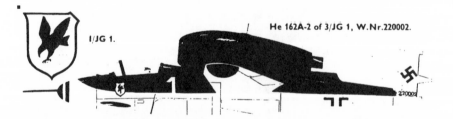

I/JG 1.

He 162A-2 of 3/JG 1, W.Nr.220002.

It was a totally new experience, flying the new, in many ways untested, single-jet-motor, Heinkel 162, also known as the "Volksjager," both Hans Berger and Karl Demuth agreed. (Courtesy Hans Berger.)

Capt. Karl Demuth (of Saint Petersburg, Florida, in 1996) stands by the tail of his 162 Heinkel jet "Hunter" plane in March, 1945. The "scores" on the tail were transferred from the Focke Wulf 190 fighter in which he earned them. (Courtesy Karl Demuth and Eric Mombeek.)

"Dr. Reuben Rabinovitch. So THAT was Harry Vozic's real name. He would be coming to dinner with me in Paris. He was a close friend to General Eisenhower, but I knew him to be a madman, as well," said Kurt. (Lute photo—courtesy of Ralph Lavoie.)

Stalag XVIIB leader Kenneth J. Kurtenbach (left) at his home in Tucson, Arizona, with the author in 1997.

Guests at the St. Wendel flying club were two ex-Luftwaffe fighter pilots, Hans Berger and Fritz Wiener, along with two American B-17 Flying Fortress crew members, Ed McKenzie and Cran Blaylock. (Courtesy Egon Keller.)

American children from the U.S. Army base at Baumholder prepare to launch their balloons, from inside the profile where the B-17 *Toonerville Trolley* had lain in 1944. (Courtesy Zimmer.)

41

Christmas in Two Stalags, Luft Three and Stalag Seventeen B

A light snow was falling on Christmas Eve 1944 in Stalag Luft Three, where the *Toonerville Trolley* pilots were being held. The snow was quickly packed hard under the thousands of army boots that continually walked the compound in the shadow of the guard towers. It had stopped by Christmas morning, but the weather turned very cold. Although bundled up in all the clothing he owned, Dick Anthony couldn't get the chill out of his bones.

Most of the little bag of wood chunks provided for the barracks stoves was used up early in the day in a futile attempt to warm the building a bit for the holiday. A few pieces were saved until evening in the hope that maybe bedtime could be made a bit more comfortable.

Of course there were no Christmas trees or gifts, but it was a real treat when Red Cross parcels were distributed. By pooling cans of Spam and C-ration crackers they made a tasty supplement to the special German Christmas ration of boiled potatoes and barley soup.

Luft Three had an orchestra, too, having received some of the instruments from Switzerland, compliments of the Salvation Army. There were some very talented musicians among the officers, and they were glad of any opportunity to play. On this Christmas day they put on a special program of traditional carols, dampening many eyes but raising spirits and helping the men to keep faith.

Dick thought it strange that there was no organized religious service. "Surely there were many prayers offered by individuals, but because of our numbers perhaps there just weren't enough chaplains to go around for everyone in all the compounds to have Christmas services," he said.

227

As did most of the others, he and Ray Raney thought about the good foods that had been enjoyed at Christmastime back home. Most prominent in Dick's mind was a pineapple upside-down cake. To prove that he had not forgotten it in the past fifty years, when I mentioned Christmas 1944 to him at our reunion in 1996 he immediately said, "Oh boy! How I liked a pineapple upside-down cake. My mother made one for me soon after I got home in 1945."

Some POWs claimed they could actually smell roasting chicken or turkey. It was most likely the odor of fried Spam, as that was the only treat available at Luft Three, if there was any meat at all.

As the holiday season ended, the men of Luft Three could hardly have imagined the hardships they must soon endure as they were driven out into the Arctic weather conditions for their march deeper into Germany.

Remembering Christmas at Stalag Seventeen, Cran and I agreed with the *Toonerville Trolley* men at Luft Three. It was just as cold there in Austria as it was to the north of Czechoslovakia in their camp. Our fuel ration for the week was a few briquets of compressed coal dust, but the supply had been used up before Christmas.

"It didn't matter much," recalled Cran. "That huge tiled stove would have taken a cord of wood to heat up."

And I added, "We couldn't have warmed that big barracks with half its windows knocked out, anyway."

We dared not take any more bed slats or structural wood for fuel, and we had been warned not to whittle any more chunks off the fence posts between the compounds. The guards would be watching, and they threatened to shoot on sight.

Someone came bursting through the door with the news that the regular curfew had been lifted for tonight. "The sky pilot's going to have a service. Come on; let's go!" he said. He may have thrown in a, "Ho ho ho," before some good Christian threw a clog at him.

Perhaps twenty of the men stirred themselves, and I joined them, wrapping my blanket and overcoat tightly around me and pulling the stocking hat down over my ears. The cold made the light snow crunch underfoot. As we walked, trails of condensed breath followed us, looking odd in the beams of the guard tower spotlights.

After we all headed for the barracks that housed the small chapel, everyone seemed to stop at the same time. All heads were tipped back, and there were expressions heard like, "Wow. Look at that!"

What we were seeing was a heaven full of stars so bright that it was breathtaking. Waves of northern lights were passing through the constellations, adding to the display. We would not have been surprised had a brighter star suddenly appeared in the East, heralding the approach of some great event.

The nightly curfew had denied us a true view of the night sky and now on this clear, cold night we were exhilarated by a sight we would earlier have taken for granted.

After the brief multidenominational service and the singing of traditional carols, we headed back with spirits refreshed. Perhaps it was best expressed by "Ace," our short, stocky Louisiana friend.

"Ah ain't felt so good since ah tripped 'n' fell into a damn watermelon patch!"

Not only was the next day another dreary one, but some awful news was relayed to us from a BBC broadcast picked up on the secret radio. The Germans were counterattacking in the Ardennes, and things were not going at all well for the American armies.

"We have begun the actions which will drive the Allies back into the Channel," was the official German report and it seemed to be confirmed. Neil Baize and I heard this as we were sharing a "D-bar" of chocolate saved from a Red Cross parcel for the holiday, thinking that it would probably be the last one we would ever taste.

42

Unforgettable Characters

"Mah real name's Frank." Ace Scarsune told me one day, "but call me thet 'n' I'll squash y'all lak a bug!" He was certainly an outstanding character in Barracks Twenty-nine. Not that he was big; in fact, he was so short that he was sometimes overlooked at roll call. He was the one who compared his good feeling on Christmas Eve with that of falling into a watermelon patch.

Although short, Ace was rugged. He claimed to have had lifts put on the foot pedals in his ball turret so he could reach them. But he could easily pick up his two machine guns at once and carry them to the armament shop. His deep, gravelly drawl was often heard above all other voices in the barracks or when standing in formation for roll calls.

Ace was raised in what he called the "betta paht of Shreveport, Loozianna," and he had worked in some of the houses of ill repute there as a young teenager, getting into many brawls. He showed off the scars on his nearly bald head as though they were earned awards.

"First two thin's ah learnt when ah joined the Air Cowah," he said, "wuz haow t'unfold a mess kit 'n' then haow t'flush a damn towlet!"

Ace claimed he had scrambled out of the ball turret and bailed out of his burning B-17 over the city of Hamburg and somehow survived falling among his own bombs. "If y'all git to the ground alive, thet ain't a real good way t' staht a friendship," he announced.

His chute had gotten tangled on a statue in the city park, and he sprained an ankle. He limped his way painfully to prison camp and many months later explained that he was continuing to limp only so he could get a Purple Heart medal when he got home.

His humor would have us holding our sides laughing, even under some pretty awful conditions. I had first become aware of him during our night in the boxcar at Frankfurt and as we headed across Austria. Over the dreary noises of suffering I kept hearing this soft, raspy, drawling voice telling stories about the seamier side of life in a Louisiana brothel. It was just incredible to me that here was a guy in this cold, stinking, crowded boxcar chatting away like he was perched on a barstool with a beer in his fist.

Ace loved to gamble with the cigarettes from his Red Cross parcel and was pretty good at it. He used some of his gains to trade for food, both with the Russians across the fence and with the German guards. He used the open window next to my bunk as his "office" to arrange some of the trades. But once when he got a bit of extra food that way I saw him pass it to one of the scrawny men who really needed it. Ace did it in such a way that it didn't seem like an act of charity, because he couldn't have lived with a reputation of being charitable to his fellowman.

Ace liked to hear Neil and me sing the old hillbilly songs, and Ace and I thought of each other as good friends. One day I called him a dirty, rotten, low-down *prince* of a guy. He thought that was about the best thing anyone had ever said about him. In return he proudly called me the "bullshitin'est dam ole Yankee bowah" he had ever known. We shook hands on that.

Ace's bunk was about ten away from mine, and that was just fine with me. One of his favorite sports after lights out was to organize a farting contest. With over a hundred men crowded into the barracks, all on a diet of cabbage or turnip soup and sour black bread there was never a shortage of contestants or fuel. At some point during the wild laughter and applause that fed his ego, Ace would simply declare himself the winner, stop the contest, and go to sleep.

When our news reader came in and finished the dispatch he was always prepared to swallow, Ace would listen with the rest of us. But afterward he would often come over to me and say, "Mac, what'n hell does that all mean anyway?" The experts in my group could always come up with some wild and wooly interpretations for him. One time he was puzzled by a word used in describing what had happened in Romania.

"When the man says they 'capichalated,' does that mean they gettin' they ass whupped?" I told him it meant they had given up and quit.

"Well, whah in the hayell dint that idiot *say* so? Ah don' know *whah* some folks cain't speak plain English."

He wore his stocking hat rolled up on his head all the time, night or day, and when someone asked him why, he said, "Ah put it on when they shaved mah haid and my damn hairs grew raht through it. It won't come off!"

Ben Phelper was a talented man. His sketches, stories, and even photographs of life in Stalag Seventeen B were something really unique.

Ben was a shot-down gunner in the 385th Bomb Group of the Eighth Air Force. Like the rest of us, he was a sergeant, but one with great talent and imagination. The books he published after the war were hand-lettered, with remarkably accurate sketches. The few now known to exist are treasured as journals of what life was like, both in the ball turret of a Flying Fortress and in Stalag Seventeen B. (In 1997, leader of the Stalag Seventeen ex-POWs Jacob Stein told me that the originals were given to the state of Texas and he would try to get release for an enlarged version for publication.)

British historian Roger Freeman in *B-17 at War* used some of Ben's material for a chapter titled "Ball Gunner—Ben J. Phelper." It was quite accurate and believable, except maybe for the part about sitting up on the rim of the radio room hatch during takeoff for a mission one day. In that book is a picture of the subject, unmistakably captioned: "Sgt. Ben Phelper."

His imagination continued to develop after the war, becoming so vivid that one could only believe he must have been talking and writing with tongue in cheek. When he died in 1993 the obituary was headed: "Phelper's Life Subject of Film." In the accompanying photo he is wearing an ex-POW cap and a wide grin.

The text says that Sergeant Phelper "joined the Army Air Corps as a lieutenant and retired from the Air Force as a colonel, but his cover story as a POW was that he was simply a staff sergeant. He was shot down August 17, 1943, while flying his 17th mission aboard a Flying Fortress, ironically on his way to being dropped behind enemy lines to begin his assignment."

Once invited to address a group of air force officers at a Texas base, Ben dazzled them with stories of how he had allowed himself to be captured by the Germans so that he could help out the boys at Stalag Seventeen B, being actually "Colonel" Phelper at the time. The adventures he related rivaled those depicted in the humorous TV series *Hogan's Heroes*. In fact, he said that the stories were taken from actual happenings in his career at Stalag Seventeen.

In one story he described the guerrilla army he kept hidden in the woods just outside the fence in Cemetery Grove, ready to attack the camp when he gave the signal. The tales with which he fascinated the air force officers were reported in their newsletter as fact. But one ex-POW with questions contacted the major responsible for the program. It was rumored that when he found out how he had been taken in, he opted for early retirement.

The wide grin on Ben Phelper's face in his obituary photo seems to be saying, "Ha ha, gotcha!"

John E. Wasche was not well known in Stalag Seventeen. If he had been then it is likely he would have been put before a German firing squad. Ex–camp leader Kurtenbach remembers John very well.

John was a gunner in my Ninety-second Bomb Group, shot down in August 1943, six months before I arrived there. He came with the others from Moosburg to open the "new" stalag in Austria in October 1943. Sometime during that period he made known to Kurt his "special talents," and when the clandestine radio was set up and receiving regularly Kurt found him to be very useful.

John was one of the two men who helped with the cooking and care of the doctors, back of the *Revier* in the compound. But what few, if any, others knew about him was that he was the guy who stuck his neck out every night to monitor the radio, picking up the BBC broadcasts. Had any German snoopers walked in on him while he was listening and taking notes, there would be little doubt of his fate.

When J. J. Katuzney dropped in on me in New Hampshire a few years ago we talked about that radio. He felt sure that the man who was responsible for it or who may even have built it came from my area. If he did, neither Ralph nor I have any awareness of it.

Kurt wrote that during 1995 he visited with John Wasche and his wife, Mary Catherine, in Minneapolis, Minnesota, and had a chance to talk about some of their experiences at Stalag Seventeen and about the many special risks they had both subjected themselves to there.

Another POW comrade who became somewhat involved in secret work was Sgt. Mark Curtis. Mark had been shot down about a year before our *Toonerville Trolley* hit the hillside in Bubach. As with Ralph Lavoie and me, and many others, we're sure, Mark was nearly trapped inside the ball turret of his Ninety-fourth Bomb Group B-17 while it was going down. In his situation, however, both pilots had been killed.

It was the top turret gunner who delayed jumping long enough to help Mark out of the turret. In my case it was the tail gunner, but Ralph says it was "the Man upstairs" who helped him. Mark Curtis came down in the flatlands of the Zuider Zee and was captured right away.

When he arrived at Stalag Seventeen he went right to the *Lazarette* barely having made it up the hill from Krems. He was suffering from what turned out to be bronchial pneumonia.

Mark was the first American soldier that the French staff at the *Lazarette* had ever seen. A news article after the war quoted him: "To say I was nursed back to health doesn't come close to describing the care I received from the French, Poles, Yugoslaves, Belgians and Hungarians who worked there." He was repatriated, but not 'til January of 1945, when a group was sent to Marseilles.

Sgt. Mark Curtis's return was to have served a special purpose. Kurt had chosen Mark to carry back information that might become very helpful to the American forces if and when they came to take our camp. "I was briefed over and over on location of bunkers, guard towers, distances, roads, and the size of the local Wehrmacht forces," said Mark, telling of his arrival in Washington, providing all of his information to an authorized interrogator, then the confirmation and evaluation processes. It was all too late. The camp at Krems was now evacuated, and the Red Army was at the gate.

43

Dr. Rabinovitch, Alias "Harry Vozic"

He was not a U.S. flyer, nor had he been shot down, but Dr. Rabinovitch played the role of Sgt. Harry Vozic for two years very well, thus avoiding arrest and probably death. Harry Vozic had knowledge of the complex system set up by French underground people, the ones who helped Allied airmen get back to England. Had the Gestapo picked him up they would have tried to extract information from him before shipping him to Dachau or executing him on the spot.

To all of us at Stalag Seventeen Harry was just another American POW, but one with some fairly good medical knowledge, thus useful at the dispensary. Dr. Reuben Rabinovitch had chosen the false name when picked up by German authorities in Paris. He was with a group of American flyers trying to avoid capture, so he decided it best to become one of them.

A Canadian, he had been completing his medical studies in France when the country was taken by the Germans. Being a British subject, he was interned in the Fresnes penitentiary. While there he organized medical services. There were other interned doctors there from Palestine, Cyprus, and other countries of the British Commonwealth.

After fifteen months in jail he faked a fall and injuries to his back, then got himself certified as close to death. Transferred to a status of home arrest, he arranged for his wife and two children to be hidden before he fled the Nazis and disappeared.

He became a member of a group of the French underground that was in contact with the Allied Intelligence Services. With them he took heroic measures helping flyers to avoid capture by the Germans. In many cases they were given forged papers, even putting some who were wounded into hospitals to be held there until they could be moved toward the Spanish border.

Over three hundred Allied servicemen went through the hands of this underground group during a period of fifteen months.

By 1943 the doctor had spent some time in a Paris prison but had been inexplicably released. However, in July or August of that year, when the Germans took some Americans captive they took Rabinovitz with them, believing him to be one of the flyers. This is how he eventually ended up at Stalag Seventeen B with Sergeant Kurtenbach and his 4,000 American prisoners of war.

Although the doctor's usefulness was limited, according to Kurt, due to the need to keep his identity secret, he was able to provide badly needed medical services for the Americans.

In a book, *Canadian Jews of World War II*, the author appears to have been convinced that the doctor's "health deteriorated greatly" before he was judged qualified for the prisoner exchange. In reality, it was his second and perhaps best performance. It was all an act.

After the war Kurt was invited to attend ceremonies at which Dr. Reuben Rabinovitz was presented with the U.S. Medal of Freedom in recognition of his unusual and valuable contribution to the cause of the Allies.

Here is what Kurt remembered about Dr. Reuben Rabinovitch, alias Harry Vozic, in a paper he prepared for the information of former POWs of Stalag Seventeen B.

It was during the summer of 1943 when Harry Vozic first came to my attention, at Stalag VIIA in Moosburg, Bavaria.

There was much turmoil in the camp at that time with prisoners entering and leaving, our men from North Africa intermingled with nationalities from all over eastern Europe and Russia. There were severe food shortages due to bombing of marshalling yards in that section of Germany, numerous escape attempts with consequent reprisals by the German staff and a general upheaval of all parts of our prison camp life.

One evening a POW came up to me, saying that he had a problem and would like to speak with me. I had not seen him before. He drew me to a quiet part of the compound, then told me his name was Vozic, that he had been a member of the French underground and had been aiding Allied airmen to avoid capture and eventually help them get back to England.

He wore typical uniform clothing of both British and American air services, stood about five feet ten, and had a ragged looking black moustache. He appeared to be older than the average flyers, perhaps in his mid to upper thirties.

As I think about him now, he bore a striking resemblance to Sydney, the psychiatrist in the TV series of *MASH*, but also a slight resemblance to Groucho Marx. His accent seemed to me to be pure "New York City."

Harry explained how he had been captured, using the story at Dulag Luft that he was a waist gunner on his first mission and that is all he knew. He knew that if his true identity became known then he would be tortured in an attempt to get information about the underground group.

He said that since all the men seemed to trust me, then he decided to unburden on me, hoping that I would assist him in evading pursuit of the Gestapo. He implied that he had friends in high places but would not name anyone.

When I asked why he had not used his own escape procedures to get out of France he did not answer directly but indicated he felt he was serving his country by continuing what he was doing.

As I recall, Vozic brought forward a couple of lads who verified he had been captured with them, but nothing beyond that. A number of POWs had come to me in just such furtive manner, relating stories about various intelligence agencies and offering help if needed. Their stories were filed away in my head and usually nothing more came of the matter. Thus it was with Vozic; accepted but then practically forgotten.

Occasionally I would notice him in the French compound at camp, which was not unusual. Many Americans were over there each day trading and visiting.

My next contact was after arrival at XVIIB. Everything was in short supply, barracks were filthy and lice-infested and there was a very real threat of "flak" typhus. We were short of medical help, supplies and personnel with any of the needed skills.

Vozic told me he had some knowledge of medical first-aid and he gave me a list of supplies that would be helpful in our desperate situation. Barracks 13 was set aside as an infirmary and we were lucky to have such men as Mark Curtis, J.J. Katuzney and others of their caliber. All were natural born freebooters and scroungers of the first water. Supplies were stolen from the Germans, passed into camp, some order began to appear and for the first time we had the ability to help the sick and injured to some degree.

Later, when Dr. Fred Beaumont arrived with some skilled staff, our principal needs were handled most capably.

Vozic stayed with the infirmary and was usually referred to as "Old Doc Vozic." It seemed to be his nature to be a leader and not a follower, which caused some problems with the doctors. They told me that Vozic was too pushy and arrogant. I had no authority in that area, so stayed out of it.

One thing I did, however, was to call him in and point out that if he was indeed who he said he was then it was becoming apparent to others and might even be noted by the German authorities.

He was fluent in German but never used that language in their presence. He seemed, however, to like to twit some guard or insult another. Their angry responses were setting him apart from the average American POW and I warned him about it several times. He would grin, agree and go back to the infirmary and be quiet for a time.

Vozic, more than any other person, was a source of embarrassment for me. Seldom a day passed when someone in whom I had the highest trust would suggest that Vozic was a spy, or perhaps was a Communist agent. What did I really know about him? they wondered. I could give them no firm answers. I felt it was good he was in the infirmary with a group who trusted him, and not in barracks where his ignorance of military matters may have done him in.

He was a madman with a sense of humor. He improvised practical jokes, kidding around a lot and helping keep spirits high. We became close friends and we had many visits and discussions, some that were highlights of my POW experiences. His knowledge of psychology seemed awesome to me, he had travelled extensively and was most capable of expressing himself. I learned that he could speak five or six languages and I utilized his abilities in meeting with various leaders of the camp communities. He would sit, looking at the center of the table, and interpret my thoughts into Russian, Polish, French or Serbian, then translate their comments into each of the other languages, then to English for me. If he had trouble with some dialect then he would use German instead, since it was not uncommon for senior POWs to have learned German.

Inter-camp relations were improved through Vozic's aid, some problems resolved, and occasionally these leaders could have their Arbeitskommandos bring badly needed supplies into the lager. Also the stage was set for some quasimilitary force to come into being should it later become necessary for our survival.

In spite of how valuable Vozic was becoming to me, he was also becoming a liability. He knew this and became more apprehensive about it, fearing that the Gestapo would eventually get him. We made the decision to get him out of Stalag XVIIB if it could be worked out.

The March 1944 notice of proposed repatriation of qualified men presented the opportunity. There were to be two categories, one would be those clearly unfit for any future duty due to missing limbs, blindness or serious injury. The second would be my list of those disabled through heart problems, partially disabling wounds or internal problems not apparent to the naked eye. These would be mine to advocate before the Commission.

We decided to get him into the hospital on the hill and get him into that second category. Through a foreign doctor we devised a plan whereunder Vozic was in his care. He would use a set of medical records filched from a desperately ill Russian soldier (who ultimately died) indicating tuberculosis of the spine. If not that precisely, then it was something else with a prognosis of certain death in a comparatively short time. His medical file was supplemented with X-ray films taken from another file.

Reports reached me of Vozic's gradual decline and his becoming emaciated and unable to leave his bed. He was such a good actor that it began to worry me, but I was assured by the doctor that all was going according to plan and I should stop worrying.

Many of the cases coming before the Repatriation Commission were so apparent that no hearing was called for. Then hearings on my list began. A simple majority vote was needed from the three German and two Swiss doctors on the board.

Thirty-two on my list of fifty-six were accepted. Germany had many wounded soldiers on active duty right at our camp and they resisted letting go several whom they thought could be useful to the Allied armies if they went home.

Almost at the end of the hearings, Harry Vozic was carried into the room on a stretcher. I was shocked by his appearance. He had a stubble of beard, the moustache he had sworn not to cut until Hitler was dead was positively long and hideous. He appeared to be emaciated and his eyes were listless and nonfocusing.

After private discussions amongst the doctors they decided

that he would go home. Now came his moment of true brilliance.

Raising himself up slightly he emphatically stated that he did not want to go home. It was better if his wife and family never saw him in this condition and he would probably never make it in the long trip across the Atlantic.

He remained so adamant that I thought to myself, "If this guy blows it then I personally will kill him when it is over!" His role was played to perfection. The German and Swiss doctors came over to his stretcher and pleaded with him to go home and he ultimately acceded to their wishes. He never thanked them but sank back on his stretcher and was carried from the room, while his certification was put into my sweating hands.

I saw him in August when I was allowed to go down to the train station at Krems and say good-bye to the repats. He had written a memo to me in one of the "Wartime Log" books given by the YMCA. It was most affectionate and signed, "Old Doc Vozic." Above the top he had written "Rube." I paid no attention to it since it meant nothing to me until much later.

44

The *Panzergeneral* and the Sergeant

Camp Leader Kurtenbach was ordered up to the *Lager Kommandant*'s quarters one day in February 1945. Major Eigl had what he considered to be a "very important visitor" there, and he wished to speak with the top-ranking American at Stalag Seventeen.

Kurt put on his best class-A shirt and was escorted through the gate, up the hill, to the *Vorlager*. Major Eigl was waiting for him.

His visitor was important indeed! It was none other than Gen. "Sepp" Dietrich, who had become known as "Hitler's Gladiator" after he had pleased the Fuhrer by cleaning up after Mussolini's disastrous attempt to invade and occupy Greece. Dietrich's full title was *Oberstgruppenfuhrer Panzergeneral Oberst der Waffen SS.*

The American armies remembered him well. His tank divisions played a big role in the December offensive we called the Battle of the Bulge. At the time of this visit to Stalag Seventeen, still ahead of him was the assignment to protect the vital oil fields in Hungary, then later take his forces into Austria to stop the Russian advance toward Vienna.

Adolf would later refer to his Gladiator in unflattering terms, since he was unable to accomplish either of those directives. As a result, Heinrich Himmler was sent to order Sepp and his officers to give up the medals they had been awarded.

Kurt recalled that at this secret conference Major Eigl appeared very nervous to be in the presence of such a high-ranking officer of the Reich. Although General Dietrich did not comment on it, he must have been quite surprised to find himself facing a noncommissioned officer as top American in this camp of 4,000 flyers.

After an introduction and exchange of greetings, the *Panzer-*

general said that what he really wanted was nothing more than to meet an American soldier. He claimed he had not met one before and wondered if the two of them might talk for a while. Eigl stayed close by and listened to the exchange.

During the discussion, Kurt says, the general told him the Russians would be stopped in their advance into Austria and that the Americans could rest assured that he would never allow them to fall into the hands of "those barbarians."

Major Eigl paid close attention to that statement. Two months later, as the Red Army approached the camp in spite of General Dietrich's efforts, it is possible that Major Eigl used the SS general's comments to justify evacuating the Americans and the German staff from Stalag Seventeen, moving them toward the west, where the Allies were advancing across Germany.

When asked by General Dietrich if things were "all right" with the war prisoners, Kurt responded that things "could be a whole lot better."

"Ja, das ist sicher!" [That is for sure!] commented the general.

But things for him were going to get a whole lot worse. There was the defeat in Hungary, then a meeting in Vienna with Heinrich Himmler before the defeat there. Himmler claimed to have brought an order from the Fuhrer reprimanding the general and his men.

The Dietrich-Kurtenbach meeting concluded, and there were no offerings or concessions. However, it may have begun the series of events that brought about the liberation of the 4,000 American airmen prisoners by the West, where their chances for survival were greater than they might otherwise have been.

It is speculated that General Dietrich was anticipating the end of the war and was at Stalag Seventeen to quietly check out a reasonably safe surrender route for himself, his wife, and their two children. We may never know whether he would have made specific offers had he not been surprised to find a staff sergeant where he expected to find a field-grade American officer or had Major Eigl not eavesdropped on the conversation.

At the postwar trials it was determined that Dietrich had responsibility for the murders of American prisoners during the Battle of the Bulge and he was sentenced to a prison term. Yet it may well have been his influence on the commandant of Stalag Seventeen that saved many of us American POWs from ending our lives in Soviet labor camps.

Although we still considered Stalin and the Russians to be our allies, we were aware of his disdain for his soldiers who had been captured by the Germans. "They are to be considered dead," Stalin declared. The Russians in the compound next to ours knew that their future was dim if the camp was overrun by their countrymen. They desperately wanted to be liberated by the Americans, but as it turned out, this would not have helped them. Politics dictated that all Russian POWs were to be returned to Russia when the war ended.

It has been claimed that many American POWs who thought they might get home sooner by heading for the Russian lines were never heard from again. In a September 1995 American Legion magazine article it is claimed that thousands completely disappeared and may have ended up in any one of the numerous Soviet labor camps.

Hitler's "Gladiator," Sepp Dietrich, and his Sixth Panzer Army failed to stop the Russians. He was captured, with his wife, at Kufstein, supposedly on his way to Berchtesgaden after going out of his way to pick her up. He surrendered to a sergeant, after all. It was a man named Herbert Kraus of the Thirty-sixth Infantry Division.

45

Those "Friendly" Air Raids

As Allied air activity increased in the Wachau Valley region, near the busy Danube River and adjacent rail lines, we dug zigzag trenches behind the latrines, on the suggestion of the German Luftwaffe commandant. They soon became wet and muddy, and there were clues that some may have used the trenches as a toilet when all the holes inside were occupied. Many of us chose to take our chances in the open, in the event of bombing attacks.

One night a line of British bombers came roaring over the camp and we were given no choice. The commandant had ordered everyone confined to the barracks. The Brits flew their night missions in single file, and the first one over dropped a huge Christmas tree flare just to the east of our fences. As it slowly drifted down on its parachute it occurred to us that this was how they marked off the target and the planes following would drop their bombs on it.

The slimy trenches began to develop an appeal. But after a while we could see that all the bombers were passing over without any bombs coming down on us. Soon the "all clear" sounded down in Krems and it was concluded that our camp was marked by the flare so that the RAF would *not* treat it as a target.

On another night we all went outside to watch the night bomber stream as they struck at the fighter base a few miles out beyond Gneixendorf. Sergeant Kurtenbach had strongly protested having the men locked in the barracks during a previous air raid, and the commandant relented. A giant fireworks display began far out in the direction of Gneixendorf, and many began to jump down into the slit trenches. They were getting a little too close.

Soon it became clear that the planes were aiming for the air base, and apparently with good accuracy. Now we all stood up and took in the spectacular sights and sounds. Sometimes one of the searchlights would pick up a bomber in its beam and the flak would explode closer to it. When a pilot was caught in the blinding light he would dive toward it and maneuver to get out of it.

At least two, however, weren't able to get out of the beam and were knocked down. It was a terrible sight to see one burning and falling apart as it fell, with maybe one or two parachutes reflecting the flames or being picked up by the searchlight beams.

As the German night fighters attacked they would create long, arcing red lines with their tracers, making fanlike patterns in the sky. The machine-gun fire from the bombers would send curving lines of sparks outward, but no sign of hits on the fighters could be seen. We saw bomb explosions in the direction of the air base and saw flames and debris shoot skyward. The thunderous booms of the bombs and the thud-boom sounds of the anti-aircraft guns made the earth shake in the prison camp compound.

It took hours for the flames and the excitement to die down, and we slowly moved back inside to our bunks to wonder if this action might have brought the end a little closer for us.

In early April of 1945 there was a bombing attack on Krems in broad daylight by B-24 Liberators of the Fifteenth Air Force in Italy. A group came directly over Stalag Seventeen from the east and toward Krems. They were high, but we could easily see the bomb bay doors opened and knew they were on their bombing run. We instinctively dropped to the ground when we saw the bombs leave the bays.

They curved slowly past the camp and disappeared behind the hill below which Krems lay and where railyards were located. The earth shook violently and we could see huge pillars of smoke and debris rising into the air. A few brainless POWs (oh, we had a few) climbed onto the barracks roof to see better and began cheering when the bombs exploded. Camp leaders and guards quickly chased them down, reminding them about the guards and staff with families there in Krems.

One barracks chief asked a couple of those cheering, "If you had a loaded rifle and some men were laughing and cheering while they watched your family being blown up, what would you do?"

Not long after the all clear there was a good response to a call for volunteers to go down and help in rescue work. We heard that the Liberators had done a good amount of destruction in the broad railyards but had mixed emotions about cars of Red Cross parcels that may or may have just arrived ready for unloading.

On a few occasions pairs of P-38 Lightnings appeared. One hovered high above while the other made a strafing dive on river barges. Smoke puffs could be seen at the nose of the diving plane, and secondary explosions came below our field of vision from our vantage point up over the brow of the hill.

These raids were morale boosters for the prisoners. Propaganda coming in from German sources about the Allies being stopped or about secret weapons turning the tide could not very well counter what we were seeing with our own eyes.

Air force historical reporting of the Krems attack witnessed by us describes it this way:

The devastating bombing raids on many German railroad junctions yards, or "marshalling yards," had made it imperative for them to rely on the smaller centers. This re-routing over-taxed the local facilities and when the Americans bombed them then terrible problems were caused by the debris from smashed rolling-stock and turned up rails.

Thus Krems had become a primary railroad center and was of great strategic importance up to April 1945, having not yet been touched by the war.

The 456th Bomb Group of B-24s which came up from Italy on the second of April made their bombing run from 18,000 feet. There was no fighter opposition and only limited flak. Their strings of bombs were released almost over the heads of the prisoners in Stalag XVIIB and most of the bombs struck the rail facilities at which they were aimed.

On the same day aircraft from Italy also hit facilities at Graz and St. Polten, in this region.

A month or more before evacuation of the camp, when the Red Army guns could be heard off toward Vienna, we group leaders were told of the military organization of which we were now a part. We were all still sergeants; however, I would now be a platoon leader. Chris, my barracks chief, was to be company commander, and the compound chief was the battalion commander. "Tell your men to be aware of the seriousness of the situation and to be prepared to follow orders, whatever might happen," group leaders were told.

In the light of a sputtering oleo burner, late into the night, my group gathered around me and we tried to predict the future. What was feared was that a force of green-uniformed Wehrmacht soldiers would march into the compound, perhaps even in the middle of the night, and line us up as though for a roll call, but with the intent of a mass execution. We never doubted that some of the Berlin authorities would not hesitate to give such an order.

The plan was that on the specific signal from the company commander I would instantly convey it to my group and we would rush the guards, assuming that all other groups would be doing the same. We would take their rifle fire but would hope to subdue them before any of their potato-masher hand grenades were tossed among us or the tower guards opened up with their machine guns. The first ones to get guards' rifles were to pick off those tower guards as quickly as possible.

Then there were men assigned who would scale the fence, climb the towers, and use the machine guns against any the patrol guards and any reinforcements that might be approaching.

We knew that casualties would be heavy, but the alternative was for us all to be dead. After months of gnawing anxiety, many of us were eager for any type of effort and the new undercurrent running throughout the camp was very exciting.

It could be speculated that it was Commandant Kuhn's decision to use us as a reason for marching away from the Russians himself that avoided the necessity for the planned revolt. He and all of his men seemed to be aware that they would soon be dead themselves or prisoners of either East or West. They chose to try for West.

46

Other Stalags Evacuated

On January 20, 1945, the Germans decided that the Russian front was moving too close to Luft Three, located sixty miles southeast of Berlin. Ten thousand prisoners were evacuated in a forced march, despite the extreme winter weather, and headed toward Nuremburg. With them were the pilots of the *Toonerville Trolley*. Dick Anthony can only shake his head and say about it, "Man, that was rough."

For six days the columns of POWs struggled through subfreezing temperatures and snowstorms, marching over sixty-two miles before cramming into boxcars to continue the journey. Some did not survive, and some have remained MIAs. Inside the infamous "forty or eight" cars they somehow existed for two days before arriving at the already overcrowded Stalag Thirteen D in Nuremberg. Held there during February and March of 1945, "we suffered not only from overcrowding and shortage of food," said Dick, "but from the cold, vermin infestation, and the never-ending air raids. The Americans hit by day and the RAF by night."

On April 14, 1945, they evacuated yet again. This time, in weather a bit more moderate, they were marched to Stalag Luft Seven A, located near Moosburg, northeast of Munich. It was the very camp from which a group of U.S. airmen had been evacuated a year and a half earlier and shipped to the camp for Russians at Stalag Seventeen B in Krems, Austria.

While the officers marched southward, four of the gunners from the *Toonerville Trolley* were on the road from Krems, moving westward toward the German heartland.

The only *Toonerville Trolley* man confined at Stalag Luft Four in Kiefheide, Pomerania, was engineer/gunner Ed Kolber. He tells about hearing the sounds of the Russian guns getting closer during January of 1945: "With only a few hours' warning, the Germans lined us up and marched us out the main gate. We were headed south and west in groups of a few hundred."

Winter weather was particularly hard on the marchers and guards as well. Ed tells about being allowed to sleep in barns at night to get shelter during the worst of it. His group existed "on the road," he says, until about mid-April, when there was no place farther to go.

"While marching they gave us some black bread and whatever vegetable they could come up with made into a soup now and then," he goes on.

"The POW leader of Stalag Four was British, and he advised us to stay with our group. We would be safer from the turmoil going on around us than we would be if we took off on our own.

"We had to be constantly on alert for American fighter planes. They were looking for strafing targets such as motor convoys and marching troops. Our route zigzagged all the way from Kiefheide to Brunswick and covered nearly four hundred kilometers in all.

"While laying over at Brunswick we discovered one night that British troops had moved in and taken over without a shot having been fired. We were no longer in the hands of the enemy."

Liberation day arrived for the Luft Three men, including Dick Anthony, Ray Raney, and Bill DePaoli, on the twenty-ninth of April 1945. Dick says, "Bursting bombs and gunfire had kept us alert all night long, and we knew that something big was about to happen!"

A P-51 came low across the camp and must have been fired upon by a guard, because he came right back on a strafing run and wiped out the guard tower. By morning not a guard could be found in the camp.

Dick goes on: "Soon a column of American tanks came rumbling across the countryside and they burst right through the high, double barbed-wire fences into the compounds. Pandemonium broke loose as the Nazi flag was replaced with an American flag and the realization set in that we were free. It was a little later when Gen. George Patton himself arrived in a vehicle marked to leave no doubt who he was. It was said that he gave

250

one of his fiery little talks before announcing that he had a date in Munich. Then he jumped into his vehicle and roared away.

"It was a scene I shall certainly never forget, probably the most important day of my life," says Dick.

47

Marching across Austria

It was a cold, damp April morning at Stalag Seventeen when we rolled off our palliasses for the last time ever. A guard stood at the doorway pounding his rifle butt on the floor.

It was still dark and I could see the searchlights from the towers all focused on the open compound. There were the usual cries of, "Raus! Raus! Appell! Schnell!" from the Germans, echoed mockingly by some of the half-awake POWs.

The roll-call process seemed more intense this morning, and some dog tags were being examined to be sure all were accounted for. Every German staff member was out and getting organized for the march. Some horse-drawn wagons were lined up and being loaded with their supplies and belongings. A few female dependents were already on board, evidently going to accompany their mates. An old guard named Schmidt had once shown us a picture of his *Frau*, a seamstress down in the village. She was short and chunky with a round, happy face. I was glad to see that he wouldn't have to leave her behind. (Unfortunately, Schmidt is said to have been one of the two older guards who did not survive the long march.)

It was announced that a motorized soup wagon had already been dispatched and would be at an appointed place ready to serve hot meals later in the day. "You will meet them each day for your meal," said the captain. The men treated this announcement the same as they had treated daily rumors that the war was over.

After several delays, we watched one group and then another march out through the main gate, and we gave each a mighty cheer. Then it was our turn. What a great feeling to be on the outside of those impenetrable fences, walking away up the dirt road past the staff quarters. "Let's stay close together," I told my group, "and check each other often to make sure we're all making it."

Those first hours severely tested the capability of each to keep up and to carry his pack. None of my group were burdened with any excess baggage. However, by midafternoon we had picked up a few items from others who were discarding their excesses.

In a group of older POWs ahead there were some who had been professional traders. As they were becoming exhausted they began to shed items. Neil spotted one tossing a rag-tied bundle to the roadside. He dived behind a guard to retrieve it and tucked it inside his shirt. When we stopped we found it contained a pound or more of elbow macaroni. We hadn't seen anything like this in over a year. Later we picked up a turnip and then a can of standard oleomargarine, the kind used to fuel our lamps in fatter times.

We cut up the turnip and ate it right away. Macaroni, however, doesn't dissolve in the mouth and is impossible to crunch up and swallow. It would have to wait until we could heat some water. The oleo had the consistency of petroleum jelly, though it was not as tasty. It did provide nourishment and each of us would dip in a finger and put some in his mouth from time to time.

There were many nonedible items being shed also as men realized that they must unburden or collapse. Collapsing might very well mean death. When I saw a wool overcoat thrown at the roadside I knew that someone had really become desperately weak. He would be cold that night.

The guards spoke and acted now as though they were our protectors. Having the same basic needs as we did, they could be counted on for at least one stop every two or three hours for rest and toilet. If a stream was nearby, then it was a chance to get a drink and to refill handmade containers. Although many emergency stops were begged because of the cases of dysentery among us, they just were not permitted. As a result some pretty nasty things happened, as some would lose control and try to drop their pants and squat while the column moved around them.

None in my group got into trouble this way, but occasionally a little tugging and pushing was required to keep one moving. I was concerned about two whom we considered old men, both over thirty. Sergeants Glenn and Kunz had known each other before the war in Detroit and were close friends and "combine partners" as POWs. That didn't prevent them from arguing much of the time. One would never let the other get ahead of him, and probably that's what kept both from collapsing during the march.

Finally, as the sun was setting, I could look ahead and see that our column was moving up into a large field, high above the Danube River. What a great sight it was to see the motorized soup truck there. It hadn't been propaganda after all, at least for day one. As we surged into the field, we formed a long, snaking line to each get a ladle of whatever was in the tub. It was very thin and there were some worms in it, but that mattered not at all. It was food.

We fell asleep where we collapsed on the ground, but as the night dampness and cold crept in we pushed ever closer together. Some of the two-man combines in my unit had sewn their blankets together to make double sleeping bags. Neil and I hadn't, but before the night was over we each bargained our way into someone else's, making them triples, then put our own blankets underneath, where much of the cold seemed to be coming from.

My last conscious thoughts before drifting off were, *Well, we've passed through many villages and somehow made it through the first day. I wonder how many more villages there will be before we either "run out of gas" or run up against the Allied armies.*

After evacuation of Stalag Seventeen on April 18, the forced march continued for eighteen days, covering about three hundred kilometers, or two hundred miles.

The first regiment out of the gate, numbering about five hundred, was at 8:30 A.M., an hour and a half later than its intended departure. This could have been due in part to the Americans' tactics of delay, hoping the Germans would just take off and leave them.

A daily log of the journey was kept by at least one keen and dedicated marcher, perhaps describing it for many of us. The copy of his eleven-page document titled *Eagles Can Walk* was marked "Author Unknown" when it came to me many years ago. Since then it has been attributed to a "Sergeant Alford" by one who knew him.

Apparently, one of the "old-timers," shot down in 1943, he had accumulated more belongings to pack than most of the "new men" of my group. He lists "two blankets, five pairs socks, half a R.C. parcel, 1/6th loaf bread, one pair long-johns, 8 packs camels, 1 box Prince Albert pipe tobacco, an overcoat and a pair of gym shoes." It appears he must have received a package from home.

Thirty-nine guards with them included "Army, Luftwaffe, Storm Troopers and Volkstrom." The log says they "stopped four times, weather fine, came through five towns nestled in the mountains. Army and SS have taken over four of the towns. People are friendly, surprising everyone. Four men passed out. We sleep in open tonight; Mac, Jim and I will sleep together for warmth. No food from 'Jerry' yet."

Alford's group, it appears, did not meet the mobile soup vehicle.

My own journal continues:

As dawn of day number two spreads across the sky I'm concerned whether it will be possible for me to get all my joints and muscles working again.

We mill around for a bit while each gets his gear wrapped about him, then get into rough alignment in the road. Our confusion is punctuated by continuous shouts from the guards, "Vall in, vall in! Schnell, schnell!"

We had been told there would be time to get water, start a fire and maybe drink a cup of something hot before starting out. Only the most naive believed it, since there was nothing whatever in the area from which we could make a fire. As soon as we are assembled into some sort of order the command is given and we move forward, advancing accordion-like until comfortable spacing develops between rows. Aching muscles and blistered feet are causing gripes and groans and those of us who are able will now and then help another who is worse off, by simply putting an arm around a waist or a hand under an armpit, giving just a little upward and forward pressure. One might take a buddy's pack and put it over his shoulder with his own.

The leaders have been able to get many of the weaker ones to the front of the column during the night, and the Germans seem to have been doing something similar. Now they can fall back some without dropping beyond the last rank, where God knows what might happen to them. One guard had said that stragglers would be put in barns and cared for, which seemed doubtful. Later, when we saw what was happening to the Jewish column we passed, then we had every reason to believe that stragglers would be shot and killed.

We are taking the back roads, looping away from the Danube and through hilly country, probably walking twice the distance we would have on the main highway. Whenever we approach what might be a primary road we become part of a crazy parade of traffic, all of which is subordinated to the military vehicles that seem to be everywhere. A truckload of soldiers careening down the road sends waves of people, horses, carts and bicycles off into the gutters like bow waves off a ship.

A few of the more vigorous POWs try to get others to stand their ground to slow down the German military traffic, but they find few whose death-wish is that far advanced.

The Germans had, I thought, made a serious attempt to plan our march so as to provide resting places, water and night stops. But with the chaotic conditions caused by the two advancing armies and all of the fleeing refugees it was impossible. Also they must maintain a space between our group and the one ahead of us.

Each day seems like the previous one and each little village seems like the last, except for differing names such as Spitz, Hofami, Krumnussbaum, Rotenhof, Ybbs, Klam and Mauthausen.

48

The Jews

One day as our ragged column was moving westward, we saw a column approaching us heading in the opposite direction. As it rounded a bend in the dirt road, we were herded out of the way, down over a small embankment.

"This is a rest stop!" our leader shouted, and the welcome words were passed back along the lines.

As my group settled down and the approaching column drew closer, we stood up, pushing as near the roadway as we were allowed. At first I thought, *They are all talking together,* but then realized it was moaning I was hearing. To me they appeared to be old men, but their ages would have been impossible to judge in their awful condition.

There were scraping and clumping sounds also, made by the wooden clogs on their feet. We stared at them as they crept past, urged on by a gray-green uniformed soldiers with iron helmets, slung rifles, and full field packs.

When one of our guards said the word, "Jude," in response to a question about who they might be I saw the yellow stars on the breasts of their clothing. None of them could have weighed more than a hundred pounds, and it was obvious that each step taken was a tremendous effort.

We had heard rumors of death camps for Jews and other "undesirables," as the Nazis called those who were being exterminated. I wondered if this group of Jews might be on the way to or from such a camp. It was moving eastward, toward the Russian advance, which seemed strange. Someone guessed they might be forced to build *Panzersperre*. These were tank "traps" or blockades like those we saw along the back roads where we had traveled. They were made from logs, earth, and stones. Someone familiar with tanks said that they probably would not slow one of ours for more than a minute or two.

Now I could hear the shouts of the guards rising above the prisoners' sounds. But there was another noise: an occasional sharp "crack" from the rear of the column.

As the column struggled past, I realized that I was hearing pistol shots. As I peered back along the road, it became apparent that each "crack" was leaving a lifeless form lying in the roadway.

Someone behind me shouted, "What the hell is this? What's happening?" Most of us just stood and stared.

"Zey are *Untermenschen*," said one of the soldiers with our group. He was a newcomer, maybe a deserter from the ragtag bands of soldiers we had seen being pushed toward Vienna. The word was new to me, but Carl explained that it meant "underpeople" or subhumans. He also guessed they might be Romanian or Hungarians, from the few words he could pick up as they passed.

Now I was seeing more of the details of their misery. Ragged, dirty clothing hung on bodies so bony and thin that it was shocking to see. My throat filled up in pity for them. After two weeks on the road with little to eat I knew that my own body was skin and bones, but could I possibly look as terrible as these men? It occurred to me that maybe I could and perhaps some of that pity was for my own comrades and myself.

Some of the Jews wore pillbox hats and some had stocking caps, pulled down almost covering their eyes. Some wore layers of pants and shirts and had other material wrapped around their feet. They were said to have stripped clothes from the dead along the route, adding it to their own to help them survive the cold nights. Most turned their heads and fixed their eyes on us as they shuffled past.

Noticing our condition as better than their own, they began to beg, with motions and words asking for anything at all we might spare them. The word I heard most was: "Cigarette." Some Americans still had cigarettes, and they began tossing a few up into the column. It was a bad mistake.

The scramble to catch the cigarettes caused some to fall down and others to trip over them. Then the guards pushed and kicked them, taking the cigarettes for themselves. They wore uniforms different from those we had been used to seeing, and I wondered if they were German regulars. The rifles or machine guns they carried were being used to prod the prisoners along, occasionally knocking one to the ground. Then he would scramble to get up and keep moving, knowing that to lie there meant death by a pistol shot to the head.

I saw such shots being administered by at least two SS men, easily recognizable by their uniforms with the death head insignia. One passed close by me and I could see the Luger pistol in his hand. He would kick at any figure lying in the road, and if it did not get up then he would bend down, place the muzzle near the back of the head, and fire. One such execution took place within a few yards of me, and I saw the head jump and a puff of dust rise from the roadway next to it.

As I felt empathy with these prisoners, it was almost as though the gun had gone off next to my own head, and I was trembling with feelings that were a mixture of frustration, rage, and fear. Some of our own guards could no doubt sense such feelings among us, and it's possible they shared them. They stayed alert, however, with their weapons aimed at us to be sure we didn't interfere.

As the dragging tail of the column finally passed, we were once more herded up onto the roadway to continue our march. The sights and sounds of the Jews disappeared around a bend in the road behind us. I tried not to look at the bodies they had left, now being dragged to the sides of the road. After a while we settled down to our regular pace, but all were much quieter than before.

Our guards shuffled along with us, not reacting to the remarks coming from within our ranks, aimed not so much at them as at their leader and his fanatical Nazi followers.

In a few hours we ran out of daylight and the cold, damp air began to creep in around us. As we filed into a field and dropped to the ground, I curled up inside my coat and blanket. I fell asleep wondering if I would ever again return to a "normal" life after these awful sights and experiences.

Who were they, those men being driven toward the east leaving a trail of their dead as we American prisoners were being marched westward? We wondered what crimes had they may have committed to deserve to be in this next-to-death state from

259

starvation, exposure, and physical abuse.

The answer may have been given fifty-two years later, when a man named Joseph Fischer, of Brookline, Massachusetts, was interviewed by a newspaper reporter. In the resulting article Mr. Fischer told of still reliving those years of forced labor for the Nazis, marching many hundreds of miles as a beast of burden, and of burying hundreds of bodies of men like himself, who had been worked to death or who had been executed by shooting.

It now seems likely that in April 1945 we saw Mr. Fischer, a Transylvanian Jew. Judging by the appearance of the men, we supposed them all to be quite elderly. Actually, he and the others were in the age group of the Americans, between twenty and thirty.

During recent excavations for a construction project near a concentration camp site in Austria, a mass grave was discovered. The news brought back for Mr. Fischer vivid recollections of a time when his own life could be taken for granted only from moment to moment. Some officials claimed that the newly discovered grave held only the remains of German soldiers who died of typhus in POW camps after the war. This did not fit Mr. Fischer's picture.

As U.S. tanks approached the area on May 4, 1945, he claimed, the surviving members of his group were ordered to drag piles of corpses of Jews into the nearby woods and to push them into open trenches for burial. It was only the arrival of the American forces that ended the ordeal for these men who, as we had observed were barely alive themselves.

The grave, found during work on a hydroelectric project, now is believed to contain the remains of Hungarian Jews, according to Simon Weisenthal, the Israeli Nazi hunter.

In the news report, Fischer said that there may indeed have been bodies of some German POWs there, but he well recalls the mass burial of hundreds of starved Jews who had been marched from Budapest to Austria in the final months of the war.

Fischer had been held at the Mauthausen death camp, which we had passed on our march, and stories of death there are as gruesome as those about Dachau, Buchenwald, and others.

The Hungarian Jews had been forced into slave-labor battalions and ordered to follow the Axis armies as they advanced into the Soviet Union. They had to carry the soldiers' belongings along with construction tools as they left Hungary in the summer of 1942 and marched a thousand miles, to the banks of the Don River, by September.

In spite of the huge losses suffered during the retreat from Russia, some Jews survived and reached Warsaw. They were just in time for the uprising against the Nazi occupiers. Some historians say it was then that the Soviets halted their advance, so as not to disrupt the uprising, which could only end to their benefit.

Escaping to Austria, Mr. Fischer and thousands of Hungarian Jews were rounded up by the SS and put into Mauthausen and Gunskirchen.

Along the way Mr. Fischer recalled seeing Nazi SS guards shoot hundreds of Jews. We American POWs from Stalag Seventeen B apparently had witnessed some of those executions and may even have seen Mr. Fischer himself as our columns passed each other.

We were passing through an area not far from Mauthausen, one of the many prison camps in Nazi-occupied Europe where forced laborers were held until they either died of starvation and/or disease or were worked to death.

One of my ex–POW comrades was interviewed for a news article in 1988, and these were his recollections:

We're marching beside a high, barbed wire fence which encloses some barracks. When we get to the barracks we hear what sounds like a hundred elephants bellowing. I look at the windows and every one of them is filled with shaved heads and sunken eyes. It's like looking at skulls, and their mouths are open and what we are hearing is their screaming.

On the other side of the road a group of men, women and children, all wearing the yellow Star of David on their coats, are being marched up and down back and forth. You can't tell if their age is fifteen or ninety. They all look like skeletons and are crying and asking for food.

When the Americans liberated this area a few weeks later

they found some survivors but mostly piles of corpses.

After about the ninth day of the march we crossed the huge bridge over the Danube at the industrial city of Linz, Austria. We were within a few miles of the huge death camp at Mauthausen, but the group in which I marched did not approach close enough to get any hint of what was happening there.

As we were entering the city, bomb damage could be seen. Some was still fresh and smoldering. The guards warned us that the people of Linz would not be friendly to American flyer POWs after several days and nights of attacks on their railyards, river dock facilities, and industries. The *Feldwebel*, who often stopped to talk with the men in flawless English, said, "I don't have to explain to you guys that your bombs sometimes miss their targets just by a kilometer or so and wipe out an apartment house or a hospital. The people are funny here; they get upset about that."

The bridge over the Danube was still intact, and we ran the length of it, then dog-trotted along the road that bordered the south bank of the river. The column stretched out for a mile, as some of the men could not keep up even though their lives may have depended on it. The leader of our column thought we may have lost a few men before we got out into the countryside again.

High on an embankment on the south side of the Danube stood an old inn, and tables were set out under spreading chestnut trees. Forty years later, as I drove over the same highway, I recognized it and we stopped there for lunch. Climbing the steps up to the patio level, we were given a table from which we could see for miles up and down the river. As I watched the boat activity, the intervening years dissolved and I saw our ragged column marching westward along the highway, unable to stop, let alone eat lunch as we were doing today. The nostalgia of the moment spoiled what little appetite I had, and we left bowls of chilled soup on the table, with only a few spoonfuls eaten.

Back in 1945 there were unexploded bombs beside the road. They were of various sizes, stacked one-on-two, without fuses or tail fins. Some had American markings and some British. The scars on them made me believe they had been dropped from airplanes, but I had no explanation for why they hadn't exploded.

My armament training led me conclude that they may have been dropped "safe"—that is, with the arming wires still attached. Had it been inadvertent or were some bombardiers saying, "Enough is enough!"?

Some of the war news would come filtering through the marching ranks to my group. I didn't know where the radio was hidden or how someone was able to stretch out the antenna within the column without it being spotted by the guards. But maybe they didn't want it shut down. It was their only source of realistic news about the war. They ignored many of the shouts of "Deutschland kaputt!" as we heard about a BBC broadcast or passed along a rumor about an American advance somewhere.

On April 24 Cran Blaylock and I, along with several others, observed our anniversary. One year ago we had leaped out of the Flying Fortress at Bubach and were made prisoners of war. Now we were each about fifty pounds lighter and a whole lot wiser about the glories of war and the nature of man.

However, one year ago we POWs were about the only Allied soldiers in German-occupied Europe. Hundreds of thousands of them were now here and fighting their way toward us.

Our anniversary party was an all-night air raid by the British. They seemed to be aiming at rail lines going into and out of the Linz industrial area. A Pathfinder dropped a flare illuminating the whole countryside, then dropped others one by one. We were in the lighted area but not in the drop zone. Flak guns were rapid-firing with dull thuds at ground level, then echoing booms overhead. They seemed to suck the air out of my mouth and ears. I curled up and pulled my coat over my head, expecting showers of shrapnel to come raining down.

The RAF was bombing "in train," dropping one at a time as they followed one another across their targets. When each bomb exploded the earth would tremble, the heavy concussions overwhelming the noise of the antiaircraft guns. Although I saw no searchlights, there were occasional patterns of red lines indicating that German night fighters were up there hoping for kills.

Next day we marched right through a Luftwaffe base. The pilots were said to be Hungarians, and someone spoke with one of them. The reason he gave for not being up battling with the

American fighters was: "We are low on benzine. We save what we have for something more important, like flying beyond the Americans' lines and then taking to our parachutes."

The weather stayed cold. "We are heading south, now," said a German guard. But to the south all I could see were snow-capped mountain peaks. Only in the west would we find warmth.

It was on one day during April that an officer made his way back along our column announcing, "I am sorry to tell you this, but your President Roosevelt is dead." It was shocking news and we trudged along in silence for a while to let it sink in. It did not seem to have been "good news" to the Germans, as we might have expected—at least at the low ranks of soldiers with us.

In a rural area somewhere west of Milch we were halted early on a gray, drizzly day. We moved off the road into the area of a small farm. Chilled and eager to rest, we began to establish our living spaces around the house and the outbuildings.

The German march leader decided he would permit us to build fires but then warned that no fuel was to come from the fruit trees or from the buildings and fences. Authority was a bit loose by now, and he must have realized that there could hardly be any fires without those fuel sources. There was nothing else.

However, we gathered wood with discretion and out of sight of the farmer and guards. A scattering of small fires began to appear amongst the shivering groups of POWs.

Near where my men had settled was a small area fenced in with rails and a dwindling number of pickets. As we were quietly harvesting a few of the pickets, Neil and I worked our way through to see what had been the purpose of the fence. It may have been built to protect a garden plot from farm animals, but now with spring barely separating itself from winter, I could see no plants of any kind, only bare earth.

On a closer look, however, I made out what seemed to be the top of a turnip, left there from the previous season. While my partner covered me, watching for roving guards, I wriggled around and scratched the earth away from the object with that all-purpose tool, the dog tag. Now I could see that what I was exposing was a large purple-topped sugar beet. I crawled back out with it and began to show our lucky find to the others.

Suddenly we heard a roaring motor, shouting, and confusion from out by the road. They were unmistakably the sounds of German authority, and I could see a big open car stopped there. Three men leaped out and were opening up a lane through the POWs, striding about the yard, with flapping greatcoats and swinging swagger sticks. They would knock men about and kick at fires and equipment as they came. Two of our guards were moving ahead of them, and another was following, all looking extremely aggravated. They kept up a steady stream of shouted commands and seemed to be headed right for where I was standing with my purloined beet.

The crazy thought came into my mind that the farmer had seen my illegal act and had called the wrath of the SS down on me. Quickly I dropped the sugar beet down the front of my pants, pushing my knees together so it would not drop below the crotch. Then moving with the others, I folded back out of the way of the charging Nazi officers without appearing to be running or acting like a thief. At the same time I was adjusting my motions so as to retain the melon-size sugar beet in the crotch of my pants.

One of my men didn't move quickly enough and was rewarded with a fist to his face, opening a bloody gash as he was knocked down. I could see the glint of a heavy ring on the hand that struck him. His partner leaped to help him.

The three Nazis charged quickly on past me, close enough so I could easily see the SS insignia on their collars. There were two German guards huddled behind my men trying to avoid drawing attention to themselves. One of them later explained that the SS had not stopped simply to harass POWs but were seeking out deserters from their own armed forces. Any soldier who looked as though he did not belong or who lacked proper identification would have simply been shot, the guards told us.

There could have been a few deserters with us, but if so they were able to play their guard role well enough to escape execution. The SS men soon completed their circle, leaving a trail of angry POWs and smoky campfire remnants. Both Germans and Americans were greatly relieved as they climbed back into their huge car and drove off down the road. The sound of their motor easily drowned out the sounds of the Americans' "Bronx cheers."

Neil lifted my arm up in the air and yelled, "Hey, they were after our damn sugar beet, but the bastards didn't get it!" There was laughter and cheering as I fished it up out of my pants and scraped off the dirt.

We carved it up and passed pieces around, as one joker called it "making like Jesus and the loaves and fishes." It was a tasty little supplement to our meager diet and the first sweetness I had tasted in weeks.

49

"Secret Weapons"

We were passing near the village of Greiskirchen. Americans of course called it "Greasy Kitchen." We must have been getting careless about watching and listening for fighter planes. We had to consider them "enemy," whether Focke Wulf or Mustang. Any marching column was fair game for the strafing Allied fighter pilots, if they could find no river barges or rail locomotives.

Suddenly there was a roaring boom right overhead and I jumped toward the roadside. As I fell to the ground, rolling over, I saw a trail of black smoke and the going-away view of a strange-looking airplane. It had no propeller, and behind it was a trail of heavy black smoke. The craft was disappearing at a speed faster than any fighter plane I had ever seen.

"What in the hell *was* that?" was the excited comment by nearly everyone in our group. They were shaking heads and pointing off in the direction where the flying smoke pipe had disappeared.

We had no answer, but concern was raised about one of the German "secret weapons" Hitler had promised to produce to win the war. We now know that two or more models of jets had been developed by the Germans and were actually in production. The example we had just seen was one of them. Messerschmitt made one, calling it an Me-262, and it had been flying against our heavy bombers.

The other production jet fighter had but a single engine. It was a Heinkel 162. Hans Berger, the pilot who had shot down the *Toonerville Trolley*, was up there flying one of them. He had miraculously survived daily confrontations with the swarms of our fighters and bombers and was learning to be a jet pilot.

Some of those experiences had been described for me by Hans Berger's friend and former group commander Karl Demuth, just before we left Florida for this fifty-second anniversary trip. With Hans and a few other pilots of JG/1, Karl had gone to a remote field in Leck to try to master the revolutionary new fighters. It was one last chance for Germany to try to stop the bombers.

The Heinkel 162 they flew was called the Volksjager, People's Hunter. Of 1,400 manufactured, only 300 were to become operational, but not one was ever used in combat.

One thing occurred to us POWs as we reflected on what we had just seen that day in 1945. If this was the type of plane that might be strafing us during our journey, then there would no longer be the sound of an approaching engine to warn us to dive for the ditch. The jet engine was only heard after it had gone past us. We stayed much more alert for the remainder of the journey.

Half a century later, in the comfort of a small German inn, almost within sight of where our B-17 had gone down, Cran and I eagerly questioned Hans Berger. We wanted to hear more about those early jets and the men who flew them, and one of them was right there with us.

Hans was glad to share his recollections with us.

"Our Volksjager was a little plane made with plywood and glue. For power it had a single BMW 003 turbojet engine mounted on top of the fuselage. It was right behind my head.

"First test flight of that model was around Christmas 1944, not far from your prison camp, at the Vienna Schwechat airdrome. An earlier model had been called a *Spatz*, or sparrow.

"We pilots at 1 JG/1 got the first planes at the end of March 1945. I had my first takeoff on March 31 in Parchim, which is about sixty miles east of Hamburg.

"We stayed there until mid-April, while you and Cran were on the march across Austria, but weren't able to fly because of the lack of fuel. On April 15 we were moved to Leck, way up near the Danish border, but the same fuel problem persisted. Although as squadron leader I was a bit privileged, I had only four more takeoffs before the war ended. For Karl Demuth, our friend in Florida, and me that was four days before the German surrender on May 8, 1945.

"I was used to sitting behind that big Focke Wulf BMW engine," said Hans. "There was a feeling of security there. In the light Plexiglas cockpit of the He-162 I felt exposed and quite unprotected. There were still many problems to be resolved, and we were flying not only as trainees but also as test pilots.

"The brief flight time of only thirty to forty-five minutes was one big problem. Stability was lacking, as was a feeling of permanency in the glued-together wings and fuselage. The plane had to be flown very gently, with no hard movements of the controls. The nose would drop quickly if proper speed was not maintained."

One example was given. On April 24 Gruppenkommandeur Dahne met a tragic end. He took off on a training flight at 4:00 P.M. in his jet and only went to about five hundred meters high. When he began a turn his plane skidded and then somersaulted. Small pieces of glass shone in the sun, and a trail of white smoke came from his turbine. The small Volksjager fluttered down and crashed in the marsh. What seemed likely was that he tried to bail out but had not first jettisoned the canopy, and his head was driven through it."

"Were there many senior pilots like you and Karl?" I asked Hans.

"No," he said. "There were many very young men, boys really. Not only the fuel shortage but inadequate training time was a big problem. Many pilots lacked the sensitivity to handle this whole new concept of flying. The jet power was fantastic!

"There were several accidents, and I knew of three who were killed taking off or landing. Our engine was started with an electric starter linked with the turbine. When I pressed that red button, then the engine would roar into life, shooting a huge flame out the rear."

He told of the awful volume of noise outside but then, once in the air, hearing only the sound of the rushing wind "just as in a glider." The most impressive feature was, of course, its high speed, up to 600 miles an hour.

"Were you ever attacked while you were making those training flights?" Cran wanted to know if Hans had ever gone against a P-51.

"No. We were far up on the coast, and how well I recall those low-altitude flights over the long, sandy beaches that stretched for miles along Amrum Island. If I had been attacked by Thunderbolt or Mustang or a Spit," Hans said, "I knew that I could escape with only a slight angle of climb. With their maximum rate of only 450 miles an hour the propeller-driven plane would be quickly left behind.

"Our orders were to attack only from a superior position over enemy fighters, then to pull up after our pass. How we regretted in those days having no time to test the advantages of the He-162 over the conventional fighters while in combat." Hans really didn't seem regretful right now, however.

Records show that all of the He-162 "People's Fighters" would end up being distributed to England, Russia, the United States, and France for testing purposes. The twin-jet Me-262, however, was used against the bombers in 1945. As we talked about it over fifty years afterward, we could laugh together picturing the B-17 navigator telling his debriefing officer, "A German fighter tore through our formation so fast it was just a streak. But how the hell it did it with its propeller gone and the engine on fire, I just don't know!"

It was claimed that the lieutenant was told he had better stop and chat with either the chaplain or a psychologist before his next mission.

50

The Stalag in the Forest

By the time we had dragged ourselves into the wooded area that someone with a sense of humor had named "Stalag Land Seventeen C," discipline had almost disappeared. Combine partners and scattered groupings were working together for mutual support and survival.

The guards appeared to be in bad shape, too. They had marched the whole distance under full pack, with little more to eat than we had, and now were ordered to begin patrolling the perimeters. Most were middle-aged or older men, and we heard that three had died during the march. At first they were shocked to see the Americans begin to strip limbs and bark in what had been a carefully managed and protected state forest. But after continuous exposure to the elements it wasn't long before they, too, were ready to use any of the resources at hand.

It was raining as I urged my group to pass beyond the early arrivals who were choking the access area, and it was raining as we claimed a spot for our campsite. Neil and I had each been Boy Scouts, and we helped the others gather pine branches and build lean-tos. No let-up in the rain was to be expected, and we added more bark to the shelters and huddled inside to share body heat and try to dry out. During the night there were some who crept among the shelters "borrowing" bark from other lean-tos, causing plenty of cursing and threats. Some didn't want to feel their way in the dark out to the slit trench, so did their toilet business right in the midst of the living area, with more cursing and threats.

Many fires had been kindled, and smoke hung in the forest like a cloud, adding to all the other the discomforts. Chris, our barracks chief, made his way around among his groups to see how we were making out, assigning men as water bearers or to help dig more latrine trenches. Incredible as it seemed, Chris said that there might be some Red Cross parcels distributed the next day.

French parcels did indeed arrive and were quickly "divvied up" while the Germans came through with some barley and potatoes.

Later, when that food had disappeared, some of the men decided to cross the guards' lines and forage for more in the surrounding area. They were well aware of the hazards of wandering around where German troops were holding out and where American troops might be advancing any moment. We were reminded that taking food needed for survival was one thing, but looting of any valuables and rape were criminal activities, war or no war.

It was several days before we heard that contact had been made with the U.S. forces that had crossed the river and were entering Braunau. Late in the afternoon a jeep came up into the camp. It had an American flag flying from a front corner, and a captain was in the right seat in full battle gear. It stopped and was quickly surrounded. When the captain stood up he looked ten feet tall. We froze into silence as he stepped out onto the hood of the jeep.

"You men are no longer prisoners of war. As of this moment you are again American soldiers on active duty!" he shouted.

Someone said later that he read the Articles of War, but if he did then few heard them. What followed can only be described as pandemonium, with cheering, screaming, back pounding, and hat throwing. There were those who just stood and grinned while others sat down on the ground and cried. What I did I cannot remember, but probably it was all those things.

After officially accepting surrender of the remaining Germans, our liberator captain drove away down the road. As the guards came filing in from their stations, they were relieved of their weapons and gear and told about their new status as prisoners of war. A few Americans, who had long memories of hardships they had suffered from certain guards, wanted to take revenge. Perhaps some did, but there were no casualties that I heard about. Our leaders took control and offered the Germans protection until they could be more formally taken care of by the American forces. I had no thoughts whatsoever of revenge on anyone. It still amazed me that all of us were still alive.

A small group of men was giving one of the German guards a hard time. When one of our guys broke it up he used some words that have stayed in my memory all these years.

"C'mon, turn him loose," he said. "You're gettin' out of the war alive if you take it easy for just a little longer. But afterward you're going to have to live with yourself for a long, long time. So why take home any extra baggage like this on your conscience?"

We were awake most of the night talking; then in the morning the sun came out. It was a whole new day, in every sense of the word.

Neil and I hadn't wanted to get too far away from the action up until now, afraid something might screw up our liberation. So far it had only been represented by one American officer and the dismissal of our guards. Now the need for some nourishment made us decide we had to do a little foraging. With two other volunteers we started out.

With Assistant Group Leader Baize and two other men I headed toward the east, mostly because few others seemed to be going that way. After walking a bit, we turned south toward Altheim. Along this road there were refugees pulling and pushing carts, wheelbarrows, wagons, and even bicycles loaded with belongings. Fear and uncertainty could be read in every face as they headed away from one enemy and toward another they hoped might not mistreat them.

We could tell that some of the men had recently been soldiers. They had thrown down their rifles, helmets, gas masks, belts, and even hand grenades beside the road and swapped uniform jackets for odd-looking shirts and coats. Some recognized us as American soldiers and averted their eyes as we walked past. Generally, with our GI overcoats and stocking caps we were able to mingle with the walkers without much notice.

We picked up rifles and a few "potato mashers" from beside the road and headed across a field toward a group of isolated farm buildings, uncertain what sort of greeting we might get.

The buildings made an open-ended square with the center area containing nothing but a pile of manure and what from a distance we thought was a flagpole. As we got closer, however it became clear it was an 88mm cannon mounted on a set of wheels.

There was a white sheet hanging out an upstairs window, and this encouraged us to move closer. As we circled to approach the open end of the yard, I could see uniformed figures moving around there and called a halt. None of us had any desire to do the infantry's work at this stage of the war, in spite of all the weapons we were carrying. They were mostly for moral support.

As we cautiously began to move away one man came running out toward us waving a stick with a white flag tied to it and shouting, "Kamerad!"

I hadn't heard that word since I had used it myself a year earlier in the field at Bubach. Suspecting a trick, we spread out and motioned for him to stop. After a few shouts and arm signals back and forth it became clear that there were some other men inside the building. He was asking us to "mitkommen" and accept their surrender.

That idea was immediately vetoed. "Nicht mitkommen!"

In our fractured German we told him to go back and tell his comrades they were welcome to come out into the field to meet us, without weapons and with hands "like this," over their heads.

He ran back. In a few minutes out marched about twenty men, all in field green uniforms. Helmets and weapons were gone, but some still wore their heavy equipment belts and carried field packs or even suitcases. There were no officers of any rank with them as far as I could tell, and they all looked either very young or very old. At a safe distance I called, "Halten, bitte," and we slowly circled them and looked them over.

With no idea what they might be carrying we told them to drop their packs, belts, and any other military gear onto the ground. Then with our "Kriegie Deutsch" language and waving arm signals we started them marching out toward the road. "Say this," Neil emphasized to the German soldiers, "and repeat it when the American soldiers approach you. 'OK, GIs, we have surrendered to the Air Corps! We are prisoners.'"

When they had gone we sneaked carefully into the farmyard, half-expecting shots from some who had decided not to surrender. That big gun in the yard troubled me because I knew our fighter planes were scouting the region looking for targets. This one might look good to a pilot who didn't want to carry home a full load of ammo in his wings. It was very quiet as we poked through the buildings.

When we stepped into the kitchen there at a table sat an elderly man and woman and a very young girl. They sat and stared at us with wide eyes and blank expressions, and I got no response to my questions: "Wo is Brot [where is bread]?" and, "Essen, essen, haben Sie Kartoffel, Ei? [Eat, eat, do you have any potatoes, eggs?]" The others added words for sausage and milk. Not even a head shake was offered, just their stares. Finally the old lady motioned with her arm and said, "Rausgehen. Rausgehen!," which sounded very much like commands we had often heard. "Get out!" she was telling us.

While I stayed and kept an eye on the family, the other three hunted around the house for anything at all to eat. I had brought in one of the beat-up suitcases dropped by the soldiers outside and opened it on the kitchen table to go through it. There were only a few bundles of letters, some wool socks, and some toilet articles. In the bottom were some loose Luftpost stamps and pfennig coins, which I dropped into my pockets along with the socks.

Even today I feel a twinge of guilt from going through some-one else's personal things and "looting" his valuable socks. The reality was, of course, that none of those men would be allowed to keep anything other than what they might have in their pockets when they were picked up, assuming that they didn't get killed during the process.

Neil yelled that they had found a couple of number-ten cans of meat and I shouted back, "Let's take it and get the hell out of here!" The three people sitting and staring at me, plus that big gun in the yard, were making me very nervous.

Someone opened a cabinet drawer and began to pull out items of silverware. "Put 'em back," I said, "but try and find a can opener or a cleaver or something." Those cans of pork had to be opened.

As we filed out the door each of us said, "Danke schön," to the three at the table. The old man gave a little smile and nodded his head, so I added, "Auf Wiedersehen."

Heading cross-country back toward our stalag in the forest,

we stopped at the edge of a field and cut open the large cans. They were imprinted with the complex word "Schweine-schmalz," which seemed easy to interpret. There had to be ham or pork inside. But as we dug into the white, fatty substance we found only a few brown shreds of meat. It was surely not pork but almost pure lard.

Nevertheless, we dug in with our fingers, each swallowing at least half a cup. The flavor was excellent and it slid down with no difficulty at all. After a rest, we abandoned our guns and hand grenades and found our way back through the woods by following the smoke and the noise. We had plenty of *Schmalz* to share with the others, who had managed to forage a bunch of turnips and a loaf of black bread. Lubricated with our lard, these familiar foods barely required any chewing. They slid right down.

It took about fifteen minutes for my stomach to rebel, and it quickly became as empty as before the meal. The others had the same experience. It was an hour before we were able to nibble on bread and turnip again, this time without the lubricating grease.

For the next two days we were firsthand observers of what happens in a battle zone when a war grinds to a stop. Jeeps, tanks, trucks, and infantrymen rushed around as though each had a specific objective in mind, while fighter planes roared overhead.

Hundreds of German soldier-prisoners and others who wanted to become prisoners hiked toward the bridge crossing the Inn River into Germany. Now and then came the sound of rifle or cannon shots, gradually becoming more distant and eventually fading away. There was little resistance to be overcome in the Braunau area. The town where Adolf Hitler was born would just as soon forget about that glory, for now.

We watched as columns of disarmed soldiers marched by. Showing his usual ear-to-ear grin, Neil remembered what he had been told often when he was first made a POW and decided it was his turn to say it. "For you *der Krieg ist* over! Nicht?"

Some C-47 Gooney Birds were coming to get us, but we had to get to a nearby Luftwaffe fighter strip to meet them.

"Trucks will be along," it was announced, "to take you to some temporary quarters in a factory just down the road. Those who want to can go ahead and start walking."

My eagerness to get on a plane had me up and walking right away. Every step I took was now clearly a step nearer home.

The factory was an aluminum foundry and appeared to have just been shut down in midshift. Machines, tools, and equipment were intact. We were given the run of the place, and my group set up housekeeping between two huge smelting machines where it was warm. We opened a case of army "10-in-1" rations, supposedly enough to make one good meal for ten men. We began on a number ten can of peaches and worked our way through biscuits and beef later.

Clothing that I was able to rinse dried quickly spread out on the warm machine tops. A collision between two fork-lift trucks resulted in a broken leg for one POW and the order to cease and desist from operating any factory equipment.

The next day as we arrived at the Luftwaffe field I could see the remains of fighter planes scattered along the edges of the landing strip. The shortage of both fuel and pilots had kept them on the ground, where some were destroyed by P-38 strafing and others by the German mechanics, frustrated that they were unable to get them into the air to fight.

While waiting my turn to board a C-47 I wandered through one of the barracks. It was cluttered with clothing, tools, books, and equipment left by Luftwaffe cadets and staff. A few items of uniform clothing were still hanging neatly against the wall, and a couple of bunks appeared to have been recently slept in. Some of the American troops had passed through seeking weapons or souvenirs, and I watched one GI looking for Nazi insignia, caps, or belt buckles, ripping some off jackets and blouses.

Walking past groups of prisoners who had just surrendered, I was impressed with how healthy and young they appeared. Most seemed to be as scared as we had been in our first hours as prisoners of war. One American GI ordered a German soldier to take off his belt so he could have it for a souvenir, leaving the soldier with no way to hold up his pants. A few of us moved in to help the new POW and made the souvenir hunter give back the belt. I had a good feeling as he put it back on and gave a little nod of "thanks" in our direction.

In a few hours the airplanes began to appear, and the cheer that went up could probably be heard in Vienna. We filed aboard

277

the C-47, and I sat on the floor with many others who were able to squeeze in. We began to roll as soon as the door was closed and were headed for what was left of Le Havre, France.

Once airborne, I stood and squeezed up to a window. I wanted to see what the giant battlefield below looked like. A few villages appeared to have been untouched, but most seemed to be devastated. Only cellar holes and chimneys remained in some, and in others sections of walls with empty window holes stared up at us. The whole population seemed to be out on the highways. Those roads not crowded with tanks, military trucks, and troops were jammed with "DPs," or displaced persons, and refugees. The Third Reich had moved millions of people away from their homelands, leaving huge numbers scattered all over Europe. Each seemed to be trying to get back to where he belonged, whether or not his village or family might even exist anymore.

Alongside many of the roadways were burned-out or wrecked trucks, tanks, cars, and wagons. It was apparent that the Allies had totally destroyed the transportation system. All along the corridor of our trip to Le Havre I saw this devastation and the crawling columns of humanity.

Moving into our "tent city," we became fully aware that we were again part of the U.S. Army. The giant bureaucracy had us in its control. It was a great feeling of security, but with it came the endless lines, formations, distributions, special notices, and orders all at the same time. There was hardly time anymore for rumors. We were overwhelmed with facts.

But some things remained familiar. We were being "cared for" by German soldiers. They were now POWs, however, and had no guns.

Ed Kolber, the wounded Toonerville Trolley engineer who had evacuated Luft Four in Pomerania and hiked for many miles, tells how he got reunited with American forces:

A German officer drove up in an Olympia automobile to surrender to the British soldiers. One of them told me to take the German's car, fuel it up at the nearby field supply, and head for the nearest American-held airfield. He had to say, of course, "You can't miss it,

Yank. The road's well marked, easy to follow, and you'll only have to motor for a few hours."

Arriving at Hildesheim, I joined with some other ex-POWs and got a plane ride to one of the RAMP camps at Le Havre. After the delousing and new clothing issue, I tried to regain the eating habit and after a while was put on the merchant ship *Marine Robin* to head for New York.

Released prisoners were officially known as Recovered Allied Military Personnel, or "RAMPS," in army shorthand. A printed brochure was passed out, welcoming us back into the ranks and explaining what would now happen.

Many ex-flyer RAMPS had enjoyed being picked up in Eighth Air Force B-17s or C-47 "Gooney Birds" for their trip to the Reims area. There they were shuttled into huge "tent cities," each named after a popular cigarette brand. Ours was Lucky Strike. Many thousands of men were being freed daily as the Allied forces swept through Germany, and the plans for identifying, evacuating, receiving, feeding, and housing them must have been almost as huge as the Normandy invasion plans.

After food, for me the top priorities were delousing and reclothing. The unavoidable red tape we encountered was at times frustrating but easily understandable.

German POWs did much of the work at the RAMPS camps, not unhappily, since they were not only out of the war now but were getting fed and housed along with us. One of the greatest pleasures I enjoyed was sleeping in a good old comfortable army folding cot, which had not only a mattress pad but also clean sheets, blankets, and a pillow. Never had these things we take for granted when we got to bed each night seemed so much a luxury.

One surprise procedure was that of payroll. Each man was given a small amount of the back pay he had coming. It was in French francs and amounted to about fifty dollars. Since there were few ways to spend money in the ruins of the towns nearby, most of it seemed to be used for gambling.

RAMPS were put aboard ships at Le Havre, where they began the voyage home, eating several times a day and slowly regaining lost weight and health. Even hearing the song "Sentimental Journey" played over the sound system all day long couldn't prepare them for the grand sight of the Statue of Liberty standing in New York harbor and the cheering throngs who awaited them on the piers.

51

The Missing Chapter

(Author's note: Those of us who evacuated Stalag Seventeen B knew little about what happened after we had gone, leaving a few hundred behind who were unable to march. At a reunion, long after the war, Kurt told the whole story. Taken from a transcription of his talk, the following is a summary.)

On April 7, 1945, when I was ordered to prepare the Americans to be evacuated from Stalag Seventeen B on the next day, I met with my leaders and senior medical officer Fred Beaumont to see how this might be done without causing insufferable hardships.

It was determined that we would place those who were clearly unable to march into two buildings, currently used as the infirmary area in the main camp. Those wounded in combat with debilitating injuries, some with limbs amputated, the blind, and many just too ill from malnutrition, dysentery dehydration, or other diseases would be held there with someone to look after them.

After deliberation with the doctors, it was decided that I would stay behind to provide whatever assistance I could for those unfortunate ones. The decision was made easier by the fact that I still had problems with wounds in my right leg, also that I was most familiar with the camp and any German authorities who would stay behind.

We believed that the Red Army would soon be approaching. The rumble of artillery could be heard in the east, and we knew that we soon would be overrun. Some of the groups of men who were preparing to march out thought that perhaps by a little foot-dragging and other delaying tactics they might accelerate the Germans' departure, but it didn't work. They weren't swayed by the attempts, and with shouting, prodding, and some use of

281

boots and gun butts they were able to push the last of the 4,250 men able to walk out through the main gate by late in the afternoon.

The commandant had told me there would be no kitchen facilities left behind. We brought some Red Cross parcels into our two barracks, Thirteen and Fourteen, for storage and security. They were to be our "kitchen" until liberation.

Left behind with my group of under a hundred Americans were about five hundred in the French and Serbian compounds. The scattering of Russians who remained were near death from disease and malnutrition.

A small contingent of German officers and soldiers was left to control the remaining prisoners. They put a single strand of wire around our two-barracks area, and one guard was stationed at the gate. At first we weren't permitted into the west compounds, where other nationalities had existed, but we were free to wander about the American compounds. No nighttime movements were permitted, and I was warned that this would be strictly enforced.

Right after the main body of American prisoners had gone I felt an extreme sense of loneliness and emptiness. This was the first time in two and a half years that I had not been surrounded by thousands of others, with all of the attendant sounds and activities. It was peaceful but unnerving to endure the silence and comparative loneliness in these hostile surroundings now so full of the unknown.

We spoke softly when we spoke at all. We went quietly about the chores of surviving and caring for those who were unable to help themselves. Realizing how fragile our existence had become, we no longer felt the comparative "safety of numbers" we had before.

We tried to get some sleep, fully aware of the growing intensity of the battles to the east. Active warfare was drawing ever closer to us.

The Red Army was now in the suburbs of Vienna, and the Austrians were insisting it be treated as an "open city." But General Sepp Dietrich [who had visited with Kurt only three months earlier] insisted on holding every inch of ground until blasted from it. According to our clandestine radio, the Austrian troops had begun to revolt against their German comrades, and their general had been shot in the back by his own troops. The revolt allowed negotiations to proceed between the Wehrmacht and the Red Army. Thus the beautiful city of Vienna was taken with very little destruction and loss of life.

The pathway was opened to the Danube River, deeper into Austria, and toward the city of Krems, which lay just down the hill from Stalag Seventeen B. We had all experienced air warfare and were about to get involved in ground warfare.

There were plenty of slit trenches available to us, but not without some difficulties in getting the sick and injured men out of and into them. As the artillery shells exploded closer each day, accompanied by illuminating star shells at night, we used the trenches.

Attacks by Sturmovik dive bombers began against Krems and its railroad facilities below us. We would see the Russian planes flash by, flip over, and dive toward their targets. There were sporadic bombing attacks by larger aircraft during the night, seeking out targets along the Danube.

Barracks Thirteen was hit by what appeared to be a 100-pound antipersonnel bomb, but we were spared many deaths and injuries when it did not explode. It remained imbedded in the building.

A week after the American POWs had left there began to appear among us many DPs. They were Czechs, Poles, and Hungarians, and they moved themselves into some of the barracks we had deserted, numbers Thirty-six, Thirty-seven, and Thirty-eight. At first only a trickle, then in larger groups they came. I didn't know whether they were simply overwhelming the German garrison left to guard us or if they were given permission to come on in.

It would have been difficult for the meager group of guards to stop these starving and desperate people. The Germans helped us to bar them from our small compound. Had they learned that we had a store of food they could easily have overcome us and taken it all.

A few of our walking wounded went over to visit with the refugees, and some watched a Polish woman give birth to a child in Barracks Thirty-seven A. They came back commenting that if that was how it happened then they would never marry and become fathers.

By April 15 the Red Army was only a few miles to our east. The Germans began moving some of their big guns in, setting them up for action. Four were placed under the trees to our south, along the roadway into the *Vorlager*. Several others were placed just outside the fence on the northern, lower side of the camp.

On both sides of the entrance road were placed several small detachments of Wehrmacht infantrymen. They appeared to be remnants of front-line troops, and I was told by the guards that they had been fighting a rearguard action the whole 1,500 kilometers of German retreat from Russia.

"Do not engage them in conversation," I was warned. "They are very dangerous." Their uniforms were ragged, their faces haggard and drawn, and their exhaustion was evident. Considering what they had gone through and what obviously lay ahead of them, they had good reason to be depressed and "dangerous."

I decided it was about time I had a talk with whoever was left behind as the top-ranking German officer. With permission and escorted by one of the older *Unteroffiziers* I passed through the gate, headed for the *Vorlager*. As we went along the road past some of the rear-guard soldiers, one called out to the guard asking who and what the man he was escorting was.

The guard's unthinking answer was that it was an American flyer who had been shot down and captured. The soldier quickly drew a pistol and cocked it. When he realized it was empty, he turned to the others and asked for bullets or another gun. Luckily, they had no interest in helping him. He shouted and raved that he was going to kill me.

"Keep moving, Kurt," said my guard with white face and clenched jaw. "Don't run, but just move along rapidly."

After we were out of sight he explained that probably the man's family had been killed by bombing and he wanted revenge. We took a different route on our return from the *Vorlager*.

The trip had been a waste of time. The German officer in charge was not about to quote the Geneva Convention and protest the bringing of artillery and fighting troops into a prisoner-of-war camp. It was not the time for casual discussion and a report to the Swiss embassy.

When I suggested that they were only inviting the Russians to attack the camp, they countersuggested that perhaps they were protecting us from the approaching Russians, whose treatment of us would be far worse than what we had been receiving from the kindly Germans.

For a time following the mass evacuation, some of our American POWs came filtering back into the camp. They would come in twos and threes, usually at night, and we made them welcome. They felt there was little hope of their surviving long enough to reach the Americans approaching from the west.

Our comrades had escaped from the march by faking an emergency toilet dash or by hiding out while stopped for the night, then not rejoining the column in the morning. They knew how to get to Stalag Seventeen B and knew there would be more compassion and security there than in the Austrian woodlands. It was cold and wet, and there were armed soldiers, DPs, and civilians wandering about ready to kill for something to eat or a warm article of clothing.

We could provide some food for them, although water was a growing problem. Our ranks had now swollen to nearly double the initial number.

The war was surrounding us. Each night the gunfire was louder and the noise and smoke from the return fire by the Germans was almost continuous. At night and sometimes in the day we helped our men get into the slit trenches where they might stay for many hours until the action subsided.

Russian soldiers approached from the river valley, attacking with rifles and machine guns wherever they found German resistance. Fire fights were going on right up to within a few thousand yards of us. It became very intense and very hard on our nerves.

During this period (on April 13) I learned on a radio broadcast that President Roosevelt had died. It was a traumatic time.

Other news seemed to indicate that the war was close to being over; however, it was not that way within our little neighborhood. Even as we heard a BBC news item stating that May 8 had been agreed upon as the surrender date, the local fighting continued. Many Germans continued to fight to avoid surrendering to the Russians, hoping against hope that somehow the Americans might get to them first.

On the morning of what was to become known as "VE Day," May 8, outgoing cannon fire from the camp was answered by incoming from down by the Danube. It continued until just before noon and then stopped.

All was silent with a single exception. At about 3:00 P.M. a German eighty-eight-millimeter shell was fired from the south edge of Stalag Seventeen B. It was the last shot of the war we heard.

As we emerged from the slit trenches there were no German soldiers to be seen. No one was near their artillery pieces, and there was no guard at our gate. We Americans, and the others who had survived at the camp, simply stood about or wandered around looking to find some clue as to the meaning of the sudden and complete silence.

There were no shouts of joy or even any conversation. The trancelike feelings persisted well into the evening, and there was little sleep that night.

The next morning a few of us ventured outside the camp area and found it quiet and peaceful. We bartered eggs from some elderly farmers who were pleasant and cooperative, even friendly. There were a few younger ones who did not seem so friendly and would not approach us. We didn't go down into Krems but stayed above the town in the hills.

Late that night a column of Russian soldiers entered Stalag Seventeen. They were Slavic soldiers and Uzbek cavalry, and they seemed quiet and well mannered. Their leader, an elderly general, took up his residence in Thirty-eight A, one of our old barracks.

After a discreet wait, I approached a soldier and asked for an audience with the Russian general. It was immediately granted.

He was seated on one of our wooden bunks with a blanket wrapped around his shoulders. As I stepped up to him, he returned my salute. He used an interpreter to ask what we were doing here and how many there were of us.

When I explained, the general told me that we were safe from harm from his men, that he had other problems, just as we had ours. He said that there was very little he could do and ordered us to stay in our two barracks buildings at night. During the day we would be free to wander where we pleased, but at night his men were ordered to shoot anyone moving around who was not a Russian soldier.

He was neither friendly nor unfriendly but mirrored total exhaustion. I went back and instructed my men about limiting their movements. No Russian soldier entered our compound or spoke with us of us during their occupation.

52

One Escapee Who Got Back In

When freedom became too dangerous to his health and welfare, Sgt. Gene Sebeck decided to "unescape" back into Stalag Seventeen. He had left in the evacuation of April 8, but then Gene and his combine partner chose to sneak away from the marching column after the first day on the road.

Fifty years later I wrote to Gene at his home in Vanderbilt, Pennsylvania, asking him to tell what happened after the two of them broke away from their German guards and were free at last.

"We took off during the night after the day's march," he said, "heading north toward Czechoslovakia. However, my escape-mate got sick and was having difficulties. We decided it best to head back to the camp and try to get inside, to join those who stayed behind with Kurt Kurtenbach. Approaching the stalag we were unsure about just how we could do this safely, and we spent the night in the 'cemetery woods' outside the fence. We had never imagined we would one day be figuring out a way to get inside those high fences.

"Next morning we decided to approach the main gate and, to our surprise, with no trouble at all were allowed to pass through."

Gene also told of his recollection about how the war ended there in the Krems area.

"On May 8th, the day it was officially over, several of us ex-POWs went down into Krems and stood on the Wilhelmstrasse watching the Russians move in to occupy the city."

He remembered it was a week later when the American column of trucks and ambulances arrived. He heard that Father Kane and Major Beaumont had somehow got to Linz to tell the Americans about the plight of the sick and wounded in the Russian-occupied area.

In 1987, after he had returned from a visit to Krems, I asked Gene about the airport runway there, supposedly built right on the site of our camp. When I visited a year later the vineyards seemed to cover the whole camp area, but others had told me about seeing the landing strip on the very site of Stalag Seventeen.

"Yes," he said, "there is a single runway on the site that would have been the area dividing our barracks, and it is used for small planes and gliders. The Luftwaffe airfield, you'll remember, was a couple of kilometers farther east. The British bombed it one night in 1944."

My hotel, on the postwar visit to Krems, was the ancient Weiss Rose hotel, on Wilhelmstrasse in the downtown area. Gene with his son and grandson stayed at the Gasthof Zum Goldenen Kreuz at the bottom of the hill on which our camp was located.

"Together we walked through the woods where our graveyard had been, but saw only empty trenches there now," he said. "I showed my son and my grandson where I had spent that night, wondering how I could get back inside of Stalag Seventeen, behind the barbed wire."

It appeared to have been General Patton's decision to get the Americans left at Stalag Seventeen back into American hands as quickly as possible, once he learned about their situation.

Leader Kurtenbach describes what happened:

"They came driving right in through the fences one morning, a convoy of ambulances and trucks. An army captain stepped out of the lead vehicle, introduced himself, and said, 'Sergeant, can you and your men get your things together and be ready to leave in one hour?'

"'Whatever things a prisoner of war might accumulate,' I assured him, 'could easily be put together in much less than an hour.' Within thirty minutes we loaded up and were on our way toward the American lines. Some French workers wanted to know if they might come along, too. They were told that any who could find space either in or on a vehicle were more than welcome to join us."

Kurt concludes, "It was a hazardous trip. The thousands of

DPs and refugees who crowded the roadways had to be convinced that they ought to make way for us, so we could move along toward Linz."

The American forces also had serious concern about reactions of the Russian soldiers who might want to block their way, but all made it safely. As they crossed into the American-held area, many of the men for the first time in over two years saw the stars and stripes of the U.S. flag flying over their heads.

"What a glorious sight that was!" remembers Kurt.

53

Hans Berger's Turn to Be a POW

During the fifty-second anniversary observances of the meeting in the skies over Germany, the Zimmer family invited us to their home for a little luncheon. It was a fine opportunity for the three flyers, who were emotionally involved, to have one more chat together. I queried the ex–fighter pilot about the "final days."

Long after his victory over the *Toonerville Trolley* near Bubach and near the end of the war, Hans Berger became captain of the Third Squadron, Jagdgeschwader One (3/JG 1). The group had been stationed at Greifswald for the "Defense of Berlin" campaign before being moved into eastern Prussia. Here is how he describes the end, for him and our mutual friend in Florida, Karl Demuth:

> During the final weeks we moved to Leck, near Husum. It was here that I was to learn to fly the Heinkel "Volksjager" (People's Hunter) designated the He-162. It was one of the very first jet aircraft ever to go into production. My Group Commander was Karl Demuth, the man with whom you spoke before embarking on your return to Germany.
>
> We were there at Leck when the British troops over-ran the area just before the war ended on May 8, 1945, and it was there we were made prisoners of war. Fifty of the new He-162s were lined up on the airfield when it was taken, never having been flown in combat.
>
> I was held as a POW for a relatively brief period, receiving fair treatment, then about three months later I was released and discharged.

The Luftwaffe of the Third Reich had ceased to exist.

Karl Emil Demuth was Hans Berger's *Staffel Kapitan*, and he, too, flew the Heinkel 162 model A-2. In one of the photos received from Hans Karl stands by the tail of his airplane. I wondered about the many "kills" scored on the tail assembly of the jet.

"There were sixteen," he explained. "However, they were transferred from the tail of the Focke Wulf 190 fighter in which I earned them." Karl had been seriously wounded just a few weeks before Hans had shot down our B-17. When Karl's plane was hit it burst into flames, and he suffered third-degree burns all over his face and on his hands and arms. It seemed miraculous that he was not badly disfigured.

As the battle lines approached, near the end of the war, Karl described some of the difficulties that he, Hans Berger, and other comrades had in getting into position where they could surrender without being killed. It was not an easy thing to do in the confusion of advancing and retreating armies.

It was the British who made them prisoners. Their prison camp was a soccer field in the Schleswig Holstein district, and their quarters for the duration was a four-man tent.

"The British allowed us to keep all of our clothing and personal gear, even including the pistol," he said, "and after a few weeks we were released." Another photo from his mementos shows him seated in front of the tent with Hans and two others, playing cards to while away the time.

Although Hans described it without passion, it must have been very difficult, after the Luftwaffe was in effect "disbanded," to go out into a world that had been so devastated and disrupted.

"I studied English," he said, "and did various work, including some time spent with the German Youth Activities (GYA) of the U.S. Army in the Heidelberg and Mannheim area. It was here I became manager of two youth centers which had been erected with American aid. In 1951, while you were involved with your P-47s in the Korean conflict, I was in the U.S. taking part in an exchange program. Over a six-month period I served in New Jersey, Illinois, Montana, and California."

When the German Youth Activities program ended Hans moved to Munich to attend school, and after graduating he became an interpreter and translator. Since 1953 he has been a lecturer for technical English at the Munich Institute for Languages and Interpreting, a Bavarian technical college.

Hans said that he continues to enjoy that work, practicing

some sports to keep fit and, with his wife, taking vacations at a cottage they own on the island of Corsica.

The "Return to Bubach" formally concluded with a farewell dinner party in a fine restaurant with about twenty people who had been our hosts or who were involved in all the complex arrangements for the visit. The group was increased by eight when the American airmen group from Ramstein Air Base who had provided the musical part of our special services at the old Niederkirchen church were invited to come along, with two wives and one little baby.

It was a time for more speeches, and when I deferred to Cran Blaylock he surprised us all by offering a toast, speaking for all of the *Toonerville Trolley* crew, present or absent, living or dead.

Klaus Zimmer could not be enticed to speak. However, Pres. Hans Kirsch was eloquent in conveying the great satisfaction enjoyed by his historic and cultural group and the historians who went to great lengths to bring about this unique gathering.

Prof. Egon Keller sat with the choral group, and while they were eating he brought them up-to-date on what the whole week had been about. They registered disbelief.

"Could it be true? Such an event that happened during the huge war fought thirty years before we were born?" they asked.

"And these three men fought each other in the skies right over where we are sitting? They survived all that and today have attended church together and are eating here with us together, tonight?"

More handshakes and autographs became necessary.

Egon interpreted both the Germans' and Americans' remarks, fascinated the choristers with his historic descriptions during the meal, and still reserved enough energy to josh me about eating Dan's meal, finally providing a fine "wrap-up" speech, appropriate to the occasion. A most amazing man.

54

"Sentimental Journey" One More Time

As we approached the airport at Frankfurt, at a convenient road-side rest area there was a huge map of the terminal and its approaches. What a great idea! Dan and I planned to suggest it to some airport authorities in the United States. Parking, however, is no more convenient here than at any other airport, in Europe or America, so we urged Klaus to drop us off at the curb in the underground area convenient to our boarding area.

A quick unloading, a heart-felt, "Auf Wiedersehen," and Klaus was on his way back to Hassel. We had enjoyed nearly two hours of conversation during the drive, reviewing all the activities he and the historical-cultural group had planned and executed for us. We graded all but the weather with very high marks. One outstanding exception was the warm and sunny day of the Rhine River tour.

Klaus Zimmer is a devoted and intense historian, and there is the characteristic of "indefatigability" that Hans Kirsch says he possesses. I had been aware that Klaus was sharing the emotions and the drama as we three World War II flyers were led through remembrances of long-ago events, events that happened before he was born. He was living every moment of them with us.

And I share with him the enthusiasm for history. Researching and writing is a wonderful avocation. To relive historic events with some who had participated in them can be tremendously rewarding.

Later, as brother Dan and I winged our way westward over the Atlantic, we could forget about jet lag and just relax. The song "Sentimental Journey," played over and over on the Liberty ship that brought me home in 1945, was not heard this time, and there would be no crowds, only U.S. Customs agents, to greet us at the terminal.

Flying down across Newfoundland seemed like a strange

sky route to Florida, and when the screen told us we were passing Portland, Maine, I seriously considered bailing out, to save
the flight northward again next week. In compact New England,
the seaport of Portland, Maine, is only an hour away from my
home in the White Mountains of New Hampshire.

But Hans Berger's friend, ex–Luftwaffe pilot Karl Demuth,
is in Florida. I am eager to talk with him once more before writing "the end" to the episodes in which he and Hans Berger were
involved during the war. Who could have dreamed that half a
century later I would become friends with two of the Luftwaffe's
jet fighter pilots of World War II?

I am well aware that time is shrinking rapidly for commit-
ting memories to paper with accuracy. We have been helped by
the gift of the published history of Jagdgeschwader Number
One, in which Karl and Hans served, as well as the many photos
and other mementos that some of us had each tucked away for
all those years.

"Do you still plan to visit Hans Berger in Munich this year?"
I asked Karl.

"Yes," he said, adding a phrase in German that I noted to ask
Dan about later. It interpreted to this universal truth: "As our
numbers grow few, each old friendship becomes a treasure
beyond value."

A German television station covering our Bubach ceremonies provided a video copy, which I found could be converted
so to be played on American VCRs. I sent a copy to Karl later, so
he could see and hear his old squadronmate talking and shaking
hands with some American flyers at the exact spot where he had
shot them down, fifty-two years earlier.

We have a picture of Karl standing with his Heinkel jet and
another in which he is shown with Herman Goering receiving an
Iron Cross award for a victory over an American Flying Fortress.
The *Air Reichsmarschall* had been unkind to his Luftwaffe pilots
after one experience when the U.S. planes had got the better of
them, actually questioning their courage. Karl remembered this
event and spoke of the reaction of his squadronmates when
Goering later visited their aerodrome wearing heavy makeup
and a strangely decorated, brightly colored uniform. Although
incapable of showing any direct disrespect to their commander

and a top ace of World War I, they shuffled their feet and avoided eye contact as a subtle indication of their disapproval. "Of course, by this time many Germans were referring to him as 'Herr Meyer,'" said Karl, remembering the comment attributed to Hermann Goering that if Allied bombers were ever able to reach Berlin, then his name would be "Meyer."

55

The Rest of the Harry Vozic Story

(As Related by K. J. Kurtenbach)

After our release and arrival at Camp Lucky Strike in France, I was taken along with security chief Joe Dilard to a hotel on the Rue Lafayette, Paris. It was occupied by the Intelligence Corps, with a couple of generals, some colonels, and their support staffs in residence. On the next day I was told by a general that he had invited an old friend of mine for dinner that night. It was a Dr. Reuben Rabinovitch, and it was to surprise him.

I stared blankly, suggesting there must have been a mistake. I knew no one by that name. They smiled at me.

One asked, "Sergeant Kurtenbach, do you know Harry Vozic?"

Him I knew. So that was his real name and the reason for his note signed "Rube." He would be coming to dinner. He was one of General Eisenhower's close friends, and I knew him to be a madman, to boot.

Joe Dillard looked at me and shook his head. "You are one lucky so-and-so," he said. "I figured you were headed for a court martial on that one."

I had acted more or less on a hunch and had not been wrong. To say it was a relief is an understatement. I had carried the burden of knowing of Harry Vozic for a long time, and it had become a fire in my belly, especially never having been able to discuss it with anyone.

Shortly before dinnertime I stepped out onto the balcony that overlooked the Rue Lafayette. Presently I saw Harry coming. He was striding jauntily along with a cane in his hand, wearing a civilian suit and sporting a mustache that was trimmed. Hitler was dead! He passed right beneath me; then when he was only ten feet from the entrance to the hotel I shouted at him in German, calling him by name and telling him to stay right there because I wanted to talk to him.

Vozic never flinched, paused, or looked around. He took a few steps, then appeared to stumble as though on a shoelace. He bent down and pretended to retie the shoe while looking back under his shoulder to where I stood. He straightened slowly, turned around, and said, "Kurt, you do that again and I will kill you. Leap into my arms you [expletive]." He ran inside, we met on the stairway, and it was a good feeling I had at that moment.

After a wild dinner he informed the generals that he would be taking me away for a few days, and they agreed. I had only some old uniform clothing, but it seemed to make no difference. Wherever we went I was warmly accepted.

Dr. Rabinovitch took me to a hospital in which he performed cranial surgery, and he told me then that he was a neurosurgeon practicing in Paris after it was made an "open city." This country boy cannot recall everything that happened in the next few days, but included was a sumptuous dinner at the home of a wealthy industrialist, a Confirmation party for a little girl, a nightclub tour on which I learned that he was a "Knight of the Wine-tasters." He was a man of amazing talents and was very relaxed while reveling in the amazement that I exhibited. He had many, many friends in Paris.

After those few days with him I was returned to the hotel and I left almost immediately to go home and then to Washington, D.C.

I learned much later that while the repatriation ship *Gripsholm* was docked at Liverpool an American colonel came on board and commenced a grueling interrogation of Harry Vozic, going on for several hours. When it was ended the two walked off the ship and he was taken to meet with General Eisenhower.

"Ike" issued an order for Dr. Rabinovitch empowering him to use any forces of the Allies for whatever he might require. He used it to cross the Channel, go down the coast with the help of an armored column, and move into Bordeaux to recover his wife and his two eldest sons, Alexander and Steven. It was a many months later, after the war ended, when he met with me in Paris.

"His great courage and exemplary devotion to the Allied cause merit the highest praise and recognition of the United States," read the certificate with the U.S. Medal of Freedom awarded to Dr. Reuben Rabinovitch in October 1947.

Epilogue

Bubach before and during the War

An important part of World War II for members of the *Toonerville Trolley* bomber crew began in the village of Bubach. It was in the Bavarian district of Germany until occupation forces redrew the lines after the war. Then it became part of the Saarland district in Germany.

The district government for the villages was in the city of Kusel, where we were officially "arrested" by police. After the war this county seat was moved to Saint Wendel. The region is generally Protestant, and its parish church is in Niederkirchen, where the special service was held for us when we returned in 1996.

In my war journal I had called Bubach "a fairytale village" because it reminded me of an illustrated story that I had read as a child, "The Pied Piper of Hamelin." The red tile roofs, flowering window boxes, and clean cobblestone streets impressed me, in spite of the trauma experienced there. The name and location of the village remained unknown to us for over fifty years, until Klaus Zimmer's letter arrived in 1995 leading to our celebrated return for the public ceremonies and festival on the Buberg, where the *Toonerville Trolley* had met its end.

Bubach is an ancient farming village of about four hundred people located in the narrow valley of the Oster River. It was founded over twelve centuries ago, and it's written history dates back to the year 1412.

It lies about 130 kilometers southwest of Frankfurt, 100 kilometers west of Mannheim, and 70 kilometers east of the German border with Luxembourg and the old city of Trier.

Coal mining and steel manufacturing provided economic support for the not quite self-sufficient farmers.

The parish Protestant church in nearby Niederkirchen is very old. The organist who provided a historic tour of the edifice after our services there in 1996 told me that he went out to the hillside to see our airplane carried in his grandmother's arms.

How the War Came to Bubach

(Based on Information Provided by Walter Harth)

Just outside the village the German command set up an antiaircraft gun emplacement during the spring of 1938. This was not in anticipation of our air attacks but for the coming war with France. There were eleven military structures, three of them placed within the village. Ordnance supporting this battery of "flak" guns was stored at the Koenigreicher Hof, but it was used only during the invasion of France in 1939 and 1940.

In a regional history developed by Klaus Zimmer it is claimed that by 1943, after several years of war, propaganda of victories by German armies was no longer accepted. The precarious situation at the battle fronts could not be hidden. Increasing numbers of Allied aircraft were being seen overhead, and it was becoming obvious that Germany was in danger of losing air supremacy in its own skies. Soldiers who came home on leave confirmed stories of the worsening situation. Economic hardships increased and doubts arose as to whether there could ever be that "final victory" promised by the Fuhrer. This was the feeling that existed when the *Toonerville Trolley* bomber brought evidence of the war right into the village itself.

At the time of our crash-landing on the hill called the Buberg, the invasion by the Allied forces was a growing threat. The people of Bubach got their first look at enemy soldiers when the Americans were taken as prisoners.

By late 1944 the pressure of the Allied armies moving in from the western front forced the moving of the district road department from Saarbruecken into Bubach. Offices were set up in the dance hall from Gasthaus Lensch, where they would stay until the end of the war.

A few children from Oggersheim in the Pfalz had been sent

away to Saarbruecken for safety from the bombings. Then they were moved to Bubach when it was no longer safe in Saarbruecken.

By March 1945 the enemy lines were very close. Battle sounds could be heard, and some American artillery shells were landing outside Saint Wendel. German army soldiers passed through Bubach each day on foot or in vehicles, coming from Saal and going in the general direction of Krottelbach.

As the last of them left the area, they destroyed the munitions stored in the Sauboesch woods just above Bubach village, close to where the American bomber had crash-landed a year earlier.

On Palm Sunday, March 18, 1945, Vicar Fauss of Niederkirchen decided that he would add a special confirmation for the seven-town region. This was for the evacuee children in the age group whose turn it would be a year later. They were from a part of the destroyed city of Ludwigshafen called Oggersheim, and their future was quite uncertain. He recognized, too, that there was a broad feeling of impending disaster and that the church had a role to play in addressing that fear. The first service took place very early in the morning, in the same church where our 1996 service was held.

During the same afternoon a German soldier while traveling to Krottelbach in a horse-drawn covered wagon was shot by a strafing American fighter plane. He was buried in Bubach.

The last German soldiers to leave town on the next day barricaded the road leading toward Saal. When they had gone, August Lensch, who lived next to the barricade, mounted a white flag on top of it. Shortly before noon on Sunday, March 18, American tanks of the Tenth Armored Division arrived at the roadblock and burst through. The infantry GIs with them searched the houses and shelters throughout the village looking for German soldiers. When they found none, they ordered the Bubach people to clear away the remains of the road barricades.

One American tank was stationed at the center of the village exactly where the four Americans from the *Toonerville Trolley* had sat as prisoners eleven months before.

A few Bubach families were moved from their homes to provide shelter for the American soldiers, but it was only for one night.

One Bubach farmer, August Cullmann, found four German officers hiding in his barn. They asked him to give them civilian clothes, but he declined. They went away, leaving their weapons behind.

An old villager says, "The Americans caused us no trouble and did not take away any of the food which we had put aside. They asked for eggs and a chicken or goose to eat, however."

After the Americans had moved on to Krottelbach the district police department was taken over by the local communists. They declared an evening curfew but were unable to enforce it.

This temporary police force was disliked by the Bubach people, and they got no cooperation. It was claimed that these ersatz police were inclined to show favoritism, and they were said to have confiscated household items and private property. The few Nazi Party members still around were imprisoned for a while.

Soon the French forces came and took control of the occupation, raising their tricolor flag at the Niederkirchen railroad station each morning and insisting that all people honor it.

Erwin Karst, a locksmith's apprentice, once passed and did not take his hat off. A French sentinel dashed out and slapped Erwin's face so that his hat flew off and his tools were dropped.

Local farmers were required to provide chickens and eggs for the French commandant.

Slowly the people adjusted to the changes brought about by the change in their government. The town came through the war without damage. However, seventeen of its soldiers died and eleven remained missing in action. Two Bubach citizens died from bombing attacks while away in other cities.

The most outstanding event of the war for the village was the crash-landing on the Buberg of the American Flying Fortress, *Toonerville Trolley*, and the capture of four of its crew: Bill Hamilton, Ed Kolber, Cran Blaylock, and Ed McKenzie.

Return to the Stalag: Kurtenbach Remembers

On the fiftieth anniversary of the release of the Americans

from Stalag Seventeen B, former camp leader Kurtenbach was invited to address a group of ex-POWs making a special return to the site. He was unable to attend, but he sent along a message to the men who were there to dedicate a plaque identifying the old camp location.

I also was unable to attend but received a note from Kurt shortly after a large group had enjoyed their traumatic return:

Ed. This address was delivered when they placed the plaque at the site of our old Stalag, read by Jim Clark, from Missouri, one grand lad you should meet some day.... Kurt.

After greetings and opening remarks Kurt quoted Winston Churchill, who knew something of the POW experience, then went on:

Your young faces and eyes met every challenge, only changing when the guns barked and comrades lay dead or wounded, when the always inadequate water supply was cut off, when the daily bread was below starvation levels and when the harsh treatment seemed never to end. But always the young faces and eyes would brighten and the always present humor would assert itself and someone would shout: "Out the gate in '48!"

Not once did these young men falter or fail to assist one less fortunate than themselves or fail to attempt to cheer up one who was in distress. Always these young men lived with hope, not only within themselves but within their own barracks, within their own battalion and the whole stalag.

When the day ultimately arrived and they were to quit the Stalag, to march to a destination unknown with all the attendant trials such as lack of water, food and adequate shelter from the weather, they went as though it was another adventure, daring their captors to break their spirit, willing to face whatever confronted them.

No, I would not see old faces and tired eyes. I would see only young faces, forever young, and bright eyes always bright. Those are the faces and eyes I have seen for the last half-century of my life.

I know that each will pause as they paused back then, remembering their fallen comrades who were not allowed to continue on into the next adventure.

305

God bless you all and may your faces and eyes be always bright, as I will always remember each and every one of you. I shall always treasure your courage in my memory.

—Kenneth J. Kurtenbach
Former Camp Leader
Stalags Seven A and Seventeen B

Kenneth Kurtenbach, whom we all knew as "Kurt" or perhaps "Joe," has since the war kept in touch with many Stalag Seventeen men and has cooperated with many researchers, historians, and degree candidates, all of whom got answers to their questions. He has provided his "lads," as he called us, with both oral and written materials when asked.

The compiler of the chronicles we have used for reference was Luther Victory, of Baytown, Texas. He was one of the early leaders of the postwar organization of ex-POWs from Stalag Seventeen, and the historical record that he published is a valuable resource. A copy was recently provided by Kurt to the U.S. Air Force Academy Library at Colorado Springs, where Gen. Albert Clark has instituted POW reference material. Some of Luther's material for the chronicles was literally "dug up" at the old Stalag Seventeen site. A number of documents were buried far below the chimney base at one of the barracks and were retrieved after the war.

Two of the B-17 *Toonerville Trolley* crew, Bill Hamilton and Irving Blank, were among those who stayed behind, too sick to join in the evacuation on that April day in 1945. Before he left, Bill looted some material from the German files, including my POW identity picture. Years later he sent it to me. When I sent a note in return it came back: "Addressee Unknown." Only through historian Klaus Zimmer's research did I learn that Bill had died soon after the picture was sent.

The pilot of my original bomber crew went MIA on the Berlin mission of April 29, five days after my own MIA.

Radio operator Dick Harding, who had been on that fateful Oberpfaffenhofen mission in another B-17, later wrote to my father to ask if there was any news about my fate. Father had not yet learned that I was a POW.

Dick safely finished his missions and was sent to the Far

East, working a C-54 radio and something new called Loran, as they ferried materials over "the Hump" to China. After the war he made a career of the air force, but as a chaplain. He retired with the rank of Colonel.

Dick and I were good friends during training at Sioux City, Iowa, and with a few other boys still wet behind the ears we drank milk shakes instead of beer when we went into Denver on pass, considering it a fantastic evening if we danced with a girl, held her hand, or maybe even kissed her good night.

After retirement Dick became a United Methodist minister while I, having lost the benefit of his fine example, became a public utilities executive.

Regarding Special Treatment of Jewish-American POWs

Had our *Toonerville Trolley* waist gunner with the "H" on his dog tag been at special risk as an American Jew in a German POW camp?

The one person who could best answer it for the men of Stalag Seventeen would be Camp Leader Kurtenbach. Some time after the war he was asked by a researcher whether the Germans had made any efforts to identify and segregate the Jews. His answer to that question was that he knew of no such efforts.

Other questions and answers were:

Q. Do you know if the Germans ever compiled a list of the Jewish-American POWs confined there?
A. Aware of no such lists.
Q. Do you recall any rumors that German military authorities were going to transfer Jewish-American POWs to civilian jails?
A. Perhaps. But it was heard about all American "Luft-gangsters."
Q. Did you ever observe or hear of any incidents where the Germans mistreated, harassed or discriminated against Jewish-American POWs? Do you remember any incidents where a German guard or officer made an anti-Semitic statement to a Jewish-American POW?
A. No.

Q. Were any of the American POWs ever concerned that the Germans might mistreat, harass or discriminate against Jewish POWs?

A. Perhaps

As one of the over four thousand POWs in the camp, I was unaware of any mistreatment or threats of mistreatment or of any attempt to determine who were Jews and who were not. We must conclude that our waist gunner, in retrospect, did not have to be concerned after he had come under Luftwaffe control in Stalag Seventeen, at least.

The researcher went on: "At Stalag Luft III, they [the Germans] attempted to produce a list of Jewish-American POWs. I believe that the stalag officers who probably had the responsibility for identifying the Jewish POWs in the camp were Abwehr, or counterintelligence service personnel."

Our three officers of the *Toonerville Trolley*, however, who were confined at Luft Three were unaware of any attempts that may have been made to take Jews from the camp or single them out.

Summing It Up . . . Men of Stalag Seventeen B

Although the Paris meeting with "Harry Vozic," for whom Sergeant Kurtenbach had provided life-saving cover, had been arranged, the principal reason for his Paris visit was for a debriefing after a long period as one of the outstanding POW camp leaders in German-occupied Europe. There would be another session when he arrived back in the United States and was ordered to report to the Pentagon in Washington. Reports had to be made and questions answered.

From other sources we learned that the War Department was interested, also, in how the American POWs had adhered to the "Code of Conduct" that all were sworn to observe.

But there was another subject, one that had not been heard of before, that of war crimes, and crimes against humanity that may have been committed, Some charges were brought before the international court convened at Nuremberg, based on statements taken from ex-POWs of Stalag Seventeen B, such as that of Ralph Lavoie.

We would be naive to assume that every one of the more than four thousand Americans in Stalag Seventeen B was content with the organization and execution of authority by their fellow Americans there. Some had different concepts of what rules prisoners should impose on themselves and each other or even those rules that were imposed by the code of conduct and the general rule of military authority.

Some took strong exception to an order to quit or reduce trading with the enemy. Most realized that they could hardly expect a positive reaction from the home front, where people were making many sacrifices for their boys overseas, on learning that not only American cigarettes but also canned meats, chocolate, raisins, butter, instant coffee, and even face soaps were showing up in the hands of the enemy and available on their black market. Some, of course, were from thefts of Red Cross parcels while in transit, but another source was "through the barbed wire."

When awareness of this had reached America, then clearly, trading was getting out of control.

Some defied the order from the "White House," as they called the camp leaders' barracks. There was an aborted attempt to enforce it by use of force, perhaps unwisely. We witnessed some fist fights almost approaching riot stage, and all of us realized that the Germans would not stand aside and permit that without bringing their own physical power to bear.

Sergeant Kurtenbach chose to modify his order. It could not have been an easy explanation for him to give during his debriefing.

The comment of one who chose not to obey, as published after the war, made me wonder whether or not he was a member of the U.S. army. On challenging the authority of the camp, his remark was, "I asked if we weren't Americans and had the right to do as we pleased."

Over the years of corresponding and talking with ex-POWs I have learned that there were many happenings about which I and my barracks mates had no knowledge. One postwar writer said that "there were traitors, cheats, cowards and even a few sexual perverts there," but provided no evidence or examples.

From our perspective in but one compound during only the final twelve months of the war, we saw none of this. Or were we just too young and naive to recognize it?

At the Eighth Air Force reunion in New Orleans in 1992, while on a panel led by author Roger Freeman, I spoke for Stalag Seventeen B while four other panel members spoke for their various POW camps.

In summary, I concluded:

The very large majority of Americans in Stalag Seventeen B were good soldiers and honorable, loyal, brave airmen of the Army Air Corps. People are still astounded to learn that such a huge number of soldiers, all of the same rank, were able to organize and govern themselves under the conditions of imprisonment by their enemy.

It was humiliating in the extreme to be intimidated every day with the enemy gun muzzles always in view. However, most would agree that they might now look back in anger and frustration but certainly not in shame for any of their actions.

Enduring the incredible hardships of crowded, unsanitary accommodations with death always a near-term possibility from gunfire, sickness, or starvation, the leaders with whom I served and with whom I have since communicated are of the opinion that these shot-down airmen managed to preserve their personal dignity, honor, and loyalty, reflecting well on their squadrons and groups, the Army Air Corps, and the United States of America.

Bibliography

Bowman, Martin W. *Castles in the Air.* Great Britain: Patrick Stephens, 1986.

Caldwell, Donald, *JG 26: Top Guns of the Luftwaffe.* New York: Ivy Books, 1993.

Daniel, Eugene L., Jr. *In the Presence of Mine Enemies: An American Chaplain in World War II German Prison Camps.* Self-published, 1986.

Durand, Arthur A. *Stalag Luft III: The Secret Story.* Baton Rouge: Louisiana State University Press, 1988.

Freeman, Roger A. *Experiences of War: The American Airman in Europe.* London: Motor Books International, 1991.

———.*The Mighty Eighth.* New York: Orion, 1970.

Gabreski, Francis. *Gabby: A Fighter Pilot's Life.* New York: Orion, 1991.

Harth, Walter. *"Die Amis Kommen!" A Documentation of the War's Ending in Landkreis.* Kreistat St. Wendel, 1955.

Hough, Richard, and Dennis Richards. *The Battle of Britain.* New York: W. W. Norton, 1989.

Jabolonski, Edward. *America in the Air War.* Alexandria, VA: Time Life Books, 1982.

McKenzie, Edward D. *Surly Bonds of Earth.* Manchester, NH: Speediprint, 1985.

Messenger, Charles. *Hitler's Gladiator; The Life and Times of Oberstgruppenfuhrer and Panzergeneral-Oberst der Waffen SS Sepp Dietrich.* New York: Brassey's Defence Publishers, 1988.

Mombeek, Eric. *Defending the Reich: The story of JG 1 "Oesau."* Translated from the French by Hans G. Berger. Brussels: 1993.

Rust, Kenn C. *Eighth Air Force Story*. IN: Sunshine House, 1989.

Toliver, Raymond F. *Hans Scharff, Luftwaffe's Master Interrogator*. New York: Aero Publications, 1980.

Victory, Luther. *A Chronicle of Stalag XVIIB*. Baytown, TX, self-published, 1980.

Zimmer, Klaus. *Des Mittleren Ostertals, Heimat -und Kultural Verein*. Ostertal: e.V., 1990.

Zimmer, Klaus, and Edward D. McKenzie. *Die Fliegende Festung bei Bubach,* 24. April 1944. Kusel: aus Westricher Heimatblätter, 1996.

Personal Correspondence, Discussions, Journals

Anthony, Richard P., former B-17 pilot and POW at Stalag Luft Three, who provided story of meeting the head-on fighter attack of Hans Berger, delaying capture, and life in Luft Three POW camp.

Berger, Hans G., former Luftwaffe fighter pilot, 1 JG/1 and POW, who provided description of preparations and the aerial attack of April 24, 1944, his military and postwar biography, and general discussions of strategies in attacking Allied bombers.

Clark, Albert, Gen. USAF (ret'd), former fighter pilot and American POW leader at Stalag Luft Three, who provided discussions of personal experiences of capture and of life at POW camp, as well as allowing examination of his major memorabilia collection at the USAF Academy library, Colorado Springs.

Demuth, Emil Karl, former Luftwaffe fighter pilot, 1 JG/1 and POW, who comments on conversion to jet "hunter" plane Heinkel 162, capture, and internment by British army in May 1945.

Gabreski, Francis, former fighter pilot ace, Eighth Air Force, who provided discussion of fighter tactics and gunnery strategies.

Katuzney, John J., former POW and medical assistant at Stalag Seventeen B.

Kurtenbach, Kenneth J., former Camp Leader and Man of Confidence at Stalags Seven and Seventeen B provided stories of how the war ended at the POW camp; Harry Vozic, the impostor POW; escapes of "Shorty" Gordon; and meeting with Gen. Sepp Dietrich.

Lavoie, Ralph E., former POW and escape shooting victim, who provided details of a major incident at the POW camp.